7-03

10642885

Honest
John
Shafroth

A Colorado Reformer

Stephen J. Leonard
Thomas J. Noel
Donald L. Walker, Jr.

Colorado Historical Society
Denver

MONTROSE LIBRARY DISTRI
320 So. 2nd St.
Montrose, CO 81401

Colorado History
ISSN 1091-7438

Number 8
2003

COLORADO HISTORICAL SOCIETY

Research and Publications Office
Modupe Labode and David N. Wetzel, *directors*

Publications Director
David N. Wetzel

Colorado History **Series Editor**
Larry Borowsky

Cover Design
Mary H. Junda

On the cover: *Nameplate, fountain pen, and governor's seal courtesy Denver Public Library, Western History Collection. Photograph courtesy Colorado Historical Society.*

The Colorado Historical Society publishes *Colorado History* to provide a flexible scholarly forum for well-written, documented manuscripts on the history of Colorado and the Rocky Mountain West. Its twofold structure is designed to accommodate article-length manuscripts in the traditional journal style and longer, book-length works which appear as monographs within the series. Monographs and special thematic issues are individually indexed; other volumes are indexed every five years. The publications of the Society generally follow the principles and conventions of the *Chicago Manual of Style,* and an author's guide is available on request. Manuscripts and letters should be addressed to: Research and Publications Office, Colorado Historical Society, 1300 Broadway, Denver CO 80203. The Society disclaims responsibility for statements of fact or opinion made by contributors.

© 2003 BY THE COLORADO HISTORICAL SOCIETY
All rights reserved
Printed in the United States of America

*To the Shafroth family—his
grandchildren, great-grandchildren,
and all inheritors of his spirit—
that they may continue to emulate
his honesty and his dedication to
government of, for, and by
the people.*

ABOUT THE AUTHORS

Stephen J. Leonard chairs the History Department at Metropolitan State College of Denver. His books include *Lynching in Colorado 1859-1919*, and *Trials and Triumphs: A Colorado Portrait of the Great Depression with FSA Photographs*.

Thomas J. Noel is a professor of history at the University of Colorado at Denver and author of numerous books about Colorado history. He also writes the "Dr. Colorado" column for the Saturday *Rocky Mountain News*.

Donald L. Walker, Jr., a Ph.D. candidate in history at the University of Nebraska, is the author of *John A. Love: The Story of Colorado's Thirty-Sixth Governor*.

CONTENTS

Acknowledgments

We are indebted to many people for making this book possible. First and foremost, Frank Shafroth, Virginia Shafroth Newton, and James Quigg Newton suggested this project and supported it in many ways. Mrs. John F. (Diana Holland) Shafroth and Stephen Shafroth also offered their generous assistance. The Shafroths have worked over the years with previous scholars on M.A. theses, Ph.D. dissertations and unpublished manuscripts that have formed the bedrock upon which other studies such as this one have been built. We are indebted to the Shafroths for making available to us Christopher B. Gerboth's manuscript "Honest John," which he produced on commission for the family in 1996 and James Newton Dickson, III's 1975 M.A. thesis from Madison College in Madison, Wisconsin.

The Shafroth Papers in the Western History Department of the Denver Public Library constitute the most important reservoir of information on John Franklin Shafroth and his family. We are grateful to the Western History Department's staff, especially Coi Drummond Gehrig, Bruce Hanson, Jim Kroll, Phil Panum, Jennifer Thom, Barbara Walton, and Kay Wisnia. We also used the reference resources in other areas of the Denver Public Library and specially thank Rose Ann Taht for assisting us with government documents. A smaller Shafroth Collection at the Colorado Historical Society's Stephen H. Hart Library was also indispensable. There we were assisted by Barbara Dey, Rebecca Lintz, Deborah Neiswonger, and photography curator Eric Paddock. David Wetzel and Larry Borowsky in the Historical Society's publications department helped us in numerous ways, including editing and reformatting of obsolete computer files. The excellent history collection at the Auraria Library, Denver, much of it developed by head bibliographer Terry Leopold, helped us put Shafroth's senatorial career in perspective. Dale Reed, archivist at the Hoover Institution at Stanford University, supplied information on Will Shafroth held in that fine repository.

Dr. Henry Wolcott Toll, Jr., Esq., M.D., kindly and expertly reviewed this manuscript, catching errors and making helpful suggestions, as well as providing interviews and encouragement. Frank Shafroth, Virginia Shafroth, and James Quigg Newton also scrutinized the manuscript and provided family information, as did John F. "Jock" Shafroth IV. CU-Denver graduate history student Don Walker did research and initial writing. Another CU-Denver graduate student, Kara Miyagishima, helped in research, editing, and formatting. CU-Denver graduate student Jamie Field wrestled with the computer, while Barbara Gibson assisted with research. Marcia Goldstein shared with us her in-progress CU-Boulder Ph.D. dissertation on Colorado women since 1893. At Metropolitan State College Denise Hull and Christopher Altvater helped with copying tasks.

Special thanks to Vi and Max Noel, who made this collaboration possible. Vi's kindness, tact, and cooking helped Steve Leonard realize that Tom Noel is a collaborator worth knowing. Max, the demon cat of Newport Street, did his part by keeping a low profile. Thomas J. Noel, coordinating editor of this book, is solely responsible for any errors and omissions, which he hopes that gentle readers will call to his attention.

— S. J. Leonard and T. J. Noel

Introduction

Back in the 1880s, when John Franklin Shafroth first ran for office, many gentlemen avoided politics, fearing that if they played in the mud they would get dirty. Mark Twain, Henry Adams, and other Gilded Age commentators lamented the corruption of America's democratic system. Boss Tweed's Tammany Hall, the machine that plundered New York City in the 1870s, still cast a baleful shadow over that city. In Pennsylvania, young Boies Penrose began his ascent to bossdom, while dozens of lesser bosses ran other cities and states. The political muck that covered most of the country easily flowed into Colorado, a booming state overwhelmed with newcomers, a place ripe for plucking. The *Rocky Mountain News*, *Denver Times*, and *Denver Republican*, as well as commentators such as Robert Gordon Dill, David Day, and James "Fitz-Mac" McCarthy, all found Colorado as politically rotten as New York or Pennsylvania.

The 1889 Denver mayoral election stank more than any other. John Shafroth, then Denver city attorney, knew only too well that election day turned into a carnival of abuses. Thanks to a $20,000 slush fund, the ruling Republican machine, intent on electing Wolfe Londoner mayor, paid $2 per vote—twice the usual stipend. Repeat voters received generous bonuses in the form of lottery tickets and free beers. The army of repeaters soon exhausted the list of "dead names," and hundreds of legitimate voters arrived at the polls only to be told that they had already voted. Gambling-hall proprietors Jefferson Randolph "Soapy" Smith and William Barclay "Bat" Masterson prepared hundreds of slips containing registered "dead names" and distributed them to unqualified voters. Handy crooks boarded up polling places, forcing citizens to push their ballots through slots to an unseen poll judge, who could easily discard votes deemed politically incorrect.

The *Rocky Mountain News* pronounced the polling "the most disgraceful in the history of Denver politics, corrupt as they have been before." Even the *Denver Republican*, while congratulating Londoner upon his victory, admitted that a corrupt gang had sullied the GOP campaign. After both city and county officials refused to review the election, the reform candidate, Elias Barton, complained to the Colorado Supreme Court. Following a trial that uncovered gross voting abuses, Mayor Londoner was removed from office in 1891, shortly before his term was to expire.

Reformers, too optimistically, hoped the state legislature could flush out the Denver cesspool. The 1889 Colorado General Assembly, under the guise of reforming Denver, put the city's firemen and policemen under the thumb of a state-appointed Fire and Police Board, which had the power to fire bad cops and to hire good ones. This sham reform merely shifted control from mercenary city officials to mercenary state functionaries. Many legislators themselves were corrupt; the Seventh General Assembly earned the infamous title "Robber Seventh" because members took state furniture home with them at the end of the session. Often these lawless lawmakers met in the White House Saloon and other such congenial places. Even the senate's committee on temperance, one senator complained, "should more properly have been called the intemperance committee as the room assigned to the committee constituted a free dispensary of many choice wines and liquors."

The Fire and Police Board proved to be the perfect tool for Robert Walter Speer. Speer stood six feet tall, weighed two hundred pounds, had a ready smile and firm handshake, and was by the early 1890s well on his way to becoming Denver's most effective political boss. As one of the three state-appointed fire and police commissioners, he cultivated voters by having policemen dispense coupons to the indigent. The poor could exchange these coupons at saloons for sandwiches, hard-boiled eggs, and other nourishment. Supposedly a charitable measure, this early food-stamp program helped both the poor and the saloonkeepers to remember the name Speer.

Speer also created "Speer Clubs," which raised money and votes, often in exchange for political favors. He manipulated appointments to the police and fire departments and the awarding of saloon licenses to grease a Democratic machine that could outdo even the Republicans. Speer's clout became apparent with his 1904 election as mayor of Denver. According to Benjamin Barr Lindsey's exposé, *The Beast*, Speer won thanks to ten thousand illegal votes.

In the also smelly 1902 state election, James H. Peabody was selected governor of Colorado. During the next two years he used Pinkerton detectives, goon squads financed by mine owners, and the supposedly neutral but blatantly pro-management Colorado National Guard to crush workers striking for an eight-hour workday and a minimum wage of $3 a day. Reaction against Peabody led the Democrat Alva Adams to victory in the 1904 gubernatorial election.

The Republican-controlled Colorado Supreme Court investigated the contest. Not surprisingly, especially in our own age of U.S. Supreme Court electioneering, the probe revealed fraud on both sides but focused on chicanery in the Democrat districts—such as Denver, Boulder and Trinidad. The justices declared Peabody the winner, overturning what had initially been a ten-thousand-vote victory for Adams. This heavy-handed judicial interference led to such an uproar, even among moderate Republicans, that a compromise was reached. Peabody replaced Adams on May 17, 1905, but resigned immediately and gave the post to Lieutenant Governor Jesse F. McDonald. The spectacle of three governors in one day drew national attention to the need for political reform in Colorado.

As abuses multiplied, the demand for reform increased. Journalists such as Upton Sinclair and Lincoln Steffens exposed the sewers that ran through American life. Reformers who came to be called progressives dedicated themselves to expunging evil wherever they found it — in saloons and brothels, in meat-packing plants, in monopolistic business trusts, in city halls and state capitols.

Colorado boasted its share of progressives, including the nationally known juvenile court judge Ben Lindsey and the women's club leader Sarah Platt Decker. Among them, one man stood out as a successful politician who could turn reform rhetoric into actual reform. He was a man of such principle that he resigned from the U.S. House of Representatives in 1904 because he felt that his election was tainted. That man was "Honest John" Shafroth. Voters, remembering his extraordinary honesty and approving his progressive agenda, elected him governor of Colorado in 1908, re-elected him in 1910, and sent him to the U.S. Senate in 1913. Their faith in him was not misplaced. More than anyone else in Colorado's history, Shafroth lifted politics out of the mire and made tangible Abraham Lincoln's vision of government of the people, by the people, and for the people.

This story of a man and his era details Shafroth's slow rise to prominence, his tumultuous years as governor, his contributions in the U.S. Senate, and his narrow defeat in 1918. It presents both a history lesson and a lesson of current relevance, because many of the evils he fought still bedevil the state and nation, despite the advances made by "Honest John" and the other reformers of his day.

John Franklin Shafroth, age nine, 1863. Denver Public Library, Western History Collection.

Chapter One
Early
Years

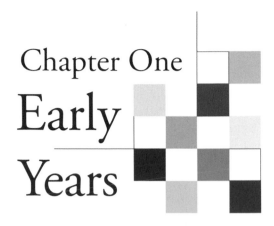

Coloradans called him "Honest John" with good reason.

On February 15, 1904, John Franklin Shafroth stunned his colleagues in the U.S. House of Representatives by resigning from Congress. His election, he told them, had been tainted with fraud. Without his knowledge, he claimed, political hacks in Denver had forged ballots in order to elect their own candidates, and his name, unfortunately, was on the same ticket. He could have kept his place in Congress through maneuvers and delays, but Honest John would have none of that. Instead he asked the House to seat his opponent and, in a voice strained with emotion, he bid his fellow congressmen goodbye.[1]

Shafroth's enemies gloated over the cracked remains of a fallen Humpty Dumpty Democrat who, they thought, could not be put together again. But his supporters mourned his resignation. Advocates of independence for the Philippines would lose a champion. Backers of federal reclamation projects and women's suffrage would lose a friend. After nearly a decade of representing Colorado's First Congressional District, Shafroth, it seemed, was politically dead.

His detractors did not notice the sparks that immediately sprang from the embers of his career. The House heard his farewell in amazed silence, with occasional outbreaks of applause. Never before had a congressman voluntarily resigned at the beginning of a term because of a questionable election. When John Franklin finished speaking, onlookers in the galleries clapped as congressmen on the floor rushed to congratulate him. So rarely did a politician put principle above power, so refreshing was this devotion to clean elections, that other statesmen, including President Theodore Roosevelt, lauded Shafroth for his sacrifice. Lewis Ludlow, a newspaper reporter long accustomed to the stench of Washington politics, marveled: "I had never seen anything like that happen before, and I said to myself, 'God must be pleased with this honest man.'"[2]

During the 1902 campaign Shafroth's friends dubbed him "Honest John," a nickname his enemies sarcastically turned against him as election chicanery came to light.[3] By resigning his seat, the congressman reclaimed his right to the title "Honest" and, with the adroitness of an expert chess player, turned sacrifice to advantage. As calculating as he was honest, Shafroth traded a minority-party congressional seat for the high moral ground. Standing upon that plateau, he was twice elected Colorado's governor, in 1908 and 1910. He used that office to push for more than a dozen progressive reforms, ranging from the initiative and referendum to child labor laws. Those achievements helped get him elected in 1912 to the U.S. Senate, where he fought for women's suffrage, the Federal Reserve system, and President Woodrow Wilson's dream of a League of Nations. Unlike Humpty Dumpty, John Franklin knew how to put himself together again, using his political skills to construct victory from the shards of defeat. Those skills were rooted in nearly a quarter-century of experience in Colorado politics—and in an immigrant family from the small town of Fayette, Missouri.

Ambition and Labor

Today a town of some three thousand people, Fayette advertises itself as a community of strong values "where everyone knows your name." The Missouri River, fifteen miles south of town, enriched the area's history and the bounty of its farms. The river drew French traders and trappers into the region in the late eighteenth century. In 1804, Lewis and Clark camped nearby on Bonne Femme stream as they headed west in search of the Pacific. Several years later Daniel and Nathan Boone, sons of the legendary hunter, started manufacturing salt at Boone's Lick. The nearby town of Franklin also profited from its river site until the mighty Missouri washed it away. Fayette, higher and dryer, was laid out in 1823 and in 1827 became the seat of Howard County. Tennesseans, Kentuckians, Carolinians, and Virginians flocked to the region, seeking cheap, fertile land and bringing with them Southern ways and slaves. A handful of immigrants and Northerners also located there, but they were too few to dilute "little Dixie's" atmosphere.[4]

John Gotlieb Shafroth, who initially spelled his name Schaffroth, was a German-speaking immigrant from the canton of Berne, Switzerland. Born on September 3, 1810, and orphaned at about age twelve, he migrated to the United States in the 1830s.[5] He bounced around in Missouri, living three years in St. Louis, then in Rocheport and Boonesville, before making Fayette his permanent home around 1840. In Fayette he had a few German-born neighbors, but his was not the life of thousands of other German speakers who congregated in ethnic enclaves in cities such as Cincinnati and St. Louis. From their early days in the United States, the Shafroths demonstrated an adaptability that would later serve John Franklin well.

John Gotlieb went into partnership with M.A. Boyd to form Boyd and Shafroth, a general store that sold everything from porcelain dinnerware and tin plates to groceries and animal feed. Boyd and Shafroth likely did well, because Howard County ranked among Missouri's richest agricultural districts. In 1860, the U.S. Census counted 446 white residents, 198 slaves, and three free African Americans in Fayette, one of half a dozen small towns in Howard County.

On November 9, 1840, John Gotlieb Shafroth married twenty-year-old Annis Aule (also referred to as Anna with a last name of Awl and Aull), who had been born in Germany. Within a few years Anna and John had five children: Sophia, William, Laura, Louisa, and Carrie. John Franklin, the couple's second son and youngest child, was born June 9, 1854.[6]

Young John Franklin learned to do chores, to obey his parents, and to be honest. As a five-year-old he no doubt watched while workmen in the town square completed the stately brick Howard County courthouse, two stories high and topped by a cupola and a weather vane. In 1860 he may have sensed the anger in Howard County, where many slaveowners condemned Abraham Lincoln's election to the presidency as a "triumph of sectionalism over nationalism--of fanaticism over patriotism."[7]

Family tradition suggests that the Shafroths, although they owned four slaves according to the 1860 census, were Unionists during the Civil War. That placed them at odds with many of their neighbors in Howard County, which contributed at least fifteen hundred men to the Confederate cause. Many joined Major General Sterling Price, one of Fayette's best-known citizens, in his futile attempts to make Missouri a Confederate state. William Shafroth, John's brother, was of military age, but his name is conspicuously absent from the list of the county's Confederate volunteers. We may infer that John Gotlieb Shafroth opposed his community's powerful Southern currents, because after his death he was lauded for "having carved out a successful career in the face of difficulties, yet having held steadfastly to the right amidst all surroundings."[8]

Fayette suffered little during the great conflict. Federal troops occupied it early in the war, but life went on much as it always had, with slave trading continuing until 1864. Most Missouri blood was shed farther to the south, but Fayette risked raids. On September 21, 1864, William "Bloody Bill" Anderson and the infamous Confederate guerrilla William Quantrell swept into town with a force of nearly two hundred men. The marauders killed an African American man near Shafroth's store and attacked Union soldiers in the courthouse and others in a log stockade. Repulsed after a stiff fight, in which they lost at least twenty-five men, the raiders fled. Mounted Union troops later trampled the corpses of the Confederates, a terrible warning to Howard County's Southern sympathizers.[9]

Normally Fayette life was neither so grim nor so exciting. John Franklin attended school, where he learned to write in a clear, legible, although somewhat cramped hand. He worked in his father's store, played baseball, and enjoyed the unhurried, semi-rural life of a small-town boy in the 1860s. His cares, however, multiplied on May 8, 1866, when his father died at age fifty-five. But John Franklin's mother was still relatively young, and he had the support of his older sisters and brother. He earned his first dollar at thirteen, working two hard days in a local print shop. Nearly half a century later he still remembered: "I think that ink roller must have weighed a ton."[10]

In 1871, John enrolled in Central College, a Methodist institution in Fayette that was then little more than a glorified high school. There he studied mathematics, Latin, literature, and physical science. In an oration he delivered on June 27, 1871, Shafroth divided people into those with low ambitions "not aspiring higher than that of a brute" and those with high aims, the literary class, who would enjoy "the true beauties that such a life possess, leaving behind a name that will exist until the stars of heaven grow dim and the sun ceases shining its golden rays upon the surface of the earth."[11]

John Franklin Shafroth aspired to be among the literary class. In 1872, after a year at Central, he transferred to the University of Michigan in Ann Arbor, one of the nation's best public institutions. He pursued a rigorous course of studies, including math, science, German, French, history, philosophy, and rhetoric. He read law books, the *Federalist Papers*, and a life of Lincoln, assembling a library of more than a hundred volumes. Some of his college papers survive, charting the trend of his thinking. His father had not been particularly religious, and that perhaps explains John Franklin's tilt toward Charles Darwin's theory of evolution. "A hundred years ago," Shafroth wrote in his college notebook, "if anyone held the opinion that the world was not created in just seven times twenty-four hours, he would have been considered an infidel." But, he said, after the discoveries made by geologists, "[t]he world looks back and wonders how ignorant she was."[12]

In nearly thirty notebook pages he detailed the life of Benjamin Franklin. He stressed Franklin's secularism, his attention to his finances, his hard work, and his interest in science, all characteristics that would mark Shafroth's life. "There is an inseparable connection," he wrote in another paper, "between Ambition and Labor—one is sure to follow the other, as night the day. Labor performs the work and Ambition prompts the person to perform the work." And for the ambitious and industrious, rewards awaited. "History will tell you," he said, "that ambition and industry raised Cicero from his obscure birth to the noblest place in the hearts of his countrymen." That was a thought John Franklin, a young man of obscure birth, kept in mind.

Reflecting upon the nature of government, Shafroth wrote: "No matter how far back a country dates its existence, if the elements of justice, reason, and right are found wanting, then it is not legitimate." Adopting a point of view not then widely held among male Americans, he argued that justice would best be served if women had the right to vote. Nearly forty years later he wrote to suffrage leader Clara Berrick Colby: "I have believed in Women's Suffrage ever since the first speech I ever made in a debating society, the subject under discussion being Equal Suffrage. While our side lost the debate, it made me a firm believer in Equal Suffrage from that day to this."[13]

Debating and playing chess were among the few extracurricular luxuries Shafroth allowed himself. "Chess," he wrote in one of his college papers, was "a study worthy of the attention of the most intellectual men." For college fraternities he had no time. "It was work, work all the day for me," he told a reporter many years later. "I can't say that I was ever a 'rah, 'rah boy."[14] By sticking to his books he raced through Michigan, graduating with a Bachelor of Science degree in 1875, three years after he entered.

Shafroth returned to Fayette to read law in the office of Samuel Major, a prominent attorney with offices above Boyd and Shafroth's store.[15] The apprenticeship system was a common way for aspiring lawyers to learn the ropes. Like most small-town attorneys, Major took almost any work that paid, including criminal cases, civil suits, real estate transactions, bill collection, and foreclosures. Shafroth proved an apt apprentice and in 1876 was admitted to the Missouri bar.

Fayette grew in the 1870s, shaking off the effects of an 1872 cholera epidemic that left fifty-three people dead. The Shafroths, who may have left town to escape the disease, were spared. The following year a railroad built a line into Fayette, helping the town grow from 815 people in 1870 to 1,247 in 1880. Nickel-and-dime business—a lien on Monday, a deed on Friday—was likely plentiful at Major and Shafroth, perhaps too plentiful for the conscientious apprentice. Major was elected to the state legislature in 1878, so most of the firm's drudgery probably fell on Shafroth, who received only a portion of the partnership's revenues. Practicing small-town law for peanuts was not a life he relished. Young and ambitious, he looked west for better prospects. A little more than half a century earlier, Christopher "Kit" Carson had left Howard County seeking his fortune in the Rocky Mountains. In 1879, twenty-five-year-old John Franklin Shafroth also went west.

Family tradition has it that Shafroth intended to go to Seattle in October 1879 to join a friend, James Hamilton Lewis. According to the story he stopped in Denver, tarried a few days, fell in love with the booming town, and decided to stay. It is a good tale, but it runs counter to Shafroth's character.[16] He was neither wealthy nor impulsive. He had included in his college notebook a story about Benjamin Franklin's wasteful purchase of an overpriced whistle, noting that Franklin had forever after remembered that costly whistle and hence avoided frivolous expenses. Making an expensive change of plans on a whim was not Shafroth's style. And Denver made good sense as his destination. It was only a thirty-six-hour train ride from Fayette. Perhaps he intended to scout Denver out and, if he did not like it, go farther west.

The contrast between Fayette and Denver must have hit John Franklin immediately. Fayette was small and bucolic, while Denver was skyrocketing from a village of 4,759 in 1870 to a city of 35,629 in 1880. Denver boasted blocks and blocks of two- and three-story brick business buildings, as well as the five-story Tabor Block, built by overnight millionaire Horace Tabor. Fayette boasted a courthouse with a weather vane, but it had no grand five-story buildings and no overnight millionaires. Anyone could see that Fayette was destined to remain a minor place. Denver, with few urban rivals within hundreds of miles, had splendid prospects of becoming a major metropolis.

Certainly Fayette had its attractions. There Shafroth had been born; there lived his loved ones. There, too, was his wife-to-be, Virginia Morrison, a young lady from a leading family. But if Shafroth were to rise in the world, to become a man worthy of Virginia, he would need a wider field for his talents. He could have stayed in Fayette, where everyone knew his name, and might in time have become a county judge. Instead he took a chance in Denver, where nobody knew his name. He gambled and won. Within fifteen years almost everyone in northern Colorado would know of John Shafroth, and within thirty years his honesty and his progressivism would spread the name Shafroth far beyond Colorado.

Denver in 1879

When Shafroth arrived in Denver in October 1879, he undoubtedly knew of the much-publicized silver discoveries at Leadville, a hundred miles to the west. Gold had initially drawn prospectors to Colorado in the late 1850s, but it was silver that energized the state in the late 1870s. Silver flowed by the ton from mines and smelters not only in Leadville but also Silver Cliff, Rosita, Ouray, and other far-flung towns. Hordes of pick-and-shovel men, mining engineers, teamsters, and financiers flocked to those mushroom camps

Serious young John Franklin Shafroth found little time for play. Taking his cue from another Franklin—Benjamin—he was a disciplined, diligent worker and excelled as a student. He posed for this photograph after graduating from the University of Michigan. Denver Public Library, Western History Collection.

to extract the ore, smelt it, ship it, and reinvest their profits. Carpenters and cooks, bankers and prostitutes, attorneys and morticians also hoped to share the bonanzas. Denver, though far from most mines, prospered by supplying and serving the mountain towns. Like Fayette, Denver was a county seat. But it was far more. The state's most populous city, it was also Colorado's capital and the center of the region's politics and commerce.[17]

Shafroth was not getting in on Denver's ground floor. John Evans, Walter Scott Cheesman, David Moffat, and other movers and shakers had been in Colorado from its pioneer days. Evans, once territorial governor, turned his talents in the late 1860s to railroad building and, assisted by Moffat and Cheesman, connected Denver to the Union Pacific Railroad. During the 1870s Moffat emerged as one of the city's most powerful bankers, while Cheesman made money drop by drop, developing water supplies for the expanding city. Evans dabbled in many ventures, including the water company, real estate, railroads, and the city's streetcar system, which he eventually passed on to his son, William Gray Evans, who later became the behind-the-scenes Napoleon of Denver's politics.[18]

Sometimes willingly, sometimes begrudgingly, local moguls admitted newcomers. They readily took in Nathaniel Hill, whose Boston and Colorado Smelter helped make their city a Western industrial center. They may have held their noses when Horace Tabor joined their ranks because Tabor, the lucky Leadville silver titan, was himself rank, carrying on an affair with the glamorous divorcee Elizabeth "Baby" Doe. But Tabor's millions assured him entree into the city's inner circles. Also welcome, as long as they did not rock the business community's boat, were refined, well-educated new arrivals with talent and intelligence—people such as John Shafroth.

Colorado's capitalists knew that business and politics went hand in hand. They looked to the nation, the state, and the city to subsidize their ventures, to protect their interests, to break strikes, to grant franchises to their water companies and street railways. The U.S. Army swept away the Indians and opened their land to cattlemen, ranchers, and homesteaders. Congress subsidized railroad companies and gave away mineral riches to prospectors and speculators. So cozy was the relationship between government and big business that sometimes the same men directly ran both. Horace Tabor was elected lieutenant governor in 1878 and later briefly served as a U.S. senator, one of many Gilded Age tycoons who hankered after membership in the exclusive millionaires' club known as the U.S. Senate. Nathaniel Hill used his money to land a Senate seat in 1878; in 1889 another Colorado smelter millionaire, Edward O. Wolcott, secured a place in the Senate. At other times the less wealthy tended the political grind. Henry Teller, a Central City lawyer, served capitalists so well that he remained in the Senate for more than thirty years.

Teller, Hill, and Wolcott, like most of Colorado's successful politicians, were Republicans. Populated mainly by Northerners, the state remained loyal to the Union during the Civil War and, like most of the Midwest and Northeast, elected Republican governors, senators, and representatives afterward. On rare occasions, a Colorado Democrat such as Thomas M. Patterson, who served in the U.S. House of Representatives from 1877 to 1879, could win. But until the economic crisis of the early 1890s unraveled the state's political traditions, the victories usually went to the Republicans.[19]

Shafroth, who had cast his first vote in 1876 for Republican presidential candidate Rutherford B. Hayes, likely was not thinking about politics when he stepped from the train in Denver in October 1879. But if he read the *Rocky Mountain News* on October 8, he might have been shocked at the allegation that local Republicans had manufactured fake ballots in order to get Richard Sopris, "a duly authorized representative of the gambling fraternity," elected mayor.[20] The Denver newspapers of October 1879 gave Shafroth a mixed view of his would-be home. In some ways Colorado seemed to be civilized, not much different from the East or Midwest. Local artists were busy at their easels: Donald McKenzie drawing a crayon portrait of Mr. Shittler, Miss Linnie Dwight "succeeding well in animal painting." Denver also had a Choral Union to present the cantata of Don Munio at Walhalla Hall, where "the critical listener will sit in rapt attention enjoying the many beauties of the whole."[21] In other ways, Colorado seemed far from the East and far from civilization. Late in September 1879, Ute Indians in northwestern Colorado besieged federal troops, killed Indian Agent Nathan Meeker by shoving a barrel stave down his throat, murdered the other white males at the White River Agency, and took Meeker's wife and two daughters hostage. And in October word reached Denver that four highwaymen had robbed two Leadville stagecoaches.[22]

Life in Denver, it must have occurred to Shafroth, would be more interesting than in Fayette. One of his first concerns was getting a job. By late October he had entered into partnership with Andrew Brazee, a former justice of the Colorado Territorial Supreme Court who enjoyed a well-established practice. A third of the firm's profits were to go to Shafroth, the rest to Brazee.[23] Shafroth's Fayette training had prepared him well, and he plunged into a heavy civil and criminal caseload. His minor cases did not warrant much notice. The *Rocky Mountain News*, however, paid attention to his adept defense of a murderer, James D. Stout, who, Shafroth successfully argued, could not be jailed because the court in which he was convicted had not been legally constituted.[24] Shafroth also sometimes put miscreants in jail. In the first court case brought by the Colorado Humane Society, he convinced the jury that a livery man named Donovan, who had whipped a horse until the whip broke, wrestled the animal to the ground, beat it, and kicked it, was indeed a cruel man.[25]

He also took an interest in the legal profession. On September 2, 1881, Shafroth and other attorneys established the Denver Bar Association. The organization's supporters said it would help attorneys get to know one another. Alfred Sayre, a Denver lawyer for a quarter-century, said an association was needed to prevent "fraud and chicanery among members of the profession."[26]

Shafroth got well acquainted with fraud and chicanery both in his private legal practice and in public practice as the deputy district attorney and city attorney. Denver harbored hundreds of prostitutes, pimps, gamblers, and opium eaters, who preyed upon the thousands of newcomers flocking into the booming city in the 1880s. Political bosses and police forged a mutually profitable alliance with that shadow world. For a price, policemen would conveniently turn a blind eye as they walked down Holladay Street, the nexus of the city's red-light district. For a price, the underworld would deliver votes and elections to would-be mayors and aldermen.

Shafroth's legal work opened his eyes to corrupt Western ways. At the same time, it gave him the financial stability he needed before he could propose to Virginia Morrison. As a lad he had appeared in a school play with Jennie, and he regularly carried her books home for her after school. Perhaps she seemed beyond the reach of an immigrant shopkeeper's son, for she was the daughter of John L. and Eliza Morrison, whose roots reached back to Virginia and Kentucky. John Morrison had served as county sheriff and judge. Had Fayette's aristocrats sported English titles, Jennie would have been Lady Virginia, daughter of Lord John and Lady Eliza. As it was, John Morrison settled for the common Southern honorific of "colonel." The Morrisons lived atop Lilac Hill. From their three-story home, a grand Federal-style edifice with nine fireplaces to chase away the winter chill, they could survey their eight-hundred-acre cotton plantation and racehorse farm.[27]

The Civil War probably reduced the family's fortunes. Virginia initially had hoped to attend Vassar but settled instead for Howard Payne College in Fayette, an all-female school adjoining the all-male Central College. With eight teachers and a diverse curriculum, Howard Payne could claim to be one of the best women's schools in the Midwest. Virginia enrolled in 1873 and received an excellent education that prepared her, after graduation, to teach in Carrollton, fifty miles northwest of Fayette.

On July 20, 1881, John Franklin wrote to Virginia's father: "Doubtless you are aware that more than a feeling of friendship exists between your daughter . . . and myself." Though his $83 monthly salary as an assistant district attorney was "not as good as I would like," his prospects were good and he was building "a little cottage." Jennie had already agreed to marry Shafroth with her parents' consent. John Morrison replied: "I have always had full confidence in Jennie's good judgment and in this the most important step of her life taken in connection with my personal knowledge of your moral worth and good character I have no reason to doubt her judgment in this case. Her ma dislikes very much having to have her so far from her."[28]

On October 26, 1881, twenty-seven-year-old John Franklin Shafroth married twenty-six-year-old Virginia T. Morrison in Fayette. Jennie was one of the strongest ties that still bound Shafroth to Fayette, and when she re-turned with him to Denver that tie was broken, although John promised Jennie's father that they would visit. In Denver, John and Virginia settled into their first home, a small, one-story brick structure with an uncovered front porch at 1536 Pennsylvania Street. In 1890 they moved to 1755 Emerson Street and lived there until 1894, when they built a stately, two-story brick home at 1537 York Street, two miles east of the central business district. There they would live the rest of John's sixty-eight years, and there Virginia would remain until her death at age ninety-five in 1950.[29]

Family and Fortune

Susan, the Shafroths' first child, was born in August 1882. She died at age four on February 25, 1886. More than three decades later, the pain of her passing still lingered. "The first of our children," John Franklin remi-nisced, "was a girl and while [Jennie] and I were both disappointed that it was a girl, the child wove herself into our hearts so strongly that would not have exchanged her for any boy. She was a lovely little girl."[30] In March 1887, slightly more than a year after Susan's death, the Shafroths' first son, John Franklin Shafroth, Jr. (known within the family as Jack), was born at 1536 Pennsylvania Street. Their second son, Morrison (known as Morry), was born in October 1888. Two more sons followed: George in August 1891, and William (often called Will) in July 1894, after they moved to 1537 York.

At the York Street house, the Shafroths spent most of their family time together in three rooms: the parlor, living room, and library. John enjoyed carpentry and, according to Virginia, "loved nothing better than building a home for his books." The house had one bathroom, the only room that could be locked. Jack once retreated there to avoid a spanking from his mother. As Virginia pounded on the door he responded: "Laugh mother, and I'll open up." She laughed and spared him the spanking.[31]

Father John, by contrast, was more willing to punish his sometimes unruly children. Years later Virginia declared, "They have their father to thank for their discipline. If I'd been left alone I'd have spoiled them. But John would have none of it."[32] Yet Shafroth was far from a tyrant papa, as a tender letter he wrote Jack in August 1891 indicates. Returning from Europe on the ship *City of Paris,* he wrote his four-year-old son: "[T]he boat I am in is very big longer than 50 of our house." "London," he said, "is a great big town and you can walk all day there and never get out of town." He said he was bringing Jack buttons for his sleeves and apologized to him for not bringing a horse, promising to do so when "mama and I take a trip."[33]

The house on York was in a substantial but not ostentatious residential district, less than half a mile southwest of Denver's nascent City Park. Many of the town's wealthiest mining kings, bankers, brewers, and attorneys lived in large mansions near the State Capitol, some two miles west and southwest of the Shafroths. John Franklin's neighbors included solid men like himself, some of whom played important political roles. Next door to the Shafroths, at 1543 York, lived Dewey C. Bailey, a federal marshal who became Denver's mayor in 1919. Booth M. Malone, a U.S. district judge, lived at 1549 York. At 1529 York, on the corner of East Colfax Avenue, resided Archibald [Archie] M. Stevenson, an attorney and Republican machine politician. Eventually Archie Stevenson came to oppose Shafroth in the public arena, but they remained friends in private. Once when the Shafroths were vacationing, their son Jack took sick, and his throat swelled shut so that he could not breathe. Stevenson summoned the family doctor, who inserted a silver tube in Jack's throat, saving his life.

Shafroth's York Street home reflected his improving fortunes and his rise in the legal profession. He and Brazee dissolved their partnership in 1882, and Shafroth entered into a new partnership with Herman E. Luthe and John Stallcup. When in that same year Luthe was elected district attorney, he made Shafroth his deputy, a position he held until 1885.[34] Then, after two years in private practice, Shafroth ran, as a Republican, for city attorney in 1887.

Democrats charged that wealthy Republican Edward Wolcott used his millions to pull strings in the 1887 election. Wolcott's partisans were accused of passing out rotten cigars at the polls to make puffing Democrats sick before they could vote. Such bizarre allegations could not derail the Grand Old Party's juggernaut. The Republican ticket gained 1,500 more votes than the Democrats and Prohibitionists combined, and Shafroth became city attorney, a position he held until 1891.

In 1887 Shafroth and Stallcup terminated their partnership, and Shafroth formed a new one with Platt Rogers, who became Denver's mayor in 1891. Besides practicing law, Rogers and Shafroth bought and sold land, collecting rents and mortgage payments. In northwest Denver, Shafroth joined with John Brisben Walker, Jr., to develop Berkeley Heights, a tract south of Sacred Heart College (now Regis University). Shafroth, either alone or in

Virginia Morrison Shafroth posed for Denver photographer John E. Beebe in 1887 with her firstborn son, John Franklin Shafroth, Jr. Denver Public Library, Western History Collection.

partnership with others, owned other Denver property, including the ground under the Kenmark Hotel at Seventeenth and Welton Streets, and four lots at Twentieth and Broadway, the basis of the family's Twentieth Avenue Realty Company. He also held land near the hamlet of Westminster northwest of Denver, more than a thousand lots in Grand Junction in western Colorado, and properties in eastern Utah and Kansas City, Missouri.[35]

Real estate speculation made sense in the booming Rocky Mountain West during the 1880s and early 1890s. Denver tripled its population in the 1880s to become the nation's twenty-fifth-largest city by 1890, with a population of more than 106,000. Farms of the early 1880s sprouted houses in the late 1880s, and the lucky landowners reaped the harvest. Economic depression in the 1890s burst the real estate bubble, forcing would-be millionaires to shelve development plans and keep their land in crops. How much money Shafroth made and lost is difficult to determine. The house at 1537 York, completed in 1894, may have represented one of the high points of his fortune. In 1907 he told brother-in-law James H. Seager that their Grand Junction investment of "long ago" would pay off, but not "big."[36]

Other ventures were busts. Shafroth owned an interest in mining property in Leadville that subjected him to a yearly liability of nearly $2,000. His investment in the Fayette Mill became a headache after his brother, William, who had tended to the business, died in 1916. On the plus side, in 1905 Rogers and Shafroth's Broadway Realty Company wisely purchased lots at the corner of Eighteenth Avenue and Broadway in downtown Denver, property that would remain in the families' hands until the 1980s.[37]

Shafroth's fortunes, like those of many Coloradans, depended as much upon what happened in Washington, D.C., as upon events in Denver. From its territorial days, Colorado had relied on the national government to help finance railroads and to make land easily available to settlers. The silver industry, the motor of Colorado's prosperity, was especially dependent on federal policies. Between 1792 and 1873 the United States had used both gold and silver for coins—in principle, at least. In fact, because silver was scarce before the late 1860s, little of it circulated. Increases in the silver supply in the early 1870s distressed proponents of the gold standard. They feared that silver producers would exchange silver for gold, leaving U.S. Treasury vaults overflowing with a devalued metal. Because most other industrialized nations insisted that debts be repaid in gold, the United States would be placed at a disadvantage, and other financial ills would follow. In 1873 Congress decreed that regular silver dollars would no longer be minted. Within a few years, new silver discoveries caused producers to hanker after the government market. In 1878 they pressured Congress to pass the Bland-Allison Act, requiring the U.S. Treasury to buy between $2 million and $4 million worth of silver each month.

That bailout temporarily saved silver, but increasing production in the 1880s continued to threaten the price. In 1890 silver producers and their allies in Congress, including Senator Henry M. Teller, again used their muscle, forcing passage of the Sherman Silver Purchase Act. This law obligated the U.S. Treasury to buy four and a half million ounces of silver each month. But even that support was insufficient. Silver's value continued to slide. Holders of silver dollars insisted that the treasury convert them at face value into gold, thereby draining the government's gold supply. During the 1892 presidential election, both Democrats and Republicans, to the chagrin of their Colorado brethren, distanced themselves from the cause of silver.

Sensing the imminent wreck of their gravy train and with it the economy of their state, Colorado's Republicans and Democrats defected in large numbers to join the People's Party of America. Commonly called the Populist Party, it largely represented the interests of laborers and Midwestern and Southern farmers. Silver mine owners did not give a tenth of a tinker's damn for labor, and they did not especially worry about farmers. But they worshipped the

John and Virginia Shafroth's four sons, clockwise from top center: John F. Shafroth, Jr., Morrison, William, and George. This photograph dates to about 1895. Shafroth Collection, Denver Public Library, Western History Collection.

plank in the Populists' platform that called for the federal government to buy unlimited amounts of silver at prices pleasing to silver producers.

The Populists did not embrace silver out of sympathy for simpering mining barons. They simply wanted an expanding money supply. Minting tons of silver into dollars would spur inflation, thereby reducing the burden of farmers' debts and increasing their crop prices. In addition, a money supply partly based on silver, a Western metal, would reduce the power of Eastern banks. Claiming to represent the "common people," the Populists cast their crusade in moral terms. Gold was evil, an instrument rich capitalists used to crucify poor farmers. Silver was good, an escape from economic slavery for farmers, a way for the West to shake off its thralldom to the East.

Colorado already had many disgruntled laborers and farmers in 1892. Joining with pro-silver Republicans and Democrats, they elected Populist Davis H. Waite governor. Events overwhelmed him and almost everyone else in Colorado. In 1893, Congress repealed the Sherman Silver Purchase Act, and the price of silver collapsed, knocking the props out from under Colorado's economy. As many silver mines closed, hundreds of angry, unemployed miners flocked from the mountains to Denver, where they camped along the South Platte River. City fathers encouraged them to build boats and float away. Denver wanted to get rid of the jobless miners because it, too, was suffering. With the value of silver plummeting, silver kings such as Horace Tabor could not pay interest on their debts. Tabor forfeited his Leadville mines and his Denver properties, including the Tabor Grand Opera House, the Tabor Block, and even his home. Old John Evans, once a pillar of stability, faced foreclosure on his downtown Railroad Building. Unable to collect on their loans, banks failed and left their depositors, large and small, penniless.

For many the economic breakdown meant ruin. For Shafroth, the tempest spelled opportunity. On September 11, 1894, as Republicans struggled to reassert their power, the party nominated him to run for the U.S. House of Representatives. At age forty, fifteen years removed from small town life in Fayette, John Franklin Shafroth was ready to enter the national arena. He had only to win an election.

Chapter Two
Representative
Shafroth

As he prepared to run for the U.S. House of Representatives in 1894, John Shafroth faced extraordinary challenges. Because Eastern Republicans had helped repeal the Sherman Silver Purchase Act the previous year, Republicans in Colorado wondered how they could win. Democrats, also burdened by anti-silver national leaders, threw most of their support to the Populists in 1894. That left the Republicans to fight a Populist-Democratic coalition.

Shafroth's opponent, Lafe Pence, a handsome, flamboyant attorney, had been elected as a Populist to the House of Representatives in 1892. Pence's incumbency and his oratorical skills seemingly gave him an advantage over thoughtful, solid Shafroth, who after an especially long speech was dubbed "Windy John" by the *Boulder Daily Camera*.[1] Solidity and thoughtfulness, however, were prized qualities in 1894. Many voters had grown tired of bumbling, brash Davis Waite, a Populist elected Colorado's governor in 1892. Although most Coloradans liked the Populists for their support of silver, the party's other demands—including fair treatment of labor unions, a graduated income tax, and government ownership of railroads, and telegraph and telephone lines—found fewer adherents. Had Waite been clever and tactful, he might have successfully promoted a few of the Populists' ideas, some of which were later embraced by progressive reformers. But Waite was neither clever nor tactful. His rhetoric—"it is better, infinitely better, rather than our liberties be destroyed . . . that we should wade though seas of blood: yes, blood to the horses' bridles!"—appalled conservatives and moderates, who saddled him with the nickname "Bloody Bridles Waite."[2]

Waite's proposal to mint silver dollars in Mexico and circulate them in Colorado met with scorn, because so-called "Fandango Dollars" trampled on the federal government's exclusive right to coin money. His ham-handed attempt to remove corrupt Denver police and fire commissioners by force, with the state militia ousting them at gunpoint, almost led to a shooting war between the state of Colorado and the city of Denver in March 1894. Although Waite called off the militia to end the bizarre "City Hall War," Republicans pilloried the governor as a hotheaded crank. Shafroth warned Coloradans that Eastern investors would shun the state as long as radicals ruled. Many business leaders agreed, including William G. Fisher, co-owner of the Daniels and Fisher department store in Denver. "We confess," said Fisher, "that we would rather have our store burglarized of $50,000 worth of our best merchandise" than face two more years of Davis Waite.[3]

Populists claimed credit for giving Colorado's women the right to vote in 1893, but Republicans retorted that they, too, favored equal suffrage. Sensible reform, they said, had always been their objective: Republicans had supported the Homestead Act, emancipation of slaves, and public schools. And, to defuse the silver issue, Shafroth promised that he would "subordinate every other question to the free and unlimited coinage of silver."[4]

Clad in silver armor and armed with the sword of anti-Waiteism, Shafroth had little to fear. Yet at times he stumbled. Golden's *Colorado Transcript*, a Democratic paper, chided him for turning up "his nose at the antics of one of his baby auditors," thereby insulting the baby's mother, who stalked out of the hall with nearly half the audience following her in sympathy. "The mothers of these playful babies each have a vote. Golden mothers do not like to have their babies snubbed by candidates."[5]

Shafroth survived the ire of Golden mothers and the barbs of Populists and Democrats, who described Republicans as "a gathering of harpies" responsible for "thirty years of accumulated filth bred from the unclean slums of their political organization, which for corruption outdoes all that can be imagined of corrupt, putrid and concentrated scoundrelism."[6] He picked up support from the American Protective Association, an anti-Catholic organization, but because of that backing he probably lost some Catholic votes.[7] In the end, Shafroth's political credits easily outweighed his debits; he galloped to victory on November 6, 1894, with 45,875 votes to Pence's 31,665.[8]

Congressman Shafroth quickly mounted his defense of silver, equating its use as money with the good of the common people. He warned that if Eastern Republicans failed to support silver, then Westerners like himself might bolt the party: "I have always been a Republican. I have never voted the Democratic ticket in my life, and yet I believe that it should be the policy of these Western states to herald to the east that we can no longer follow party domination if it is not in accordance with our convictions."[9] Shafroth met with silver partisans in Salt Lake City in May 1895 and asked them to back whichever party favored silver in the 1896 presidential election. Seven thousand people applauded his proposal, but convention delegates voted it down. Shafroth, marching ahead of more timid Republicans, told the *Denver Republican*, "[I]f the Democratic party puts a free silver candidate in the field for president, and the Republican party does not, that it will be the duty of the Republicans of this state to support the Democratic nominee."[10]

In December 1895, Shafroth introduced a bill mandating the coinage of silver, but it failed. In February 1896, he declared: "The remonetization of silver will do more than any other legislation to alleviate the sufferings of mankind, to give employment to the laborer, to permit business to be operated upon stable markets, to allow the tiller of the soil to get some little return for his work, and to produce an era of prosperity unequaled in the history of the world."[11]

Silver: Principle Above Party

Although Shafroth's oratory had improved since his days as "Windy John," most Republicans rejected his arguments. By the spring of 1896 both Teller and Shafroth were distancing themselves from the anti-silver Republicans. For the aging Teller, the journey may have been easy, for he was ready, he said, to retire. For Shafroth, abandoning the party that had elected him might have ended his political career, especially since Edward Wolcott, Colorado's junior Republican senator, was lukewarm in his support for silver.[12] Shafroth faced a difficult choice: either break with his party or renege on his campaign promise to fight for silver. Moved by principle and an astute sense of Colorado politics, Shafroth decided to remain true to his silver pledge.[13]

Republicans met in St. Louis in June 1896, nominated William McKinley for president, and taunted silverites with the chant:

Gold, gold, gold—
I love to hear it jingle.
Gold, gold, gold—
Its power is untold,
For the women they adore it,
While the men try hard to store it.
There is not a better thing in life than
Gold, Gold, Gold.[14]

Sickened by the jingle, Teller and other silver partisans, including Shafroth, split from the regular Republicans and formed a third party, the Silver Republicans. Shafroth suggested to Teller that he run for president, but Teller, knowing that a single-issue splinter group could not win, thought it wiser to support the Democrats if they should nominate a pro-silver candidate. Shafroth then attended the Democratic National Convention in Chicago, where he urged delegates to select a pro-silver man. On the fifth ballot they did so, nominating William Jennings Bryan. "You shall not press down upon the brow of labor this crown of thorns," Bryan thundered. "You shall not crucify mankind upon a cross of gold."

In Bryan, Colorado's Democrats, Populists, and Silver Republicans found a true champion: a congressman from Nebraska who understood the West, defended silver, and spoke with a voice so powerful that thousands could hear him. Many Coloradans, mired in the depression that had begun in the early 1890s, regarded Bryan as more than a candidate; he became a savior. Conservative Easterners, damning additional coinage of silver as fiscal suicide, despised "The Boy Orator of the Platte" as much as Westerners and Southerners loved him. By spending lavishly and campaigning hard, the gold bugs won enough electoral votes in the populous Northeast and in portions of the Midwest to make McKinley president. In Colorado, though, Bryan was magnificently victorious, racking up a hundred-thousand-vote margin over McKinley.

In their 1896 Colorado victory, the Democratic-Silver Republican-Populist coalition temporarily erased old party lines. Rivals in 1892 and 1894 became friends in 1896. Over the next eight years, as the silver issue slowly faded, old political divisions would re-emerge. But the shakeup of 1896 fundamentally altered Colorado politics. Some of the defecting Silver Republicans would never return to the Grand Old Party, and many voters would no longer automatically vote Republican. As a result, after 1896 Republicans could not assume that Colorado was a safe haven. Between 1876 and 1897 Democrats held the governorship for only four years. Between 1897 and 1919 they held it for twelve years, four of them being the back-to-back terms (1909-1913) of Democrat John F. Shafroth.

Shafroth profited from the new political structure he had helped build. Having embraced Bryan in 1896, Shafroth was embraced in turn by Colorado's Democrats and Populists in that year's congressional elections. He defeated the regular Republican nominee for Congress, Thomas E. McClelland, in one of the most lopsided victories in the history of Colorado, gaining eight votes for every one his opponent received. By siding with Teller and the silver interests rather than with Wolcott and the Republican establishment, Shafroth demonstrated both his principles and his political acumen.[14] Teller remained senator until 1909, when he was replaced by Charles J. Hughes, Jr., another Democrat. Wolcott lost his Senate seat in 1901 to Democrat Thomas M. Patterson.

During his years in Congress, Representative Shafroth fought for Colorado by constantly championing the cause of silver. Colorado Historical Society, Denver Post Historical Collection.

During the waning years of the nineteenth century, silver remained a core issue for Shafroth. His speech to Congress of May 26, 1898, was widely praised by silver's friends. Two years later he observed: "The man who thinks the silver question is dead does not understand the fundamental principles of that issue. It is bound to continue as a leading issue as long as there are creditors and debtors in the world, and as long as the Republican Party legislates for the money standard advocated by the capitalist class."[15]

Had Shafroth focused on silver alone, his career would have been short. But as the silver issue tarnished, he found other causes and made other alliances to keep him in the good graces of Colorado's voters. In 1896 he ran as a Silver Republican and won. He gained re-election in 1898 and 1900 by styling himself a Silver Republican/Fusion Democrat. In 1902 he enjoyed Populist support while running as a Democrat. He would stay with that party for the rest of his life.

Temperamentally John Franklin was far more at home in one of the mainline parties than he would have been in a third party such as the Populists. Although terms such as "the capitalist class" rolled easily from his tongue when he spoke of Eastern gold bugs, during his years in Congress he faithfully represented Colorado's capitalists. He consorted with Populists because of their stand on silver, but Congressman Shafroth, attorney and real estate investor, was no radical. His rhetoric simply reflected that he was a Westerner representing Western businessmen against Eastern businessmen, whom Shafroth and many others in the West saw as exploitative, colonial overlords. For him the question was not whether the West would be developed, but rather who would benefit from that development.

When the Union Pacific and Central Pacific railroads begged for a federal bailout, Shafroth opposed the handouts.[16] He knew that his constituents, Western shippers, hated the big railroads for imposing high freight rates. When President Grover Cleveland listened to conservationists and ordered some 21 million acres of Western land set aside as forest reserves in early 1897, Shafroth and other Westerners condemned the order, arguing that federal lands should be left open to timber cutters, miners, ranchers, and farmers. Colorado, which included large numbers of timber cutters, miners, ranchers, and farmers, generally applauded that anti-conservation position. "No state," historian Michael McCarthy notes, "was more collectively against conservation than Colorado."[17]

Shafroth favored conservation when it promoted development. He joined Nevada's Francis Newlands in lobbying the federal government to spend revenues from federal land sales in Western states for water conservation projects.[18] Years later, Colorado congressman Edward Taylor praised Shafroth for his work on behalf of the 1902 Newlands Act: "Without his irrepressible and tenacious persistence . . . it [the Newlands Act] would not have been enacted."[19] Shafroth also wanted the federal government to protect timber on federal land by creating thousand-foot-wide fire breaks and punishing people who set forest fires. Timber cutting, he argued, destroyed far less forest than did fires: "A forest fire will sweep over that country and in one week's time will do more to destroy the timber than all the cutting you can do in years."[20] Just as he recognized the commercial value of the forests, he saw the significance of the ancient cliff dwellings at Mesa Verde, both as historical assets and as tourist attractions. His efforts to create a national park at Mesa Verde came to fruition in 1906, after he left Congress.[21]

Had Shafroth simply stuck to those Western issues and the dying cause of silver, he would have quickly blended into the gray soup of lackluster congressmen whose porcine portraits fill the pages of historical tomes. The biography that accompanied his picture would have mentioned his unsuccessful crusade for silver. It also would have told of his lesser failures, including his scheme to redesign the U.S. flag so that the stars representing the thirteen original states would encircle the stars of the other states, which together would form a large star. He argued that the new arrangement would allow each state to identify its own star. The *Washington Post*, though, thought the idea laughable. It imagined a patriot from Ohio, dying in battle, looking at the new flag and gasping: "Fourth star counting from the apex star of the interior star, going to the right, I die for you."[22] Whatever its theoretical merits, Shafroth's fancy banner, like his silver standard, never caught on.

On the plus side, Shafroth's biography would have praised him for saving the honor of the United States by winning a chess game. He loved chess. "It is," he wrote, "the most beautiful game of which the mind of man has conceived."[23] His skills proved invaluable in 1897, when the British House of Commons challenged the U.S. House of Representatives to a chess match pitting five members of Parliament against five congressmen. One of the U.S. competitors, Robert Bodine of Missouri, invited Shafroth to join the team. Shafroth begged off, saying he had not played since his college days, but Bodine insisted. He knew the Colorado representative was a good player, Bodine confessed, because years earlier, when Shafroth had played a young woman in Missouri by postcard, Bodine had secretly dictated her moves— and Shafroth had won the game. Thus cajoled, Shafroth joined the team.

The U.S. players sat at a chessboard in Washington, D.C.; the British, at one in London. Moves were transmitted 3,500 miles via the Western Union and Anglo-American companies' undersea telegraph cable. At the conclusion of the fourth game the British had two victories and the United States one, with one stalemate. Shafroth opposed John Howard Parnell, brother of the Irish statesman Charles Stewart Parnell, in the last match on June 1, 1897. For fifty-eight moves, the opponents jockeyed their pieces without seeing the whites of one another's eyes. Then, with his position untenable, Parnell gave up and sent congratulations to Shafroth. The victory enabled the United States to even the overall tally at two games apiece with one stalemate, leading to the net result of a draw.

Afterward, Speaker of the House Thomas Reed, known as Czar Reed because of his autocratic ways, summoned Shafroth and said: "The next time you want to give one of those raging sixteen-to-one silver speeches, just give me notice and I will let you in."[24] The cable company also gave Shafroth a gold-plated rook with a piece of cable visible through its glass top. Untroubled by the irony of being a silver man with a gold trophy, he proudly displayed the rook on the fireplace mantle in his Denver home.[25]

Back on the legislative playing board, Shafroth helped engineer the creation of the National Bureau of Standards. It won him praise from Henry Pritchett, president of the Massachusetts Institute of Technology, for being "one of the most important pieces of legislation with which you have had to do."[26] Unheeded at the time, but adopted three decades later, was Shafroth's proposal to shorten the period between November elections and the seating of a new Congress.[27]

Even with his support for the National Bureau of Standards and his role in passing the Newlands Act, Shafroth's legislative record was thin. But by forcefully raising two of the most important issues of the late nineteenth century—issues that would reverberate well into the twentieth century—John Shafroth assured himself a place in the history books.

Women's Suffrage and Anti-imperialism

The role of women in the nation's political life, and the role of the United States in the world, were monumental questions during Shafroth's tenure in Congress. Bull-like, he met both head on. His stance on women's rights probably helped him in most of his political contests in Colorado; his anti-imperialism may have hurt him.

His commitment to women's suffrage benefited him at the polls when he first ran for Congress in 1894, because the previous year Colorado's women had gained the right to vote in all elections. At that time only one other state in the nation, Wyoming, accorded them that right. There were far more women in Shafroth's congressional district than in all of Wyoming, so he represented, at least temporarily, the largest body of women voters in the United States. That made him a natural spokesperson for equal suffrage. In 1895, during his first congressional term, he proposed a measure calling for a constitutional amendment to give all U.S. women the same voting rights as men. It read, in part: "[T]he right of citizens of the United States to vote shall not be denied or abridged on account of sex." Susan B. Anthony lauded his efforts and encouraged him to introduce a similar bill in 1900.

John Franklin consistently testified to the success of women's suffrage in Colorado. Virginia backed him by rebutting the popular claim that political squabbles between husbands and wives would wreck homes if women could vote. "I've no patience," she told a national women's magazine, "with the false attitude anti-suffragists strike when they assert that giving women the ballot causes them to destroy the peace of the home."[28]

Women voters arrive at a Denver polling place. Shafroth staunchly supported women's suffrage, which Colorado implemented in 1893. As a member of the U.S. House and, later, the U.S. Senate, he regularly introduced bills for nationwide women's suffrage. The cause finally prevailed in 1920, after Shafroth's retirement, with the ratification of the Nineteenth Amendment. Colorado Historical Society.

The simple yet revolutionary statement in the Declaration of Independence that the legitimacy of government rested on the consent of the governed provided one of the bulwarks of Shafroth's pro-suffrage stance. It was also key to his anti-imperialism, a position that put him at odds with the expansionist sentiment that dominated national thought. Blaming Spain for the destruction of the U.S. battleship *Maine* in Havana harbor, the United States declared war on Spain in April 1898. Shafroth, a firm believer in the Monroe Doctrine's dictum that Europeans should stay out of the Western Hemisphere, supported the war. But he and others, including Henry Teller, recognized the greed that lay behind the lust for conquest.

U.S. industrialists realized that England, France, and other European powers had assured markets for their products by snatching up colonies. In a monkey-see, monkey-do frame of mind, the United States—the world's largest manufacturing nation—hoped to create its own empire by plucking up choice pieces of Spain's ill-secured possessions. After a few months of what the United States regarded as a "splendid little war," Spain capitulated and ceded Cuba, Puerto Rico, the Philippines, and Guam.[29] In a separate action in July 1898, the United States annexed the Hawaiian Islands, which had earlier been wrested from their native ruler by U.S. businessmen. By early 1899 the United States claimed a satrapy of more than eight million people spread over a hundred thousand square miles.

Acquiring that vast and far-flung empire proved easier than governing it. Most Americans, cheered on by market-hungry industrialists, reveled in the war victories and took pride in the newly won islands. Others—including Eastern intellectuals and writers, along with some Southerners and Westerners—argued that by subjugating people outside the United States, the nation violated its own basic principles. In April 1898, Henry Teller, in one of the most effective shots fired in the anti-imperialist crusade, persuaded Congress to pass the Teller Amendment, which barred the United States from retaining Cuba. On June 14, 1898, Shafroth addressed the House of Representatives and voiced his opposition to the annexation of Hawaii, warning that history "records the downfall of every nation that ever undertook to realize the dream of universal empire. Let us profit by their example."[30]

Unwilling to heed that warning, Congress also ignored Shafroth's arguments about the stupidity of trying to defend the Philippines, the cost of maintaining the islands, and the dangers to American liberty posed by running an empire. "It was truly said," he told the House, "that the Republic could not endure half slave and half free, and I believe it cannot endure half republic and half empire."[31] But President William McKinley dismissed the anti-imperialists' logic and mired the United States in a "dirty" war to subdue the Filipinos who insisted on independence.

Sweltering in Philippine jungles and frustrated by fighting an unconventional war, U.S. commanders let their troops resort to torture, trickery, and the killing of prisoners. Shafroth condemned "the actions of those officers who disgrace their uniforms by murdering prisoners of war, burning barrios and villages, and torturing men to extort information against their own people."[32] "Is it right," he asked on another occasion, "for the administration to violate the fundamental principles of the Declaration [of Independence]? Is it right to treat men as unequal before the law? Is it right to

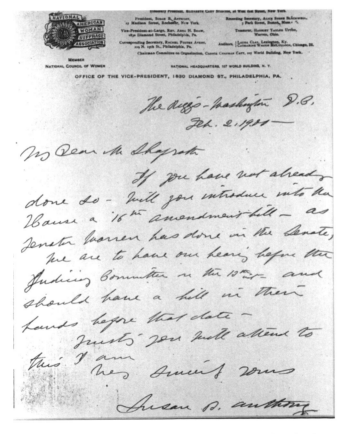

A letter from Susan B. Anthony to Congressman Shafroth, dated February 2, 1900. Anthony counted Shafroth as one of her strongest friends in Congress, and Shafroth prized his alliance with the famed suffragist, whom he once praised for "the uplifting of womanhood." Frank Shafroth Collection.

forcibly annex a people without their consent? Is it right to subjugate a people who are struggling for liberty, and independence?"[33] When empire mongers insisted that the United States should never pull down its flag, Shafroth retorted: "The American flag should be pulled down from every place were it should not have been planted."[34]

Theodore Roosevelt, who was elected McKinley's vice president in 1900 and succeeded him as president after McKinley's assassination in September 1901, believed in planting flags and saw the world in simple terms. Filipinos were Apaches, and the anti-imperialists were unpatriotic, even disloyal, for daring to question U.S. policy.[35] Shafroth, who witnessed the problems in the Philippines during a 1901 congressional tour, responded: "[T]he true patriots are those Americans who love their country too well to let it do wrong; too well to suffer it to violate the principles of the Declaration of Independence; too well to allow it to repudiate government of the people, and by the people; too well to be wrecked upon the rocks and shoals of colonial empire."[36] When he returned from the Philippines in October 1901, he told the *Denver Times* that the islands were of no use in opening the China trade, the cost of governing them was high, U.S. officials there drew princely salaries, the archipelago gave the U.S. no revenue, and it would be "necessary to keep troops in them permanently."[37] Finally, as if those were not reasons enough to get out, he complained that he had not had a good cup of coffee since he left the United States.

By insisting that he was "for the republic forever, and the empire never," Shafroth ran political risks in Colorado. In 1901, one thousand Colorado volunteers were still stationed in the Philippines, fighting to put down an independence movement that Shafroth compared favorably to the American Revolution.[38] Moreover, Colorado-born Brigadier General Irving Hale, who had helped conquer the islands in 1898 and remained there commanding volunteers, was a hero to many Coloradans. To buttress his anti-imperialist stance, Shafroth appealed to Colorado's self-interest by pointing out that the state's sugar industry would be jeopardized if cheap Filipino, Cuban, and Hawaiian sugar were to flood the U.S. market. That sensible argument hardly harvested the votes that Shafroth's defense of silver once did, because in 1901 the state's sugar beet industry was still in its infancy. Shafroth may have picked up a few friends among the anti-English Irish when he condemned England's war against the Boers in South Africa.[39] And in response to those who charged that he was not sufficiently attuned to U.S. commercial interests, he could point to his support for construction of a fortified canal through Nicaragua.[40]

Election 1902: "A Brave and Honest Man"

Sugar, Nicaragua, and Irish friends were not enough to save Shafroth in 1902. His anti-imperialism was only one issue in the campaign, yet the close election might not have been so close had he sung the virtues of empire. Shafroth won the praise of national anti-imperialists such as the suffragist Carrie Chapman Catt, one of the people Theodore Roosevelt belittled as "professional goo goos."[41] Unfortunately Shafroth could not count on large numbers of "goo goo" votes in Colorado, although wealthy Denver businessman Henry M. Porter commended Shafroth for his opposition to empire.[42] Many of Shafroth's former supporters deserted him in 1902, leaving him with such a thin edge that he could not claim a clean victory.

Shafroth had won by a margin of eight to one in 1896, the first year William Jennings Bryan ran for president. He easily beat Charles Hartzell in 1898 by a vote of 43,311 to 18,850. In 1900, Bryan ran for president again, and again he took Colorado, although he received nearly seventy thousand fewer votes than in 1896. Shafroth also saw his margin of victory slip as he defeated Republican Robert Bonynge in 1900. Bonynge, the *Denver Republican* had argued, could do more for Colorado than Shafroth in Congress, because Bonynge belonged to the same party as the president and the congressional majority.[43] Moreover, by 1900 silver—the cause that had helped propel Shafroth to power—was no longer as potent an issue as it had been in 1896 or 1898. Many silver miners had taken other jobs or left the state. Many silver barons like Horace Tabor were ruined, dead, or both. Dollar signs tell the story: between 1881 and 1890 the value of Colorado's silver output exceeded that of gold by more than $100,000,000. Between 1901 and 1910, gold bested silver by more than $160,000,000.

Republicans in Colorado's First Congressional District nominated Bonynge again in 1902. For the fifth time, Shafroth prepared to run. He still had the good will of a handful of old Silver Republicans, the remnants of the Populist Party liked him, and he won the endorsement of the Democrats, a blessing that turned out to be mixed. By getting the Democratic nomination, Shafroth automatically garnered Democratic votes, but he also picked up the support of the "Savages," a motley collection of slum lads willing to break almost any rule for political advantage.

To their friends in Denver's saloons, brothels, and shabby apartment houses, the Savages were merely boys "true to the people of their ward." As Edward Keating, once a Savage himself, explained it: "When the Democrats were in power we got our share of the patronage. There was no civil service system, so we were able to parcel out the jobs to those we considered 'deserving.'"[44]

He added: "If the city's government neglected the ward in any way, we raised a row and generally the row produced results."[45]

To their enemies those Robin Hoods were "pirates" whose "only creed is to win, for the sake of the spoils, and to win by any means." A decade earlier, said the *Denver Republican*, the Savages had been "as tough a set young boys as city life ever produced. . . . They organized parties for fighting and stealing and general ruffianism. They were the hoodlums of the downtown streets, the terrors of the corner grocery men. They drained beer kegs at the back doors of saloons, and smoked cheap cigars in the hay mows of livery stables."[46]

The hay-mow set grew up and took to politics. Having learned their larceny lessons well, they became adept at stealing elections. In the 1902 contest, said the *Republican*, the Savages were in "full control."[47] The *Republican* charged that one Savage, the Arapahoe County clerk, printed up plenty of extra ballots, "two and a half for every voter in the county."[48] Savages kept Republican judges from watching the polls in certain precincts, particularly in downtown Wards F and H. Then the thieves voted the extra ballots. They did it clumsily and stupidly, said the *Republican*, sometimes making "600 ballots at a time run exactly alike."[49]

Shafroth's 2,792-vote margin over Bonynge in the 1902 election left him on thin ice. If the Republicans could shake the results in just a few wards, they could claim victory. The new Congress did not meet until December 1903, so Bonynge had to wait until early 1904 to press his case. A congressional subcommittee slowly reviewed the ballots. They hired a handwriting expert, David N. Carvalho, to check the results in twenty-nine precincts. He determined that more than 5,000 illegal ballots had been cast, 4,761 of them Democratic and 780 Republican. After examining ballots for three days, Shafroth himself concluded that it was impossible to resolve which were legal and which illegal. Colorado law voided the entire vote of a precinct if illegal votes were cast there, and it was clear to Shafroth that at least some illegal votes had been cast in precincts where he had done well. Throwing out those precincts meant that he would lose the election.

Unclean elections were then as common as unclean streets, and few congressmen of either party questioned the process that put them in power. Representative James R. Mann, chairman of the House Committee on Elections, said that had Shafroth decided to stay in Congress even some Republicans would have supported him, thereby assuring his retention.[50] Had Shafroth wished to tough it out, he could have retained his seat. Instead he did as he had done in his crusade for silver and in his support of independence for the Philippines—he put principle first.

On February 15, 1904, in a short speech, he told his colleagues in the House of Representatives that despite his efforts to keep the 1902 election clean, ballot irregularities cast doubt on the validity of his victory. He resigned his seat and asked Congress to seat Robert Bonynge. Impressed with his honesty, congressmen from both parties congratulated him as onlookers in the House gallery burst into applause. President Roosevelt commended him, and Justice David Brewer of the U.S. Supreme Court wrote: "Only a brave and honest man would do as you did. Such actions make one proud of his country and sure of its future."[51]

"Honest John's" future was not as certain. Democrats praised him for his honesty. Republicans sneered at him, portraying his resignation as a forced bow to the inevitable. The Cripple Creek *Star* compared him to the Irishman accused of murder who was asked how he pleaded, guilty or not guilty. He replied: "I can't tell until I hear the evidence."[52] After hearing the evidence, said the *Star*, Shafroth had to plead guilty. Yet Shafroth, in pleading guilty, adroitly left the impression that others were guilty while he was himself innocent, an honest man hurt by a bad system. Honesty, in his case, was the best policy—and the best politics.

Honest John handed his congressional seat over to Robert Bonynge on February 15, 1904. The Denver Post's editorial cartoonist lamented Shafroth's resignation the following day. Colorado Historical Society.

Shafroth's resignation may have improved his family life. His children no longer had to shuttle between classrooms in Denver and the District of Columbia. However, that constant uprooting may have helped weld the Shafroths into a cohesive, self-reliant family unit.

In his college notebook at Michigan, Shafroth had included Benjamin Franklin's advice that a large family kept children from becoming spoiled. In his case, the four Shafroth boys helped the family deal with the tragedy of young George's spinal tuberculosis. Doctors had no effective cure for the painful malady, which caused the spine to collapse upon the spinal cord, making invalids of its victims. Often, as in George's case, patients were encased in plaster jackets to support the spine, but the treatment rarely worked. "[I]t may be that no one on earth can help him," Shafroth sadly admitted.[53]

George bore his affliction gracefully and patiently. His elder brother John, known in the family as "Jack," carried George, who was often paralyzed, around on his back. In one of George's diary entries he recorded his appreciation: "I am getting better all the time and can walk about all over the house. Jack has been the best fellow in the world to carry me on his back. I'll pay him back when I am a rich man."[54]

As he left Congress in 1904, John Franklin Shafroth, just short of his fiftieth year, still had plenty of ambition. He had been injured by the 1902 election, but the damage was not beyond his skill to repair. His opponents saw his resignation as proper punishment for being involved in a tainted election, and they hoped voters would not forget the taint. His friends viewed it as the righteous action of a principled man, a man worthy of again holding high office. How the electorate would regard it remained to be seen.

In the summer of 1904, only a few months after he resigned from Congress, Colorado Democrats nominated Shafroth for an at-large seat in the House of Representatives. Shafroth, who had never held statewide office, had to run in every Colorado county against the incumbent, Congressman Franklin E. Brooks, whom *The Denver Post* called "a nonentity of so little personal weight that it seems cruel to aim a blow against a man so small."[55] In November, little Franklin Brooks beat John Franklin Shafroth.

For the next four years, from 1904 to 1908, "Honest John" wandered in a political desert as dry as any arid plain in Colorado. His resignation gamble in 1904, it seemed, had not worked. His acumen as a political chess player had apparently failed him. But his ambition and his stubbornness still drove him. In an amazing reversal of fortune, John Shafroth would resurrect his political career, restore his halo of honesty, and gain the power he needed to put many of his principles into practice.

Chapter Three
Becoming
Governor

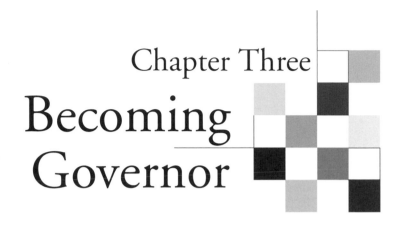

R esignation, missed opportunity, and defeat made 1904 one of the worst years in John Franklin Shafroth's political life. In February he resigned from Congress. Soon there was talk of his becoming the Democratic candidate for governor. He brushed that speculation aside, saying he lacked the money to campaign and needed time to rebuild his law practice.[1] With Shafroth's blessing, Alva Adams, a former governor, received the nomination instead; in November 1904, he defeated Republican James H. Peabody. In the same election, Shafroth, who might have been elected governor had he run for that office, lost his bid to become congressman-at-large. As he sifted through his career at the end of 1904, he held little more than an impressive collection of newspaper clippings.

By March 1905, fortune's turning wheel had eased the pain of 1904. Shafroth's resignation had earned him praise as "Honest John," a title of honor in an era of political dishonesty. His race for the at-large congressional seat made him known outside of Colorado's First Congressional District. Even his defeat had a silk lining, for had he been elected he would have lacked any real power in Congress, because the Republicans not only dominated the legislature but also, in the person of Theodore Roosevelt, held the White House.

Had Shafroth been elected governor in 1904, he would likely have suffered Adams's unhappy fate and been removed from office. The 1904 election ranked among the most corrupt in a long line of corrupt Colorado contests. The bully boys of Denver's downtown precincts and their allies—pimps, prostitutes, and police—stole votes to secure the election of Democrat

Robert W. Speer as mayor. That greatly pleased "Napoleon Bill"—William Gray Evans, the head of the Denver Tramway Company. Evans backed Speer, and in turn Speer favored Evans and his friends among the city's old power elite, including banker David H. Moffat and Walter Scott Cheesman, who controlled the Denver Union Water Company.

Seeing that thousands of fraudulent votes helped elect Speer mayor and Adams governor, the Republicans cried foul and insisted that Peabody deserved the governorship. But their hands were also dirty, because they, too, had stolen votes and intimidated voters.[2] In southern Colorado, where huge coal companies dominated the economy, Delos Chappell of the Victor Fuel Company told his workers they had a choice: vote Republican and keep their jobs; vote Democratic and lose them. After an investigation involving more than 2,000 witnesses and 180,000 pages of testimony, the Colorado General Assembly removed Adams from office. The Assembly briefly made Peabody governor on the condition that he resign, then raised Lieutenant Governor Jesse F. McDonald, a Republican, to the governor's chair. The fiasco of having three governors in twenty-four hours made Colorado a national joke. Lucky John Shafroth, in the meantime, sat on the sidelines being honest.

The Election of 1906

As Alva Adams left office in 1905, he diagnosed the cancer that ate away at the state: "Colorado is a province of the fuel company, the smelter trust, the tramway and allied corporations."[3] Sickened by the subservience of the major parties to the corporations, reformers proposed numerous remedies, many borrowed from the Populists of the 1890s. In its drive toward reform, Colorado hardly stood alone. Across the nation, men and women who came to be known as progressives—Robert LaFollette in Wisconsin, Woodrow Wilson in New Jersey, Hiram Johnson in California—fought to restore government to the people.[4]

Progressives thought the so-called Australian, or headless, ballot, would lead to more honest elections. Political hacks found it simple to steal elections in part because ballots allowed voters to vote for all members of one party by simply writing in the name of the party at the top of the ballot. By forcing voters to vote for individuals, rather than parties, the progressives hoped to allow reformers, regardless of their party affiliation, to win elections. In addition, progressives favored direct primary elections, in which candidates would be nominated by the party at large, not just by those insiders who attended political conventions—and who were all too easily manipulated by men with money. The reformers also wanted to give citizens the power to initiate laws through a petition and election process. This would enable the public to bypass state legislatures—which, like political conventions, responded more readily to moneyed interests than to ordinary people.

Another reform, the referendum process, would allow citizens to repeal laws they did not like and to vote on measures referred to them by the legislature. Enactment of recall laws would serve the same purpose by empowering voters to remove elected officials before their terms ended. In addition, proponents of change wanted to amend the U.S. Constitution so that the people could directly elect U.S. senators, rather than have them selected by state legislatures.

Robert W. Speer, mayor of Denver from 1904 to 1912 and from 1916 until his death in 1918, "bossed" Colorado's anti-reform Democrats. Speer, who worked with Republicans and business interests to realize his vision of Denver as a "City Beautiful," opposed Shafroth and other reform Democrats trying to end corporate control of Colorado. Colorado Historical Society.

Colorado's Democrats and Republicans both had progressives within their ranks, but their reform voices were often silenced by wealthy corporations. In 1904, Democrats pledged to support initiative and referendum laws, but before they could deliver on the promise Republicans in 1905 ousted Alva Adams. In 1906, Democrats again nominated Adams for governor, while Republicans turned to Henry Augustus Buchtel, a Methodist preacher and the chancellor of the University of Denver. Buchtel, a model of pious rectitude and a great fund-raiser for the university, was much beholden to the Evans family, whose support had helped build his institution.

The Democrats were doomed in 1906. Even before their nominating convention met in September, the party in Denver split between Speer's operatives and the reform faction. Shafroth sided with the reformers, who included U.S. Senator Thomas Patterson and Patterson's law partner, former governor Charles S. Thomas. At the convention, which Shafroth attended, the reformers angered Speer and his delegates by refusing to seat them.[5] Alva Adams received the gubernatorial nomination but had to run without much support from Speer's machine. Even worse from the Democrats' standpoint, two formidable third-party candidates—William D. Haywood and Benjamin Barr Lindsey—entered the contest. Together they siphoned away thousands of votes that otherwise would have gone to the Democrats.

William D. "Big Bill" Haywood, secretary-treasurer of the Western Federation of Miners, had no chance of becoming Colorado's governor—he sat in an Idaho prison, accused of conspiring to assassinate that state's former governor. Colorado's Socialist Party nominated Haywood in abstentia after anti-labor operatives kidnapped him in Denver in February 1906 and hauled him off to Idaho, where he faced trial on trumped-up charges.[6] Unskilled workers and miners loved him and held him up as a martyr, but most Coloradans regarded the vitriolic labor leader as a dangerous radical.

Confined to his cell, Haywood campaigned not at all. But Judge Benjamin Barr Lindsey, nationally known for his work to save Denver's delinquent children, conducted a dynamic reform campaign. In November he took 18,014 votes, and Haywood received 16,015, for a total of more than 34,000. Alva Adams desperately needed those votes because, added to his 74,416, they would have made him governor. Instead Buchtel, with 92,602 votes, won the election.[7]

Republicans also won control of the General Assembly in 1906, gaining the power to elect Colorado's next U.S. senator. In early 1907, insensitive to the clamor for reform, they sent Simon Guggenheim to the Senate, replacing Thomas Patterson. Guggenheim, Benjamin Lindsey said, "was a man of many good qualities," but "there wiggled into his brain the maggot of ambition to be United States Senator."[8] The maggot convinced Guggenheim that he was fit for the Senate. He was, after all, a multimillionaire smelter tycoon. His money had helped elect Republicans to the Colorado legislature in 1906, and in 1907 he demanded repayment. Guggenheim told his fellow Republican, John W. Springer, that he "intended to get" the Senate position "even if it cost him a million."[9]

Guggenheim epitomized all that reformers considered rotten in Colorado politics. His ability to buy votes devalued the votes of the people. And, what rankled as much, his money came from the American Smelter and Refining Company, a giant industrial octopus that, like the major railroads dominated by Eastern financiers, held Colorado in economic bondage. Many Populist issues of the 1890s—especially the East's domination of the West, and big money's domination of the people—still mattered to Coloradans in the early twentieth century. As in the 1890s, the debate was not simply between rich and poor or West and East but also between competing business interests.

Nor in the clash of developers versus conservationists, smelter owners versus mine owners, and small businessmen versus large utilities should the power of personalities and political loyalties be overlooked. Indeed, as much as any other single factor (save his own abilities), Shafroth's support from *Rocky Mountain News* editor Thomas Patterson and U.S. Senator Henry M. Teller advanced his career. Both of those men found in Shafroth an antidote to Republican Guggenheimism and Democratic Speerism. Once a Republican, never a wild-talking radical, a thoughtful person, a man well known for his honesty, a champion of women's suffrage and thus dear to Colorado's women voters—Shafroth had all the attributes needed by a candidate for high office except good looks.

As they prepared for the 1908 Colorado gubernatorial campaign, Democrats once again talked reform. Patterson did so out of long-term conviction. Others, wanting to attract the votes that had gone to Lindsey and Haywood in 1906, wore their reform robes awkwardly because at heart they cared far more about winning than reforming. For Honest John it was the right time to run for governor. In 1907, he had participated in a national public lands convention in Denver. There he and other delegates pilloried Gifford Pinchot, the nation's chief forester, for putting restrictions on the use of the federal forest domain. Anti-conservation Coloradans applauded Shafroth for beating up on Eastern bureaucrats, but his brief public reappearance was not in itself enough to rekindle his political star. Somehow he had to emerge from the shadows or risk permanent eclipse.

A Winning Hand in 1908

From the time of his first election until he stumbled in 1902, Shafroth had almost automatically been re-elected to Congress. The public, appreciating his ability and applauding his defense of silver, did not demand that he spend much time or money campaigning. In 1904 leading Democrats, including Teller and Patterson, had pressured him into running for Colorado's at-large congressional seat. Defeated in that race, and largely absent from the public stage thereafter, he found that he had to wrestle for office in 1908. *Denver Post* scribe Hugh O'Neill, his pen dipped in cynicism, later commented: "Believing devoutly in the creed that the office should seek the man and not the man the office, he [Shafroth] waited some patient and fruitless years for further marks of public favor and, finding in the end that the office sought him not, he made a virtue of ambition."[10]

Ambition prompted Shafroth to seek the governorship in 1908, but it was his good sense of timing, his hard work, and a certain measure of luck that brought him victory. Luck dealt him a king early in the game and later delivered four aces. The king came in July 1908, when the Democratic Party held its national convention in Denver's new City Auditorium and nominated William Jennings Bryan for president. Trounced in 1896 and again in 1900, Bryan had little hope of defeating the Republican candidate, William Howard Taft. Yet the aging "Boy Orator of the Platte" remained a "Peerless Leader" in Colorado. He and Shafroth were old comrades from the silver crusade, and during the convention Bryan stayed with the Shafroths, making it clear that the king was on Honest John's side.

Thomas Patterson gave Shafroth his first ace by touting him in the *News* a week before Colorado Democrats were to meet in Pueblo for their state nominating convention. Reporter Alfred Damon Runyon wrote: "Now, of course, we all know that Shafroth couldn't be anything but honest if he tried, and the nickname is superfluous; but he got it years ago, and the indications are it will always stay with him."[11] At the convention, Shafroth got his second ace from Denver mayor Robert Speer. In 1908, as in 1906, two Denver delegations, both claiming to represent the city's Democrats, went to the state Democratic convention. In 1906 the reformers, among them John Shafroth, sent Speer packing. In 1908 the Speer faction, John Shafroth among them, sent the reformers packing. In both cases, Shafroth sided with the winners.

Had Honest John become a political chameleon—a reformer in 1906, a machine politician in 1908? Shafroth was not being dishonest in 1908. He attended the 1908 convention as a member of a Denver delegation that the *Rocky Mountain News* castigated as corporation lackeys. However, that delegation also included former governor Charles Thomas, a reformer, and the widely respected judge Robert W. Steele, as well as Shafroth. Clearly there was not an absolute division between the two camps. Shafroth belonged to the Speer delegation in name only. His heart, events would prove (and Speer's animosity toward him would show) still lay with the reformers. Shafroth's being part of the Speer delegation made sense for the reformers, as a kind of insurance policy against a Speer sweep. And the arrangement likely suited Speer as well because, for the sake of appearances, he needed an honest person or two in his tent, which was largely filled with party hacks.

At best it was an uneasy and strained alliance. Shafroth had helped ax Speer's slate at the 1906 convention and, in 1908, snubbed the mayor by not inviting him to dinner with William Jennings Bryan during the Democratic National Convention. Speer, it seems, planned to damn Shafroth with faint office by getting him nominated to the Colorado Supreme Court, a sedate black hole from which few politicians went on to higher places. Shafroth, who knew a kiss of oblivion when he was offered one, shunned the nomination.

The newly opened Denver City Auditorium hosted the 1908 Democratic National Convention. For the third time, the Democrats nominated Shafroth's friend William Jennings Bryan for president. A few months later—also for the third time—Bryan lost in the general election. Colorado Historical Society.

Speer then stumbled. Wheeling and dealing at the convention, he traded votes he did not have and made promises he could not keep. After being tricked by Speer, Cripple Creek gold king Jimmy Burns shouted in the lobby of Pueblo's Grand Hotel: "Mayor Speer is a double-crossing cur."[12] Another Speer double-cross victim, Atterson W. Rucker, had hoped with Speer's support to be nominated for governor; when Speer failed to help him, Rucker threw his votes to Shafroth. Combining these votes with ones he had picked up on his own, Shafroth won the gubernatorial nomination. As the dust cleared and the flies landed in Pueblo, Shafroth, at least minimally acceptable to Speer and well liked by Patterson and the reformers, could count on the support of a united Democratic Party.[13]

In his biography of Senator Henry M. Teller, Elmer Ellis gives another insight into the 1908 convention. Former governor Charles Thomas and Teller, suggests Ellis, cobbled together a compromise between Speer and the reformers to keep the Democrats united in their support for Bryan. The Speer forces got one prize: the convention's endorsement of Charles Hughes, Jr., to replace Teller, who had decided to retire at age seventy-eight. As their prize, the reformers got John Shafroth nominated for governor. It was an odd combination. Hughes, a corporate attorney, was firmly linked to David Moffat and William Gray Evans, the moguls who backed Speer, while Shafroth represented anti-corporate reform forces. But the Shafroth-Hughes alliance, no matter how strange, made political sense because it unified the Democrats.[14]

Like the origin of the toothpick, the ins-and-outs of the 1908 Colorado Democratic convention may never be known. Ultimately, the secrets of the convention mattered little in comparison with its result: John F. Shafroth's re-emergence on the political scene. For the citizens of Colorado, what ultimately mattered most was the Democrats' embrace of progressive reforms. If John Shafroth made good on the Democrats' platform promises, then his attendance at the 1908 convention with the Speer delegation could be easily forgiven. If, on the other hand, he turned out to be a Speer hack, he risked the progressives' enmity.

The Democratic platform constituted Shafroth's third ace. This fourteen-point manifesto called for reforms ranging from municipal ownership of utilities to state regulation of railroads. The platform makers decried the railroads' practice of giving free travel passes to politicians; they objected to the imposition of grazing fees on federal land; they opposed the creation of giant business combines known as trusts. During an era in which the wealthy and the upper middle class were falling in love with automobiles, the Democrats touted good roads. And in a day when individual depositors often lost their money if a bank failed, they demanded a law protecting bank deposits. They endorsed William Jennings Bryan for president, and they criticized William Howard Taft for favoring duty-free admission of sugar from the Philippines. And, in step with national progressives, they called for the direct election of U.S. senators, the use of the headless ballot, the creation of a direct primary system, and the introduction of amendments to the state's constitution allowing for initiatives and referendums.[15]

Republican infighting gave Shafroth his fourth ace. Meeting in Denver in September 1908, the Colorado Grand Old Party alienated some of its crusty stalwarts and many of its feisty progressives. William Gray Evans, a Republican despite his alliance with Speer in Denver, was barred from the convention; delegates refused to give him a vote and told him to sit in the gallery. Henry Buchtel, the incumbent Republican governor, was also exiled. If they had embraced reform and nominated a progressive, the Republicans might have capitalized on their break with Evans and Buchtel. But, seemingly intent on losing, the delegates nominated Jesse McDonald, a man *The Denver Post* described as "a worm," an embarrassment to the party because many Coloradans saw him as the thief who had stolen the governorship from Alva Adams in 1905.[16]

Holding an apparently unbeatable hand, Shafroth and the Democrats still had to bet it wisely. Money was a problem. Shafroth asked Lafe Pence to speak. Pence, Shafroth's opponent in the 1894 congressional election, was by 1908, like Shafroth, a Democrat. Shafroth admitted to Pence that the party needed more funds, "as the price of a hall and a band costs from $50.00 to $100.00 a night, and as the candidates agreed not to solicit from the corporations."[17] Despite limited resources, Shafroth traveled widely. Campaigning in the Arkansas Valley in mid-October, he hearkened back to an old theme in his political career, warning of the threat imported Filipino sugar posed to Colorado's sugar industry.

In Denver, Shafroth was well known and could count on Speer's support. To attract votes in the hinterland, he and other Democratic candidates pooled their money and, for $1,250, hired an engine and a three-car train for a six-day whirlwind tour. Slated to stop in more than thirty towns, from Florence (thirty miles west of Pueblo) to Durango (more than 330 miles southwest of Denver), the "Red, White and Blue special" brought the office-seekers local and statewide publicity. On October 19, 1908, as the train prepared to leave Denver, the *Rocky Mountain News* promised: "[T]here will be no let up in the warfare that this band of Democratic giants will wage." Shafroth, suffering from a severe cold for much of the trip, waged war hoarsely. At Florence, he explained the merits of the direct primary. In Salida he accused President Taft and the Republicans of being spendthrifts. In Ouray he promised voters that Democrats would pass bank guaranty laws to protect individuals' accounts. In Monte Vista he attacked national Republicans for conservation policies that kept homesteaders off of some Colorado land. Bonfires lit Harrison Avenue in Leadville as the candidates rode through a snowstorm to speak to a large crowd at the Elks' opera house. A band welcomed them to Montrose. In Durango, "a band and torch light procession paraded the streets."[18]

Damon Runyon, then a twenty-four year-old *Rocky Mountain News* reporter, traveled with the politicos and ballyhooed the trip. Runyon, later renowned as a syndicated New York columnist and the inspiration for the Broadway musical *Guys and Dolls*, praised the comforts of the cars, which included "Ballyclaire," once the private conveyance of the president of the Denver & Rio Grande Railroad. Echoing the *News'* strong pro-Shafroth line, Runyon praised Shafroth: "People like him instinctively. . . . Big physically, his mentality is big."[19]

As election day approached, the *Rocky Mountain News* predicted victory for the Democrats. The campaign had gone well. Republicans tried to drown Shafroth as a cat's-paw of the Denver Union Water Company because he had done legal work for the company, but Shafroth shook off the charge.[20] When a black cat wandered onto the stage while Shafroth was speaking in Pueblo, a local wag shouted: "Bad luck."[21] But the feline left the candidate unscratched. On November 3, 1908, he was elected governor, beating Jesse McDonald by nearly twelve thousand votes. Shafroth's son, George, wrote in his diary: "Hurray, Pa was elected easy."[22]

The other members of the Shafroth family soon found that they, too, had been elected. "Ma got her picture in the paper," George noted on November 8, "and she says she doesn't like it." The same day, George, who had not left home for fifteen months because of his spinal tuberculosis, went out to dinner with the family. Profiling the Shafroths in the January 15, 1909, *Denver Times*, reporter Thomas Hunter noted that Virginia was not politically active, although she belonged to several women's groups, including the Monday Club and the Round Table Club. "Mrs. Shafroth," Hunter wrote, "admits that she takes little interest in the uncertain game of politics other than consuming desire to see her husband realize his ambitions."

Much of the Shafroths' family life centered around their four sons, two of whom were by late 1908 away from home. Jack, the eldest, had recently graduated from the U.S. Naval Academy and was aboard the *U.S.S. Virginia*, a battleship with the Great White Fleet, steaming around the world to demonstrate American sea power. Morrison, son number two, was halfway through his college career at the University of Michigan and planning to become a lawyer. William, the youngest, was at East High School, from which he hoped to graduate at age fifteen.

George, age seventeen, had not been able to attend school for two years. Imprisoned in a plaster cast, he stayed in his room, read voluminously, visited with friends, and followed the adventures of his brothers. From Colombo in Ceylon [Sri Lanka], Jack posted a letter to George in mid-November 1908: "So you feel pretty good do you over being the governor's son? Well so do I."[23] Unable to attend Shafroth's inauguration on January 12, 1909, George previewed his father's speech the night before and pronounced it "a good one all right."[24] Whether or not Shafroth turned out to be good for Colorado, however, would depend not on the opinion of an admiring son but on John Franklin's ability to raise politics above the level of Jesse McDonald and Henry Buchtel—to make the reforms promised by the Democrats into realities.

Shafroth poses in July 1908, a few months before being elected to his first term as Colorado's governor. Colorado Historical Society.

Chapter Four
Reform
Battles

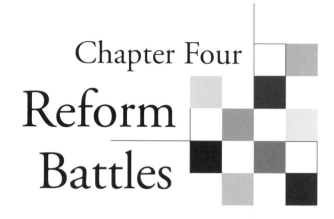

A governor's salute—seventeen guns fired from the Colorado State Capitol grounds—heralded John Franklin Shafroth's inaugural on January 12, 1909. Previous governors had delivered outdoor addresses on the Capitol lawn to shivering onlookers, most of whom could not hear the speakers. Sensible Shafroth gave his address in City Auditorium, where eight thousand people sat comfortably in warm seats from which they could easily hear him. The new auditorium was almost sacred space for Democrats. Mayor Speer had built the edifice, which opened shortly before the national Democrats arrived in mid-summer 1908 to nominate William Jennings Bryan for president. Standing in the House of Speer, and beholden to Speer at least in part for his election, Shafroth delivered a reform message that the mayor and his allies did not want to hear. Initiative, referendum, direct primaries, headless ballots, direct election of U.S. senators, laws to protect individuals' bank deposits, and railroad regulations—the new governor vowed to keep all of these Democratic campaign pledges.

Honoring those promises was to prove far more difficult than making them. For the first time in Colorado's history, Democrats controlled the governor's office and both houses of the state legislature—but Shafroth did not control the Democratic legislators, many of whom were anti-reform. The *Denver Republican*, miffed at not seeing a Republican in the governor's chair, gleefully and accurately predicted trouble for Shafroth as he wrestled with a divided party: "It will be interesting to watch the two divisions work at cross purposes."[1]

Government Economy: "Apple Pie" John

Even before he took office, Shafroth signaled his reform intentions by refusing to accept the free passes that railroads customarily handed out to officials. And, telling the party leadership that he was his own man, he refused to submit his patronage nominations to the "organization" for approval.[2] Among Shafroth's appointments, that of Thomas J. Tynan as warden of the state penitentiary at Cañon City proved to be particularly fortunate. Tynan, a traveling salesman for the Denver-based Morey Mercantile Company, had no background in prison management. Yet what he lacked in experience, he made up for in common sense. "Seven hundred idle men and more than a score of idle women" bothered him "because it was unbusinesslike and wasteful."[3] So he put the prisoners to work building roads and farming.

The idea of saving money while reforming criminals appealed to Shafroth, who had promised voters an economical administration. A frugal and careful man in managing his own affairs—he did not put electricity into his home nor enjoy a desk phone there until 1909—he believed the state should be run the same way. In his inaugural address he quickly disposed of one expensive notion by opposing a proposal to build an extension onto the State Capitol.

Shortly after he took office, Shafroth banned state agencies from engaging in lobbying. It was "preposterous," he said, for bureaucrats to use public funds to influence legislators who, in turn, appropriated funds to the bureaucrats. In his inaugural address he urged creation of a single board to oversee higher education in the state. And, although that idea fizzled, he tried to get the universities and colleges to cut down on course duplication and otherwise reduce costs. In a move which raised parsimony to the level of stinginess, Shafroth saved thirty dollars by keeping the National Guard band from playing at the New Year's Eve reception at the State Capitol.[4]

Costly meals rankled the governor as much as pricey music. Shafroth had a good appetite himself, something he once demonstrated by downing 485 slimy morsels in an oyster-eating contest. Still, he saw no reason for state employees to feast at public expense. Late in 1909 he set allowances for state officers at fifty cents per meal in Denver and seventy-five cents outside the city. Traveling officials, he argued, should be able to subsist on a meal of an egg, or a serving of roast beef, and a piece of apple pie. When one functionary presented a bill for $1 to cover a meal on a train, Shafroth discovered that the sybaritic bureaucrat had ordered a twenty-five-cent pineapple dessert. "But you could have eaten pie," scolded the governor. "By Jimny," responded the man, "I didn't want pie."[5] Poking fun at Shafroth, the *Denver Republican* nicknamed him "Apple Pie" John, a tag it reiterated for years.

Colorado's state auditor, Roady Kenehan, Sr., a "brawny man, a pleasing and convincing talker and logician," supported Shafroth's penny-pinching with all the vigor and vengeance of a zealot accountant.[6] A native of Ireland, Kenehan came to Denver in the early 1880s. He learned the value of a dollar by toiling as a blacksmith and horseshoer and learned how to keep track of the dollars by serving as a union official. On becoming auditor, he posed as a Samson among profligate Philistines. Like a Samson with a good sense of public relations, he decided to snatch headlines as he shook up government.

Kenehan would not, for example, pay for two telegrams sent out of state to recruit employees for the penitentiary. He argued that those were unnecessary expenditures because Colorado had persons qualified for the positions. And the "Blacksmith Auditor" refused to reimburse a member of the State Board of Charities who had exceeded guidelines by eating a meal costing $1.15. Colorado's secretary of state, James B. Pearce, also a

John Shafroth arrives at the Colorado State Capitol for his inauguration as governor on January 12, 1909. Colorado Historical Society.

MONTROSE LIBRARY DISTR
320 So. 2nd St.
Montrose, CO 81401

Democrat, disagreed with such petty cost-cutting, saying: "I never calculate the price of my food when I am eating. Allowing such mercenary matters to enter into what would be an enjoyable occasion spoils my appetite."[7]

Shafroth himself occasionally felt Kenehan's hammer. When in the summer of 1909 the governor left the state to accept an honorary degree from his alma mater, the University of Michigan, Kenehan docked him $13.86 a day because Shafroth was absent on a private trip. Honest John reluctantly swallowed that nit-picking, although he contended that his salary was fixed at $5,000 a year and could not be reduced by the auditor. Unabashed, Kenehan again pared Shafroth's salary for the days he spent with other governors and President Taft on a Mississippi River steamboat trip.[8]

At its worst, Shafroth and Kenehan's economizing drive was short-sighted. In 1909 the General Assembly appropriated $5,000 to inoculate children against diphtheria, which killed about one hundred youngsters each year. Shafroth axed the measure and saved the money, suggesting that it made as much sense to provide those funds as it would to give doctors free horses and buggies.[9] At its best, Shafroth's frugality cut down on the pork-barrel expenditures that legislators used to win favor in their home districts. He vetoed nearly a hundred bills for piece-meal road improvements, insisting instead on statewide road planning, which he helped initiate through establishment of the Colorado Highway Commission in 1909. Kenehan and Shafroth's attention to details occasionally netted a stinking fish such as state boiler inspector Edward J. Whitney, who had kept three sets of books in order to hide $25,000 in embezzled funds.[10]

While he watched the budget closely, Shafroth was far-sighted enough to fund important state projects. Colorado grew and prospered between 1900 and 1910, adding nearly 26,000 people a year to reach a 1910 population of 799,024. Early in the decade, lawmakers hesitated to spend. With Shafroth's blessing the Seventeenth General Assembly made up for their predecessors' stinginess by approving nearly a million dollars for state institutions, including money for buildings at the University of Colorado, the state reformatory, and a home for the "feeble-minded" in Arvada.[11]

Had Shafroth spent his time vetoing road bills and scrutinizing meal costs, his money-saving quest would have made him look silly. Had he simply presided over an administration that improved state institutions, he would have been lost in the crowd of the state's many average governors. He had not been elected to haggle over nickels nor to catch errant boiler inspectors but to make sweeping changes. It was in accomplishing those reforms that he was to assure himself a premier place among the state's chief executives.

Reform Skirmishes

At his inauguration, Shafroth anchored his administration on the bedrock of the reform platform upon which he and other Democrats had been elected. Those pledges, he told the audience, "constitute a contract between the people and us and should be faithfully kept."[12] Keeping faith with the people, however, was not a priority for many old-line Democrats. Men such as the president pro tem of the State Senate, weather-beaten William H. "Billy" Adams—also known as the Duke of Conejos County—had no reason to pass a direct primary bill, which could have destroyed the party convention system that put them in office. Such politicos saw no merit in curtailing the corporations that supported them and their associates, nor in diluting their legislative power by allowing for initiatives and referendums. Unconvinced by the musings of reform-minded intellectuals, they boasted of their homespun habits. Adams once turned down an honorary degree, explaining, "[T]hose things are for people who read books. I just read newspapers."[13] Nor were Democrats alone in opposing reform. Many Republicans voted with Billy Adams.

The anti-reformers' task was simple, and they knew how to accomplish it. Shafroth would be governor for two years, but he had to redeem the platform pledges between mid-January and early April 1909, when the legislature was in session. The Seventeenth General Assembly would only meet for a total of ninety days during Shafroth's administration; not until January 1911 would lawmakers convene again. By then, the anti-reformers calculated, Shafroth would no longer be governor; he had said he would not run again unless his personal finances suddenly improved a great deal.[14] At any rate, no one had ever been elected to back-to-back gubernatorial terms since Colorado became a state in 1876.

Adams, after more than twenty years in the legislature, fully merited his reputation as "the greatest obstructionist who ever sat in the legislative halls of this state."[15] By delaying and maneuvering, by passing weak laws and emasculating good proposals, by trading votes and making deals, he and his allies planned to thwart the progressives. The issues were not the ones that usually kept lawmakers busy—appointments to state positions, judicial district boundaries, and appropriations for prisons, schools, and roads.[16] The reformers proposed nothing less than a peaceful revolution, a series of measures designed to change who ruled—to restore government to the people.

Borrowing parts of their creed from the Populists, the Herculean reformers of the Progressive Era sallied forth to slay the hydra-headed monster of boss politicians, underworld kings, and corporation moguls. Decades later, some historians came to view Speer and other cigar-chomping big-city bosses in a less moralistic, more forgiving light, casting them as friends of the urban poor. Speer, after all, built an elegant bathhouse in a Denver slum, created parks and a zoo, and even proposed a city bakery to lower the price of bread. But those noble deeds hardly satisfied early-twentieth-century reformers, who castigated the Speer-Evans machine as the embodiment of evil.

The saints, by their own definition, were the reformers, who came to be known as progressives. Among this disparate crew of men and women, which the *Rocky Mountain News* dubbed the "Young Turks," stood the brilliant lawyer Edward P. Costigan, who would eventually make a substantial mark in Colorado politics. Thomas Patterson, an old Turk, and his stable of writers at the *Rocky Mountain News* vigorously advocated reform, while George Creel, a "sin slayer who lived in a cosmos of black and white," fought the good fight at *The Denver Post* and, later, the *News*.[17] And the feisty bantamweight dynamo of reform energy, Judge Benjamin Barr Lindsey, focused national attention on Colorado's corruption in 1910 with the publication of his muckracking classic, *The Beast*. Women, including club leader Sarah Platt Decker and journalist Ellis Meredith, did their part, organizing precincts and preaching reform.[18] Decker headed the Colorado Federation of Women's Clubs and personally staffed that organization's lobbying office in the Colorado State Capitol. When the women were temporarily evicted from the Capitol, Governor Shafroth let them use his office.

Among those strident fighters for the right, John Franklin Shafroth, cautious and cerebral, was less a flashy gladiator than a massive glacier, inching deliberately and inexorably forward. With the religious rhetoric of crusaders, Shafroth and the other progressives, as Theodore Roosevelt later put it, stood "at Armageddon" and "battle[d] for the Lord."[19] And with equal fervor, born of their instinct for political and economic self-preservation, the opponents of change fought for the status quo.

At the beginning of the 1909 legislative session, Harry L. Lubers, like Billy Adams a stick-in-the-mud rural legislator, was elected Speaker of the House, and he appointed his mossy ilk to key committees. Progressives had some power on important committees in the State Senate but, outmaneuvered by Adams and other stand-patters, could not muster the votes to overcome the combination of reactionary Democrats and Republicans.

On February 13, Shafroth tried to persuade Lubers to get a direct primary bill passed in the House. A week later, reform Democrats invited William Jennings Bryan to lecture legislators. No doubt some stodgy solons squirmed in their seats when Bryan diagnosed the failure of reform: "The progress of Democracy has been slow because there are too many Judases among the apostles of Democracy . . . . If there are those among you who have changed your minds since election regarding your platform you should be conscientious enough to resign."[20]

Lawmakers applauded, but the sly Judases remained busy filibustering, feinting, dodging, and otherwise sabotaging progressive proposals. Shafroth worked behind the scenes to counter these tactics. Finally, his patience exhausted, he went public on March 22, two weeks before the Assembly was slated to adjourn. The platform pledges, Shafroth lectured the Democrats, must be honored: "To concede that a public official may willfully evade, or openly violate a party pledge upon which he secured an election is to surrender the vital principles of representative government." For those who wished to abandon the platform, Shafroth repeated Bryan's draconian order: "He should resign his seat now." Adding threat to pressure, the governor urged political organizations in the counties to "meet in mass assembly and demand that [legislators] vote for these party measures or resign." And if that did not do the trick, the governor warned, "I expect to call an extra session of the General Assembly."[21]

Ignoring Bryan and spurning Shafroth, balky legislators whiled their time away. Members of the House invaded the Senate and with adolescent glee threw wet sponges at the senators, for which crime they were required to buy the soggy solons cigars. Lawmakers found time to attend the circus then in town. As the session wound down, the junior Ciceros spent twelve hours debating establishment of a home for persons with limited mental capacity. "Why a home for mental defectives," joked an onlooker, "when we have this?"[22] After ninety days in session, the Seventeenth General Assembly adjourned in early April, having scuttled the direct primary bill, the headless ballot, a bank deposit guaranty law, an eight-hour workday for miners, a statute limiting women to eight hours of work a day in certain occupations, and constitutional amendments to allow initiatives and referendums.[23]

Perhaps out of some sensitivity to public opinion, the Assembly passed a few forward-looking measures, among them a statute, which Shafroth crafted, forbidding all campaign donations and limiting the amount candidates could spend on their races. Instead, campaigns were to be financed with public funds, thereby breaking the money strings with which the wealthy made politicians dance.

That an anti-reform legislature would embrace such a sweeping reform law is hard to fathom. A cynic might guess that the anti-reformers liked the bill's greatest flaw. By basing campaign appropriations on each party's share of the gubernatorial vote in the previous election, the measure made it exceedingly difficult for a new third party to rise. Using 1908 as a base, Democrats and Republicans were slated to get $32,230 and $29,700, respectively, in the 1910 election, while Socialists and Prohibitionists would receive less than $2,000 each. New parties would not be eligible for any funds until they racked up votes for their gubernatorial candidate, something that, lacking money, they would find hard to do.

Perhaps anti-reform legislators voted for the statute because they correctly judged that it would not survive court review. The disciples of the status quo breathed easier when the Colorado Supreme Court, in a unanimous decision, declared the campaign finance law unconstitutional in 1910. Even many progressives were happy with the decision, because they were trying to field a third party in 1910 and would have been severely limited by the new campaign finance rules.[24]

The Factory Inspection Act also initially turned out to be a fireless dragon. It set up a state Department of Factory Inspection and gave inspectors the right to enforce laws regarding the employment of women and children. On the surface that sounded like real reform. In truth, there were no laws regarding the employment of women and children, so the inspectors had little authority except to make inspections and issue reports. They used that power to focus attention on unsafe and inhumane factory conditions, and in 1911 the General Assembly finally enacted a law protecting working children.[25]

Nibbling at the edges of reform, the lawmakers made it illegal for pimps to hold prostitutes in virtual slavery and authorized a home for persons of limited mental ability. Sensitive to the evil of having unlicensed barbers snipping away throughout the state, the lawmakers established a Board of Examiners to regulate them. And the Assembly redeemed one of the Democratic platform pledges by establishing a highway commission to plan the state's road network.[26]

Shafroth's son George shared his father's frustration with the General Assembly. "They are a sore bunch," George wrote in his diary. "It is the punkiest legislature I ever saw."[27] Stubborn Shafroth refused to give up. "We have lost a skirmish," he said. "That's all. The real campaign is just beginning and it can have but one ending—a complete triumph for the cause of reform."[28] His big gun in that campaign was his threat to call a special session of the Assembly, but even that was of limited use because the special session would comprise the same lawmakers who had skillfully sabotaged reform in the regular session. And, as the mossbacks constantly harped, an extra session would cost money.

The 1910 Special Session

When he beat John Howard Parnell in the 1897 chess match between the U.S. House of Representatives and the British House of Commons, Shafroth pondered his moves carefully, usually taking all the time he was allowed. During 1909 and 1910, in his high-stakes game with the Assembly, he followed the same strategy. By delaying the special-session call, he bought time to plan his moves and drum up support. Legislators could be pressured, editorials written, mass meetings held. All the while Shafroth kept the old guard off their guard—sometimes saying the special session would likely occur at one time, then shifting the target date.

As the clamor for the extra session rose through 1909, Shafroth delayed, thinking it best to hold the session close to the 1910 elections in order to pressure legislators who would be running again soon after the General Assembly met. By early 1910, however, it appeared that he might have waited too long. Both Auditor Kenehan and State Treasurer William J. Galligan sided with the anti-reformers. Whimpering about the nearly $60,000 they estimated the special session would cost, they vigorously urged Shafroth to change his mind. He refused, explaining: "What would be the use? I would call them in, ask them if they wanted an Extra Session, and when they said 'no,' I would say, 'Well there is going to be one anyway.'"[29]

In March 1910, many Democratic newspaper editors asked the governor not to summon a special session unless he could get legislators to promise in advance to pass the progressive measures. Thomas Patterson of the *Rocky Mountain News* backed Shafroth, predicting the death of the Democratic Party if it failed to support reform. Party leaders, however, remained deaf to Patterson's warnings and Shafroth's pleas. In April, anti-reformers among the Democrats convinced the party's central committee to pass a resolution asking Shafroth to forget the special session.

Abandoned by his own party's leadership, Shafroth shot back: "The salvation of the Democratic party depends upon our keeping faith with the voters. I will call the legislators together to redeem those pledges. I will call the extra session for some date in August."[30] Under that cloud, the anti-reformers continued to arm-wrestle the reformers. In May 1910 the apostles of the status quo suffered a broken wrist.

That month witnessed a rare combination of heavenly happenings: the return of Halley's Comet after an absence of three-quarters of a century, accompanied by a total lunar eclipse. As amazing as those celestial marvels was the temporary defeat of Boss Speer and William Gray Evans. Reformers, by a narrow margin, scuttled the Denver Union Water Company's attempt to secure a twenty-year franchise on favorable terms. The setback disheartened the Speer-Evans combine, which reputedly had wasted $750,000 on the franchise campaign. "Amazed, confused, baffled, impotent," said the *Rocky Mountain News*, "the bosses stared at each other desolately."[31]

The progressives did more than outfox the Denver Union Water Company. They also persuaded voters to approve the use of the initiative and referendum in local affairs, thus giving Denverites the right to block city council ordinances.[32] The old guard's groans reverberated beyond Denver. If the Goliaths—Speer and Evans—could be crushed on their home turf, then might not the reformers—led by their determined David, John Franklin Shafroth—rout the anti-reformers in the General Assembly? Sensing that the time was right to strike, Shafroth on July 14 announced that the special session would convene on August 9, 1910.[33] That was only twelve weeks before the 1910 elections, a frightening prospect to anti-reform legislators, who would have to face voters soon after the session ended.

Shafroth greeted the legislators on the afternoon of August 9. Keeping in mind the old adage that more flies can be caught with honey than with vinegar, he praised lawmakers for their accomplishments during the regular session in early 1909. He thanked them for passing the campaign finance bill, for creating a highway commission, for establishing the state factory inspector's office, and for approving a $100,000 museum across Fourteenth Avenue from the State Capitol for the State Historical Society. Those measures and others, he said, entitled the Seventeenth General Assembly to claim "the best record of any in the history of the state of Colorado."[34]

"As proud as I am of these achievements of this general assembly," the governor continued, "I feel that it would be a shame if such an excellent record should be marred by the failure to redeem the pledges made to the people."[35] A tenacious bulldog with a big bone, Shafroth would not let go. The pledges, he said—as he had said before and would say again—must be redeemed. Initiative and referendum amendments to the state constitution must be put before the people. Shafroth also challenged the special session to pass measures providing for the headless ballot, the direct election of U.S. senators, the direct primary system, voter registration, a public service commission, and a state railroad commission. He insisted on a bank guaranty law to protect depositors, but he backed away from a proposal to require strong banks to contribute to a fund that would be largely used by weak banks. Instead, he gave bankers a choice: They could either contribute to a fund to protect depositors in any failed bank, or they could purchase a surety bond to protect their own depositors.

The special session could only address the items the governor put before it. By centering attention on eight issues, Shafroth assured that voters would hold the legislators responsible for their action or inaction. As in the regular session of January-April 1909, the anti-reformers initially dominated the 1910 special session, but their power had weakened. For sixteen months Shafroth, Patterson, Creel, Costigan, and other reformers, both Democrats and Republicans, had beat out their message so loudly and so consistently that even the ward heelers of Denver and the cracker-barrel politicians of the hinterland had to listen. Early in the special session, reformers took control of the House of Representatives. In the Senate, Billy Adams kept reformers at bay until August 26, when the Democrats agreed to allow a full Senate vote on Shafroth's initiative and referendum proposal.

Why the anti-reformers allowed that fateful vote is unclear. Shafroth was leaning on Adams; perhaps he or a couple of his friends buckled. Or maybe Adams, a master of maneuver, was merely engaging in a temporary, strategic retreat. Allowing the two measures to come to a vote did not guarantee passage; as constitutional amendments, they required two-thirds approval in

As this Denver Post *cartoon of August 9, 1910, suggests, Governor Shafroth had to crack a few whips during the 1910 special session to get the reform legislation he sought. Colorado Historical Society.*

the Senate and the House before being sent to the people for final ratification in a general election. Adams knew he had Republican allies in the Senate. If they voted with him and the other stand-pat Democrats, his record as the legislature's greatest obstructionist would remain unblemished. And if Adams held the line in the Senate, Honest John Shafroth's reform career, indeed his political career, would likely come to an end.

Shafroth had faced several critical turning points in his political life. In 1896 he put support for silver before party loyalty and bolted from the Republican Party. It was a wise and well-timed move. In 1904 he resigned from Congress. That too was smart and well timed. In late August 1910, Shafroth again faced a do-or-die moment. Once again, his adroit moves and sense of timing served him well.

In 1908, Shafroth's association with William Jennings Bryan had helped him become governor. In 1909, he tried unsuccessfully to use Bryan as a goad to promote reform. In 1910 the governor got help from a new player— one as powerful as a queen, though he wore the trappings of a knight. His benefactor, ironically, was a Republican: Theodore Roosevelt, ex-president of the United States. Like a big wind, Roosevelt blew into Denver for one day on August 29, 1910, and within a week, after the dust settled a little, the governor knew that the great Roosevelt gust had blown the reform cause considerable good.

Chapter Five
Reform at High Tide

T heodore Roosevelt, a fact of nature like canyons, mountains, and mesas, mesmerized Americans not simply because of what he did but also—mainly—because of what he was. He was energy, drama, and fun, chuckwagon dinners, African safaris, and torchlight parades, a larger-than-life figure worthy of remembrance on Mount Rushmore. Although many Coloradans disagreed with his conservation policies, they admired Roosevelt for his energy, enjoyed him as an entertainer, and appreciated him because he loved the West.

In 1909 Roosevelt turned the presidency over to William Howard Taft and went to Africa to kill lions, tigers, elephants, and most anything else unlucky enough to cross his path. When rumors reached him suggesting that Taft was not a worthy successor, Roosevelt returned home. In the summer of 1910 he raced around the West and Midwest giving speeches. Still nominally a Republican, he staked out a position to Taft's left, a position he could use to shape the Republican Party, a position he might use to mount a bid for the presidency, a position that eventually aligned his ideas with many of those held by Shafroth and other progressives.[1]

Roosevelt arrived at Denver's Union Station a little before 11 A.M. on Monday, August 29, and was greeted by Governor Shafroth, Mayor Speer, and other dignitaries. Thousands cheered as the former president rode in a horse-drawn carriage through downtown. The Rough Riders, Teddy's own troops from the Spanish American War, put on a grand show for their commander, who reached out and shook hands, by one account, at the rate of 118 grips a minute. The Colorado National Guard, veterans of the Civil and

Spanish American wars, and regular Army troops strutted, accompanied by seven bands. Veterans of the Civil War battle of Shiloh rode in a convoy of a dozen automobiles, along with newspaper reporters and bigwigs such as Senator Charles Hughes, Jr. Sheriffs and their deputies paraded on horseback, giving TR a taste of the vanishing West—a taste that momentarily turned sour when a clumsy lawman dropped his gun, sending a bullet into the leg of Sheriff I. A. Williams of Delta County. The police assumed Roosevelt had been shot and rushed to protect him, relaxing moments later when Sheriff Williams hobbled from his horse.[2]

After the parade, Roosevelt, Shafroth, and Speer motored to Overland Park in South Denver for a chuckwagon lunch. There TR ate steak from a tin plate, feasting on the publicity. "Cameras to the right of him, cameras to the left of him," photographers shot pictures of every bite he took.[3] In midafternoon he spoke at the auditorium and later addressed the legislature. Organizers of the day's festivities snubbed Judge Ben Lindsey, Colorado's most vocal and famous gadfly, but Roosevelt spied him in the crowd and exclaimed: "Here is the man I've been demanding to see all day." The high priests of the status quo milled around helplessly as Roosevelt accorded Lindsey a place of honor on the speaker's platform.[4]

The sight of Teddy hobnobbing with Lindsey distressed Republican bosses, who rightly feared the effect Roosevelt might have on state legislators. Dr. Hubert Work, chairman of Colorado's Republican Party, gathered Republican senators at the Brown Palace Hotel shortly before Roosevelt was to address the General Assembly. There Work denounced the initiative and referendum as "un-American, un-Republican, contrary to arithmetic, calculated to destroy representative government."[5]

Shafroth and the reform Democrats had been wooing Republicans for months. As Ben Lindsey put it: "The real struggle is not between the two old parties . . . It is between the people and privilege."[6] The May 1910 defeat of the Speer-Evans machine in Denver had been engineered by Democrats and Republicans united as the Citizens' Party. In June, Lindsey and others formed a third party embracing reformers of all political persuasions.[7] Shafroth had been through the rough mill of party breakup in the 1890s, when he had joined a coalition of Republicans, Silver Republicans, Populists, and Democrats. Unraveling established parties was a risky step, one he probably preferred not to take but was willing to chance.

In his August 9 message at the start of the special legislative session, Shafroth quoted Abraham Lincoln, the greatest of Republicans, in asking the lawmakers to make "'government of the people, for the people, and by the people,' a reality."[8] In mid-August, with time wasting away, the *Rocky Mountain News* warned Republicans that if they did not allow reform, "they put themselves in a hole, and pull the hole in after them."[9] George Creel, writing in *The Denver Post* on August 18, characterized anti-reform Republicans as "corporation coolies, perfectly trained to fetch and carry, lie down, roll over and play dead." Inside the legislature, Republicans such as John B. Stephen of Colorado City urged their colleagues to support reform. Outside the legislature, progressive Republicans such as Merle D. Vincent of Paonia and Edward Costigan of Denver agitated for change.

At 4:15 P.M. on August 29, 1910, Theodore Roosevelt entered the packed House chamber in the Capitol to nervous cheers. Reformers hoped he would say what they wanted. Anti-reformers feared he would say what they did not want. And Roosevelt himself faced a dilemma with horns as savage as a rodeo bull's. If he sided with the reformers, he might split the Republican Party. If he sided with the anti-reformers, he would alienate his supporters among Republican insurgents.

During his August 1910 visit to Denver, Theodore Roosevelt positioned himself— rhetorically and, here, literally—between Mayor Speer (left), a conservative anti- reform Democrat, and reform-minded Governor Shafroth, who fought Speer's machine. Denver Public Library, Western History Collection.

Seeing one woman member of the Assembly among the sea of men, Roosevelt broke the tension by beginning his remarks: "Lady and gentlemen." He continued: "I have been asked to speak to you about your troubles. To relieve the obvious nervousness of gentlemen, I will say that I am not going to do it. Of those who made the request of me to do so each radically differed from the others as to what I should say."[10]

Brave Roosevelt, courageous Teddy, thrust out his jaw, clenched his teeth, and straddled the fence. Reformers applauded his attack on the U.S. Supreme Court because they, too, believed the courts, particularly in Colorado, were enemies of progress. Anti-reformers rejoiced when Roosevelt told the audience to "distrust the demagogue and the visionary." Then, in the same sentence, he warned against the "hidebound conservative, who though honest himself, proves himself the greatest friend of corruption by carrying his opposition to reforms to an extreme."[11] After fifteen entertaining minutes, Roosevelt left the bully pulpit—his reputation as a semi-loyal Republican more or less intact, his reputation as a budding progressive not too badly tarnished.

The speech gave Shafroth only weak ammunition. But later in the day Roosevelt, speaking at a banquet, praised Merle Vincent, a young progressive Republican who hoped to be nominated for governor. The signal was obvious: Roosevelt, pal of Merle Vincent and Ben Lindsey, favored the reformers.

Shafroth got even better news two days later, on August 31, when Roosevelt delivered a major address in Osawatomie, Kansas. Warmly embracing progressive ideas, including direct primaries, regulation of public utilities, and the initiative, the ex-president gave the speech Shafroth wished Roosevelt had given in Colorado. "No man," said TR, "should make a promise before an election that he does not intend to keep after election, and if he does not keep it, hunt him out." Roosevelt likely intended that shot for President Taft. It also wounded those Colorado legislators who failed to keep their pledges.

Why did Roosevelt give that speech in Osawatomie rather than in Denver? Perhaps, out of courtesy and caution, he did not want to attack the troglodytes among Colorado's Republicans on their home turf. Perhaps his own ideas were still evolving, and his association with the Colorado progressives stiffened his backbone. Or maybe he held his fire until he could stand at Osawatomie, sacred to the memory of anti-slavery crusader John Brown, and announce a new crusade.

Roosevelt's Kansas address kept the progressive whirlwind spinning in Colorado. *The Denver Post* reported the speech on the evening of August 31; the *Rocky Mountain News,* on the morning of September 1. Throughout the day of September 1, Senate Republicans stampeded into the reform camp.

Their support, added to that of reform Democrats, gave the initiative and referendum measures the two-thirds majority needed to pass. Other legislators, both Republicans and Democrats, thinking it wise to vote with the victors, quickly changed their positions. Senator Billy Adams suddenly spouted reform. Senator Horace T. De Long, a Republican obstructionist, underwent a similar miraculous conversion, prompted perhaps by a telegram he received from thirty-five constituents in Grand Junction: "Vote for the initiative and referendum tomorrow when it comes up for third reading, and do your best to help its passage, or don't come home."[12]

Roosevelt made several moves that helped swing the balance in Shafroth's favor, but Shafroth himself engineered the progressive victory. By calling the special session, by timing it immediately before the 1910 state party conventions, and by steadfastly insisting that Democrats live up to their platform pledges, the governor laid siege to the anti-reformers.

Initiative and Referendum: "The Greatest Piece of Legislation"

On August 31, the same day TR spoke in Kansas, as reform hung in the balance in Colorado, Shafroth, a master of timing and strategy, made another bold move. He announced that he would accept renomination for governor. That stroke, coupled with the blows already struck by Roosevelt, unhinged many anti-reform legislators, who envisioned their political careers in ruins if they had to run in November against a powerful ticket led by Shafroth. Roosevelt alone may not have converted them; faced with Roosevelt plus Shafroth, they reluctantly passed the initiative and referendum measures.

The governor's decision to run again seemed to contradict his earlier statements. On the day of his inauguration, January 12, 1909, he had declared he would not seek a second term, and he repeated that position in December 1909. Being governor of a "great state," he complained in April 1910, was "not what it is cracked up to be. I've got to get out once in a while to do a little business on the side to make ends meet. It's an awful expensive job being governor."[13] In 1904, Shafroth had refused to be considered for governor because of the damage that years of public service had done to his finances. As governor he earned $5,000 a year, far less than he could have earned practicing law. Money mattered to him; public service, principles, ambition, and the game of politics mattered more. And, needing the threat of a second term to press his agenda in the legislature, Shafroth decided to make do with that $5,000 salary for two more years. By couching his statements about re-election in terms of his personal finances, rather than political or philosophical principles, Shafroth left himself free to change his mind. Nor did running for a second two-year term put him at risk with the voters, who often re-elected legislators to additional terms.

Shafroth's decision to run again, coupled with the Roosevelt tornado, induced the reluctant legislators to approve the initiative and referendum amendments on September 1; if the voters assented, the measures would become part of the state constitution. Informed of the victory, the governor danced a few jig steps and declared that the extra session had been well worth the cost. The initiative and referendum, he believed, held the key to all other reform. If the General Assembly failed to do the people's work, the people could use the initiative process to create their own laws. If lawmakers passed bad laws, the people could use the referendum process to repeal them. On September 2, as he signed the initiative and referendum proposals (which voters would decide on in early November), he crowed: "This is the greatest piece of legislation enacted by the General Assembly of Colorado since the constitution of the state was adopted in 1876."[14]

Having handed Shafroth and the progressives a major victory, the stand-patters regrouped. In early September they passed a weak railroad commission bill that failed to give the commissioners the power to fix rates; then the session recessed, as lawmakers and the public turned their attention to the state nominating conventions.[15]

The Democrats met September 14 in Denver. Shortly after Shafroth announced his candidacy, an anonymous Republican leader admitted: "I do not think we have a man in our ranks who has a ghost of a chance against him."[16] Yet Shafroth's strength and popularity worked against him among powerful Democratic wire-pullers, who backed Dr. Benjamin L. Jefferson of Routt County for the party's gubernatorial nomination. Speer's Denver machine named its usual roster of party hacks to the state convention and insisted that they support Jefferson.

Reformers in Denver fielded their own slate of delegates. When they asked to be seated at the convention, the ubiquitous Billy Adams, chairman of the convention, allowed Speer's minions to vote against the upstarts. Speer's 284-member block kept their seats but could not control the convention. Many Democrats from outside Denver backed Shafroth, giving him a thin 27-vote margin over Jefferson, out of 1,001 votes cast.

The Republicans met in Colorado Springs, where delegates split between moderates who backed John Stephen and a handful of super progressives supporting Merle Vincent.[17] Taking a short step away from its right wing, the Grand Old Party overwhelmingly nominated Stephen and adopted a moderately progressive platform. Stealing some of Shafroth's thunder, they endorsed fair railroad rates, direct primaries, and direct election of U.S. senators. Old-guard Republicans wanted the convention to condemn the initiative and referendum constitutional amendments, but the delegates ducked the issue and made no recommendation on the proposals.

When the conventions adjourned, public attention refocused on the General Assembly. Many legislators, ignoring their parties' convention platforms, still resisted reform. Shafroth wanted a direct primary law that would bypass party conventions and allow registered voters to elect the nominees for the general election. The legislature's compromise bill would allow party conventions to nominate candidates, who would then run in the primaries with top billing over those who petitioned their way on to the ballot. The governor accepted that half-loaf as better than none, and the bill became law.

Shafroth would not, however, swallow a rotten voter registration act that allowed one person to register many others without their signatures. Thousands of fake votes could have been created that way in order to rig primary elections. Shafroth vetoed the bill in hopes that the next General Assembly would pass a better one.

He was more pleased with the Assembly's passage of a statute, slated to take effect in November 1912, that provided citizens with some control over selection of the state's U.S. senators. The U.S. Constitution assigned that task to state legislatures. To give the people more of a voice, Colorado lawmakers crafted a procedure that allowed voters to indicate who they wished to send to the Senate. The measure required legislative candidates to pledge themselves to one of three courses of action: to support the senatorial candidates the people preferred, to support the candidates the political parties selected, or to make no commitment of support. Legislators who failed to ratify the people's choice risked the people's ire. It was a cumbersome system, and not foolproof. Yet it was better than nothing, so Shafroth agreed to it. He also accepted the crumbs of the Assembly's weak railroad regulation bill, hoping to strengthen it later.

The special session of the Seventeenth General Assembly adjourned in mid-October, after seventy-one days, having achieved only a fraction of what the governor wanted. If Shafroth were to make his half-loaves into whole loaves, if he were to accomplish other reform goals, he needed voters to approve the initiative and referendum constitutional amendment. And he needed to be re-elected. By running for governor again, he assured that the progressive juggernaut he had helped launch would not stall, that the momentum picked up in 1910 would continue into 1911, 1912, and beyond.

Shafroth's Second Term: Legislative Morass

As in 1908, Shafroth barnstormed the state in 1910 looking for votes in such out-of-the-way places as Fraser, Granby, Hot Sulphur Springs, Yampa, and Oak Creek. Jokingly known as "Whispering John" because his "whisper" could be heard a block away, he used his loud voice, the "voice of the bull of Bashan," to good effect.[18] At Castle Rock he spoke despite a howling blizzard. Blamed for spending more than $70,000 of the taxpayer's money on the special session, he responded in Leadville: "George Washington did not stop to consider the cost of the revolution: Abraham Lincoln never thought of the expense of abolishing slavery."[19]

While Shafroth vicariously rubbed shoulders with Washington and Lincoln, the Democrats reminded voters that the Republican nominee, John Stephen, had helped elect Simon Guggenheim to the U.S. Senate in 1907, a triumph of big money over little people. "Shafroth," said George Creel in *The Denver Post* on November 3, "is the one candidate that seems able to rise above petty partisanship, peanut politics and shabby treacheries—the one office seeker with ideas above the salary, the patronage, and the pickings." Shortly after he made that endorsement, Creel resigned from the *Post,* a victim of a shabby treachery—his bosses double-crossed him by backing some of Robert Speer's cronies for key Denver jobs.[20] Shafroth missed the peppery Creel's support, but by early November the governor's candidacy hardly needed additional seasoning. With the backing of the Democrats and the endorsement of three reform parties— the Progressives, the Citizens, and the Platform— incumbent Shafroth had little to fear.

In desperation, the *Denver Republican* accused Shafroth of bankrupting the state.[21] Most voters did not bite on that one. Nor were many women hooked by Republican assertions that if the initiative measure passed, men might use it to repeal women's suffrage. On November 8, 1910, Shafroth was easily re-elected, securing 115,627 votes to Stephen's 97,648. The initiative and referendum amendment carried by a margin of more than 60,000 votes, out of more than 117,000 cast.[22]

The governor was to need those tools in order to outmaneuver the new General Assembly. Although he won a splendid victory in November, many anti-reform legislators were also elected. When the legislature met in early January 1911, Billy Adams again became president pro tem of the Senate, and George McLachlan, a Denver representative and an ally of Robert Speer's, became Speaker of the House. "The Denver machine," lamented the *Rocky Mountain News,* is "securely seated in the saddle in both the senate and the house and determined to use its power to the utmost to block the passage of the platform pledges of the Democratic Party and all legislation inimical to the corporations."[23]

Undaunted by the surly mood of the Eighteenth General Assembly, Shafroth outlined his mandate in his inaugural address on January 10, 1911. He reminded the majority Democrats that they had pledged both in 1908 and in 1910 to pass legislation establishing headless ballots, a bank guaranty law, and an effective law to control railroads. Those unfulfilled pledges, he said, must be kept.

More than that, Governor Shafroth served up a medley of new and old ideas. He wanted a better voter registration law than the measure he had vetoed in 1910. He regretted that the Colorado Supreme Court had struck down his campaign finance act and urged the legislature to pass another. Once again he asked lawmakers to frame legislation to control public utilities. He wanted to reorganize state prison and charitable organizations by

On November 6, 1910, two days before Shafroth's re-election to a second term as Colorado's governor, The Denver Post *depicted Honest John atop a tidal wave of reform. Colorado Historical Society.*

establishing one board of control. The two-year terms of state officials, he judged, were too short; he proposed amending the state constitution to give the governor and other elected state executives four-year terms. At the same time, he wanted to give citizens the power to hold special elections to recall corrupt or incompetent public servants.

Much of Shafroth's reform thrust before 1911 centered on structural political changes that would give citizens greater control of government and reduce the power of large corporations. In 1911 he went further, calling for socioeconomic reforms. In keeping with national progressive sentiment, he asked the state legislature to support amendment of the U.S. Constitution to allow imposition of a federal income tax. Such a tax, he said, was fair because "when a man by the protection and advantages given him by a benign government, is enabled to make an income over and above the cost of supporting himself and family, he owes to his country the duty of contributing part of the wealth so acquired for the maintenance of that government."[24]

The governor also called for laws to protect coal miners and to compensate workers injured on the job. When Shafroth took office in 1909, coal miners worked at their own risk, exposed to explosions, tunnel collapses, and other hazards. In January 1910, seventy-five died in a blast at Primero, west of Trinidad. In October and November, disasters at Starkville and Delagua killed more than 130. George Creel charged that the Colorado Fuel and Iron Company might have saved the miners' lives had it spent $10,000 on a ventilation shaft instead of using its money to buy legislators.[25]

Refusing to accept responsibility for their workers' deaths, the owners blamed poorly trained laborers for the disasters. Labor leaders reproached the owners for maintaining an inexperienced work force; when competent miners struck for better wages and conditions, companies regularly recruited unskilled workers to replace them. Men in suits in boardrooms in New York and Denver preferred poor, uneducated, and unorganized immigrant laborers—Italians, Greeks, Hungarians, Mexicans, Russians, Japanese, and Slavs among them. One miner bitterly recalled: "If a mule was accidentally killed, boy you got hell . . . if a man got hurt they'd say, 'Oh well, they'll hire another Mexican.'"[26]

Terrible ventilation in the dusty and gaseous mines, inadequate timbering to support tunnels, and frighteningly narrow underground passages all contributed to miners' deaths. Beholden to the owners for their jobs, sheriffs and coroners usually turned a blind eye to unsafe conditions and blamed the miners for accidents. One pliable inspector noted: "[M]iners unless restrained will often commit suicide and endanger their fellow workmen."[27]

Shafroth, like many others, saw through the companies' flimflam. In the wake of the 1910 disasters, he appointed a commission headed by Victor C. Alderson, president of the Colorado School of Mines, to study the tragedies and to recommend remedies. The governor also set up a commission to study workingmen's compensation plans. "The United States," he told Colorado's lawmakers, "is the only civilized country which places the burden of the risk of employment upon the individual employee, who, as a rule, is a person of small means, and often driven by actual necessity to engage in dangerous occupations."[28] A workers' compensation act, the governor insisted, was the right way to help the helpless.

Many working Coloradans said amen to that. But many legislators, beneficiaries of coal kings' campaign contributions, hesitated to offend their patrons. In early February 1911, the Alderson Commission recommended increases in the number of mine inspectors, standards for shoring up mine shafts, and regulations covering the types of explosives and the amount of dust allowed in mines. To pay for the inspectors, the commission proposed a state tax of a cent per ton of coal mined. Even such moderate recommendations were unacceptable to mine owners and their lackeys in the State Senate. The House of Representatives supported the commission's recommendations, but the Senate emasculated the bill. Passed on May 6, 1911, it was so weak that Shafroth vetoed it at the request of labor leaders.

If the 210 corpses at Primero, Starkville, and Delagua could not shame legislators into taking a small progressive step, it is little wonder that they slaughtered most of Shafroth's other reform proposals. They neglected headless ballots and campaign finance reform, and they refused to give citizens the power to recall officials. They would not permit the railroad commission to fix rates, nor would they stop the railroads from doling out free passes to lawmakers. A cynical Denver legislator dismissed the platform pledges as "a scheme to catch votes, tricks to get office; and he who thinks a party is under obligation to keep those platform pledges is a fool."[29]

While progressives lost most of the time, they sometimes won. Thanks to Ben Lindsey, Colorado enacted a child labor law that prohibited children under fourteen from working and capped the work hours of fourteen- to sixteen-year-olds at forty-eight per week. Legislators allowed a commission to study workingmen's compensation and passed an improved voter registration statute. A voter registration law, somewhat better than the 1910 version, was passed. Legislation prohibiting companies from coercing workers who joined unions received the lawmakers' nod. So did a public health measure that may have saved more lives than the mine safety act would have—a law prohibiting the use of shared, unwashed drinking cups in public places. Ironically, the governor's office itself fell afoul of that rule by providing a drinking glass near its water cooler. Informed about that outlaw glass, Shafroth's messenger, Oliver T. Jackson, locked it away.[30]

The 1911 Assembly took another reform step by creating the Colorado Tax Commission. The new body could not increase taxes, but it could assess some properties for the purposes of taxation, and it could look at county assessors' books in an effort to make taxation equitable among the counties. During the next few years the commission revealed gross inequities in the ways counties assessed property, finding only "five of the sixty-three counties in the state to be assessed at full value."[31] The commission also raised assessments of some properties. Trackage of the Denver & Rio Grande Railroad, assessed at less than $15 million in 1911, was valued at more than $40 million in 1917.

Legislators squabbled endlessly over Shafroth's proposal for a law protecting individuals' bank deposits. Unable to resolve this issue, they referred several statutes to the people for their consideration at the next general election. However, the Colorado Supreme Court struck the proposals off the ballot because a quorum had not been present when the House of Representatives agreed to refer the measures.

The legislature's failure to redeem most of the campaign pledges was compounded, and perhaps partially caused, by the death of U.S. Senator Charles Hughes, Jr., on January 11, 1911, just as the legislative session began. Ordinarily the Democrats, who controlled the General Assembly, would have filled the remaining four years of Hughes' term with a leading Democrat. Circumstances in early 1911 were not ordinary. Shafroth was perhaps the most electable man for the job. His friends appreciated him for his reforms; his opponents hoped to get him out of the governor's chair. He, however, had no intention of abandoning his reform fight in exchange for four years in the U.S. Senate, so he refused to seek Hughes' post. Two ex-governors, Alva Adams and Charles Thomas, hungered for the job. Robert Speer also wanted the seat, and the Denver machine, which had put Hughes in the Senate, wanted Speer to have it. He could also, it was rumored, count on Republican support because he had promised the Republicans city patronage jobs.[32]

The mayor had two problems, though. Reformers and many Coloradans outside of Denver despised "Boss Speer." Moreover, he had no brother, whereas Alva Adams could count on a loyal and well-placed sibling named Billy. As president pro tem of the State Senate, and hence the single most powerful man in that body, Billy Adams could reward Alva's supporters and punish his enemies. He could not, however, despite an uneasy alliance with the reformers, get Alva the votes he needed to be elected to the U.S. Senate. Nor could Speer, facing a combination of Adams and reform forces, secure a majority.

For more than three months the legislators remained deadlocked. When they adjourned on May 6, 1911, they had failed to enact Shafroth's major proposals, and they had failed, despite 102 attempts, to select a replacement for Hughes. Lieutenant Governor Stephen R. Fitzgarrald ended the session on an appropriately negative note: "I am about to bring down the curtain on the most disgraceful proceedings that ever marked a Colorado joint session. Democracy has failed to do what she promised."[33]

Reform Triumphs

Ardent reformers wanted Shafroth to blast the stand-patters, to demand that they resign as he had in 1904, to threaten them with a special session as he had in 1910. *The Denver Post* demanded: "Take the Asses by the Ears, Governor Shafroth, and Let them Know where you Stand."[34]

There was no doubt as to where Shafroth stood. He continually, forcefully, and unequivocally repeated his position. In March 1911, he branded the Speer forces "[t]raitors to the people."[35] When, in mid-April, the General Assembly passed a bill allowing racetrack betting, he called it a "violation of the constitution and the moral law."[36] He told lawmakers that if they overturned his veto, he would not appoint racing commissioners unless the Colorado Supreme Court ordered him to do so. In a close vote, the Assembly failed to override Shafroth's veto. In late April, the governor reminded the legislators that they had been in session "longer than any previous session for thirty years, and yet not one platform pledge has been placed by this legislature upon the statue books. Is there any excuse for this failure?"[37]

Shafroth stood fast for reform, but he refused to call for a special legislative session. He explained to Edward T. Taylor, a fellow Democrat and one of Colorado's congressmen, "[I]f an extra session is called, it would make the differences within our party so great that I do not believe we would have a ghost of a chance of electing anybody a year from this fall."[38] Always the chess player, Shafroth was looking ahead to the 1912 election, a contest that would determine the next governor, the next General Assembly, and two U.S. senators from Colorado. Had he split the Democrats in 1911, he would have clouded the cause of reform and damaged the prospects of the party's candidates, including himself, in 1912.

Moreover, the situation in 1911 differed from that in 1910. In 1910, Shafroth had to call the extra session to get any reform. In 1911, thanks to the initiative and referendum, he no longer needed the General Assembly. If the people wanted reform, they could have it, no matter what legislators wanted. When he needed, as he did in 1910, to risk splitting the Democrats, he was willing to do it. When he did not have to take that risk, he avoided it.

So when Denver attorney Benjamin Hilliard pressed Shafroth to "take the legislature and shake it over the pit of hell," John Franklin declined.[39] He did not roast opponents; he outthought, outmaneuvered, and outlasted them. He had grown up in Fayette, Missouri, a community divided between Union loyalists and Confederate sympathizers. Pro-Union himself, he fell in love with the daughter of one of the town's leading Confederates. To survive in that atmosphere before, during, and after the Civil War, Shafroth had to get along with people with whom he disagreed. That trait served him well in Denver in the 1890s, as he cobbled together a coalition of Republicans, Populists, and Democrats to elect him to Congress. He knew that yesterday's political enemies could be tomorrow's friends. In 1894, Shafroth, then a Republican, defeated the Populist Lafe Pence; in 1908 Lafe Pence, then a Democrat, supported his fellow Democrat, John Shafroth.

During the 1908 campaign, *Rocky Mountain News* reporter Alfred Damon Runyon had commented on Shafroth's lack of rancor toward his opponents: "He bears no malice in a political fight, and he never belittles an opponent in private conversation."[40] Once, in an intra-party fight, Shafroth's own personal secretary, William Malone, opposed the governor. Afterward, Malone offered to resign. Shafroth magnanimously responded: "I don't see why he need resign. I do not demand that any man under me shall believe as I do politically."[41]

Being a gentleman did not make Shafroth weak. His civility was laced with stubbornness. The governor's intelligence, brinkmanship, and ability to compromise when necessary made him the most effective of Colorado's progressives and among the most successful in the nation. Reformers in Wisconsin, Oregon, Oklahoma, Kansas, Missouri, and many other states lent him ideas and encouragement. While Governor Shafroth talked of workingmen's compensation and public utilities regulation in Colorado, Governor Woodrow Wilson campaigned for the same things in New Jersey. Shafroth borrowed his bank guaranty proposal from Texas. By presenting more than a dozen reform ideas clearly, simply, and forcefully, Shafroth gave Coloradans an opportunity to consider the best that national progressivism had to offer.

He was no lone crusader. Thousands of Democrats and Republicans across Colorado and across the nation fought the daily skirmishes, created the climate of opinion, and did the precinct-level work that allowed the progressives and Shafroth to succeed. The reform battalions included Thomas Patterson, Benjamin Barr Lindsey, Charles Thomas, George Creel, Edward Keating, Edward Costigan, Merle Vincent, Benjamin Hilliard, Ellis Meredith, Tully Scott, Onias Skinner, Sarah Platt Decker, Alma Lafferty, Robert Steele, James Causey, Philip Hornbein, even at times Alva Adams, among many other Colorado journalists, legislators, attorneys, politicians, and civic leaders. Given the closeness of the contest between the forces of Speer, Evans, the Colorado Fuel and Iron Company, and other big corporations, on the one side, and those of Shafroth, Patterson, small businessmen, and working people on the other side, every soldier was important to the reformers' cause. Among them all, however, there was only one general—Shafroth, mover of pawns and queens, knights, and rooks.

The Seventeenth and Eighteenth General Assemblies failed to redeem most of the Democratic platform pledges. Still, in his farewell address on January 13, 1913, Governor Shafroth listed more than a dozen reforms enacted during his four years in office. Some, such as the direct primary, the preferential ballot for U.S. Senate, the child labor bill, and the statute creating the Colorado Tax Commission, resulted from legislative action. Many others became laws because of citizen initiatives.

The 1912 election gave Coloradans their first chance to pass their own laws under the initiative system, and they made the most of the opportunity. Early that year the *Denver Times* tallied more than thirty potential statutes, many of them proposed by a group of reformers organized as the Direct Election League. Edward Keating, president of the State Land Board, pushed a measure to "allow the state to mine and sell its own coal," a blow to giant coal companies. The State Federation of Labor pondered a proposal mandating a maximum eight-hour day for all workers. Ditch companies dreamed up means to finance canal digging through state purchases of irrigation bonds. Some of those ideas, including dollars for ditches, were ditched. Many others, thanks to thousands of signatures on petitions, made it onto the ballot.[42]

In an eleventh-hour attempt to destroy these initiatives, anti-reformers found a friendly Denver district judge, Harry E. Riddle, who declared the initiative and referendum measures invalid because they allegedly had not been properly advertised before the 1910 election. For a moment the anti-reformers again had hope, because if the 1910 initiative law were invalid, then none of the citizen-sponsored measures could be considered in 1912. That hope evaporated on September 23, 1912, when the Colorado Supreme Court unanimously overturned Riddle's ruling, just in time to allow initiated measures to appear on the November ballot.

At the general election of November 5, 1912, voters erupted in reform. They gave themselves the right to recall certain judicial decisions and the power to recall officials. The General Assembly would not approve of the headless ballot, so the people approved it themselves. They sanctioned the Direct Election League's proposal allowing the state to pay poor mothers to care for their own children, rather than institutionalizing those children. They passed an eight-hour-a-day work law for women engaged in certain "exhausting occupations." They tried to pass an eight-hour workday law for miners, a law referred to them by the legislature, but failed because opponents put a sham proposal with a similar title but different provisions on the ballot. Both measures passed, so neither could go into effect until the legislature in 1913 adopted the reformers' eight-hour measure.[43]

Other Shafroth reforms would become law after he left the governorship. In 1913, the legislature passed a coal-mine inspection law and created a public utilities commission. The same year, the states ratified the Sixteenth Amendment to the U.S. Constitution, authorizing the federal government to levy a national income tax. A few months later, ratification of the Seventeenth Amendment allowed the direct election of U.S. senators. Coloradans had to wait until 1937 before the federal government guaranteed their bank deposits. And not until 1958 did they follow Shafroth's suggestion and elect a governor for a four-year term.

As he left the governor's office early in 1913, Shafroth was asked by a *Denver Post* reporter to name the greatest of his many accomplishments. He selected three: the initiative and referendum, the direct primary, and the new system for selecting U.S. senators. Historians have rightly remembered him for those reforms and more. Had his career ended in 1912, he would have been assured a place of honor among Colorado's chief executives.

John Franklin Shafroth had scaled mountains he probably never imagined during his boyhood in Fayette. His hair had grayed and his girth had expanded, but neither his reform spirit nor his ambition had cooled. Congressman for ten years, the only man yet elected to consecutive terms as Colorado's governor, he had another, logical rung left on his political ladder. That step led to the United States Senate.

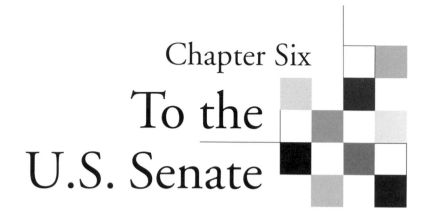

Chapter Six
To the
U.S. Senate

L ike Benjamin Franklin, John Franklin Shafroth was a methodical man. So he probably made a mental list of the plusses and minuses of running for the U.S. Senate in 1912, if only to justify to himself what he wanted to do anyway. The plusses were many. None of Colorado's previous chief executives could touch his record as a reformer. His appeal, however, did not rest solely on his sterling reform record. By promoting highways, tourism, and dryland farming, he earned the thanks of the state's businessmen. By opposing federal conservation policy, he gained the support of ranchers. Women liked him for advocating their causes. Organized labor favored him. By 1912 his friends were legion, and his opponents, bobbing like corks in the high tide of reform, were in disarray.

There were also minuses on his list. Old-guard conservative Democrats could be counted upon to oppose him. Reformers were not united in his support. Additional years of public service would take a toll on his finances. His health, too, might suffer. Between early 1909 and late 1911 he had added sixteen pounds to his ample frame, forcing him to exercise, walk to work, and consider cutting down on apple pie. Serving six years in the U.S. Senate would essentially end his legal career, because he would be sixty-four at the end of his term. But the law had rarely occupied him full time. After nearly ten years in the House of Representatives and four eventful years as governor, he enjoyed power, influence, the public stage, and the satisfaction of dealing with vital issues. He saw scant advantage in trading that for sunset years spent drafting wills and contracts. As for his extra pounds, Shafroth was philosophical: "You know some people say that extra flesh makes people worry. But I don't believe it. I am inclined to think it's lack of worry that makes people fat."[1]

Going to the Senate in 1912 would be less of a financial sacrifice for him than running for governor had been in 1908, for by 1912 his needs were reduced. Son John, well established in his naval career, married Helena Fischer in late April 1911.[2] Morrison had finished his undergraduate work at the University of Michigan, where Will was still an undergraduate. And, tragically, son George was gone.

On April 5, 1911, at age nineteen, George died of heart failure. His years of confinement in a plaster cast, necessitated by his spinal tuberculosis, had taken their toll. Educated mainly at home, he was studying law at the time of his death. "Don't bother about me mother," he had said to a worried Virginia. "I can be as good an office lawyer as anybody. A man does not need to be an athlete for that."[3] Although he had been incapacitated for some sixteen years, his sudden death shook the family, causing Morrison to cut short his legal studies at Michigan to return to Denver and join his father's law practice. The legislature adjourned for part of a day out of respect to the governor and his family, who waited for the arrival of Morrison and Will before burying George at Denver's Fairmount Cemetery.

George's death may have influenced Shafroth to run for the Senate; perhaps he needed a change of scene and a new challenge to occupy his mind. Virginia also might have wished to escape from the house at 1537 York, which had been both George's refuge and his prison. Thirty years after her son's death, she still lamented his passing: "I often regret the fact that medical science wasn't as far advanced then as it is today. If they had known then what they know now, George would probably be still alive."[4]

Shafroth could tick off many other reasons to run. He was well known. He had paid his political dues. For four years he had cut ribbons, crowned apple queens, and performed all the other ceremonial duties expected of governors. More important, he kept a good part of Colorado's business community happy. Businessmen hankered after the tourist dollars they could harvest if Colorado became, as Shafroth proposed, "a playground for the world."[5] He told the 1912 Good Roads Convention in Pueblo that Switzerland—which had no Black Canyon of the Gunnison, no Royal Gorge of the Arkansas—raked in a hundred million dollars a year from touring visitors. With good roads, he said, Colorado could do the same.

Late in 1911, Denver's Chamber of Commerce estimated that the state's counties had spent more than a million and a half dollars on roads that year. Already, the Chamber reported, a motorist could travel all the way from Cheyenne, Wyoming, to Pueblo on a serviceable road. The *Denver Republican* wanted to see an east-west passage through the mountains, running from Denver over Floyd Hill to Idaho Springs, then to Empire, then over the existing Berthoud Pass road to Middle Park "and on toward the Pacific Coast."[6] The Chamber of Commerce estimated that six thousand people had driven into Colorado in 1911 and predicted the number might balloon to forty thousand in 1912 if Colorado improved its roads.[7] By pushing for a state highway commission and by employing prisoners to build roads, Shafroth won the gratitude of motorists and business interests.

But Shafroth got little gratitude from Roady Kenehan, the persnickety state auditor. In his daily search for misplaced pennies, Kenehan nearly drove Shafroth insane. "He is after me all the day," said Shafroth, "with his complaints and discoveries. I can't attend a board meeting or give attention to the business of the office, but he chases after me to tell of some new graft he has found. Much of it is inconsequential, but it all takes time."[8] Once Shafroth and Kenehan argued so vehemently that both started shouting, pounded the

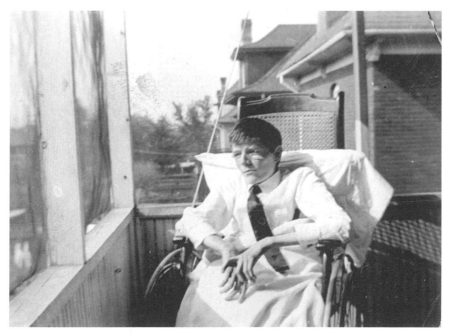

George Shafroth, shown here on the sunporch of the family home at 1537 York Street, suffered from spinal tuberculosis for most of his life. Schooled at home, he kept a diary that offers insight into a compassionate family. Denver Public Library, Western History Collection.

table with their fists; when that did not settle things, they shook their fists under each other's noses until Kenehan stalked out, slamming the door behind him.[9] But Kenehan's parsimony made Shafroth's administration look good. So did the governor's own moderation. His reputation for saving the taxpayers money was worth thousands in goodwill when he ran for office.

While attentive to the details, Shafroth also grasped the larger aspects of the state's finances. Colorado owned more than three million acres of land, but some of it stood in danger of losing its value because neighboring owners were lapping up water supplies. Rather than see the tracts become waterless wastes, the governor and the State Land Board (of which he was a member) sold them. The sales made the state money—more than $3.3 million for 287,340 acres between 1909 and early 1911—and attracted new settlers.[10] And Shafroth financed state spending without adding to taxpayers' burdens.

By selling state lands and by advocating dryland farming, Shafroth aimed to open vast reaches of eastern Colorado to settlement and development. He knew that businesspeople in crossroads farm towns wanted the bank deposits, the hardware and grocery sales, that development brought. Neither they nor Shafroth pondered the folly of farming land that could turn to dust in dry years. To them it made good sense to plow up eastern Colorado—land with little rain—trusting that, with hard work and a little luck, newcomers could make a good living.

Oliver Touissant Jackson, a Denver caterer, was among those hopeful and eventually disappointed would-be farmers. Hoping to establish an African American agricultural community in eastern Colorado, he approached the state land board in 1906 but was rebuffed. "I found it difficult," he said, "to get people in the land office to pay much attention to a negro. So I decided to go into politics myself."[11] Jackson supported Shafroth in 1908. In gratitude, Shafroth appointed Jackson as his messenger and helped him scout out tracts in eastern Colorado. After scouting land in Larimer and Elbert counties, Jackson selected 320 acres in Weld County, thirty-seven miles southeast of Greeley. There, in 1911, he set up Dearfield, so named because its fields were dear to its people. As was the case with many plains hamlets, the settlement enjoyed a few good years, particularly between 1915 and 1918, when war in Europe sparked demand for U.S. crops. But declining prices in the 1920s and drought in the 1930s destroyed Jackson's dreams, along with those of Dearfield's settlers and many other dryland farmers. By 1948, the year of Jackson's death, he and his niece were Dearfield's only residents.

Ultimately, Coloradans' misspent ardor for dryland farming helped lead to the bust and dust of the 1930s. In the short run, that enthusiasm earned

Shafroth votes. Similarly, his fight against federally managed national forests seemed ill-advised in the long run. In the first decade of the twentieth century, however, his crusade against Eastern conservationists, who often seemed oblivious to the West's needs, made him popular with Coloradans.

When Theodore Roosevelt visited Denver in late August 1910, he was accompanied by Gifford Pinchot, the former chief forester of the United States. Many Colorado ranchers loathed Pinchot, who had greatly expanded the federal forests. He preached that "the cow and the tree" could harmoniously dwell in the same peaceful kingdom.[12] But stock growers disagreed. They wanted free, untaxed use of the public domain for their cows and sheep.

Shafroth believed in conservation, if conservation meant "prevention of waste."[13] He also believed in development. When prevention of waste could be hitched to development, he was a conservationist. In 1902, for example, he helped secure passage of the Newlands Act, which set up the Bureau of Reclamation to conserve water for use in developing Western farms. But when conservation required Coloradans to pay use fees for federal grazing land that they had previously (although sometimes illegally) used for free, Shafroth was no conservationist. Just as he had fought Eastern financiers who opposed silver coinage in the 1890s, he fought Washington functionaries whose forest management policies seemed to threaten Colorado's development in the early twentieth century. His heart was with the cattleman, whose old song was being rewritten:

Bury me not on the range
Where the taxed cattle are roaming
And the mangy coyotes yelp and bark
And the wind in the pines is moaning
On the forest reserve bury me not
For I would never would then be free;
A forest ranger would dig me up
In order to collect his fee![14]

In June 1907, Shafroth, then a private citizen, joined Senator Henry Teller in staging a mass meeting in Denver, at which Westerners denounced Pinchot's policies.[15] As governor, Shafroth sent Elias Ammons, a rancher and harsh Pinchot critic, to a national conservation conference Pinchot had organized. In another slap at the conservationists, Shafroth appointed Roady Kenehan, a former prospector, to chair a gathering to promote free mining on public lands. Backing away from Pinchot's more zealous conservation measures, President William Howard Taft removed some land from the national forests and fired the chief forester. Shafroth and the other Western anti-conservationists could claim some credit for and reap some votes from that.

Shafroth also won kudos from ranchers and farmers for laying siege to the ivory towers being built at Colorado's agricultural college in Fort Collins. Practical people complained that instead of examining alfalfa roots, their sons were studying the roots of ancient Greek verbs. Instead of starching shirts and mixing aspic, their daughters were learning dance steps "from a second rate dancing master." In an editorial unnerving to the dancing masters and the Greek professors, Denver's *Rocky Mountain News* declared: "We need hogs that will make more bacon and less lard." Shafroth agreed and put pressure on the college to till its agricultural fields.[16]

Many farm folks liked Honest John, a man who had grown up in a country store in a country town; a man who played chess and read books but did not put on airs; a big, ungainly, sometimes disheveled man, someone a lot like themselves. Many women liked him, too, because of his consistent and forceful defense of their right to vote. When anti-suffrage forces charged that corrupt women in Denver committed fraud in the 1902 election, he defended the women.[17] Henry A. Buchtel, Shafroth's predecessor as governor, was less gallant and astute. "Only the dregs of womankind vote in Colorado," he reportedly said, angering thousands of women voters.[18] Shafroth, by contrast, pointed out that in the 1908 Denver municipal election "for every one woman who attempted to sell her vote, there were ten men who succeeded in doing it."[19]

In courting the women of Colorado's precincts and wards, Shafroth acted both out of conviction and good political instincts. He appointed Helen L. Grenfell, a prominent Democrat, to the board that controlled the state penitentiary. Subscribing to the notion that prison administration was outside the proper sphere of a woman's activities, one newspaper charged, "'Honest John' . . . is making an ass of himself."[20] Mule-like, Shafroth would not back down. Speaking to the Equal Franchise Society in New York City, he asked who had made the "sphere" in which women were supposed to operate. He answered himself, as *The Denver Post* of December 4, 1909, reported:

> "Man made it!" he thundered, "Man! Man even went so far as to say that women's sphere was ordained by God. I can remember the time . . . men said that slavery was a divine institution. But the slaves are free. Did God have a hand in that? The right of women to vote in Colorado is as fixed and as immutable and as certain to last through the ages as that slavery will never again exist in the United States."

That was sweet oratory to the ears of Colorado's women, who also thanked Shafroth for declaring: "The arrogance with which men assert that women have a sphere to which they should be confined must be galling to women of thought and action. Why have men the right to determine woman's sphere without even consulting her?"[21]

Women backed Shafroth because he said what they wanted to hear and because his reforms helped them achieve their goals. Two of the initiated measures put before voters in November 1912 directly benefited women: the women's eight-hour law, and the statute allowing the state to subsidize poor women who wanted to take care of their own children. Moreover Shafroth, like many women, was a devout prohibitionist. In 1914, the Women's Christian Temperance Union and other anti-liquor forces would use the initiative to outlaw the sale of intoxicating liquor in Colorado, a measure that went into effect in 1916.

Working people, both men and women, also voted for Shafroth. The Republican Party's labor record was a long and rarely interrupted plunge from bad to worse. It hit one of its frequent low points between 1903 and 1905, when Governor James Peabody ruthlessly used the Colorado National Guard to crush strikes and arrest strikers. "Anybody but Peabody" became the cry of union men throughout the state. Shafroth's 1908 victory over Republican Jesse McDonald rested, in part, on labor votes and support.

Shafroth repaid his debt during his gubernatorial terms by backing eight-hour workdays for coal miners, improved mine safety, laws limiting child labor (which helped older workers by reducing competition), workingmen's compensation, and a statute prohibiting employers from firing workers who joined unions. When in 1911 Boulder County coal mine owners demanded that Shafroth dispatch the state militia to protect strikebreakers, the governor instead sent his son Morrison to check out the situation. Morrison reported: "I don't think they need any National Guard up there, they'd just create a war."[22] So Shafroth refused to send troops. Later he reputedly told Rocky Mountain Fuel Company president Edwin E. Shumway, "You had better sign up with the union. If you sign up you will have no further trouble. You will get better service from educated men. Why don't you sign up."[23]

Though opposed to deploying the National Guard as it had traditionally been used—against labor—Shafroth willingly employed it, or at least the threat of it, in other, uncommon ways. When a La Junta mob gathered in July 1911 to lynch Bob Harris, an African American accused of murder, Shafroth quickly announced that he had troops ready to protect the prisoner, a well-publicized warning that helped save Harris's life.[24]

With considerable wisdom, Shafroth refused to deploy state troops on December 14, 1911. Late that evening he received a call from Thomas Patterson, one of his major supporters, requesting that Shafroth send soldiers to the Denver County Courthouse, a few blocks from the State Capitol. Henry J. Arnold, the Denver County assessor, a darling of the reformers and an enemy of Speer's, had barricaded himself in his office when he learned that Speer planned to replace him. Speer's henchman, George Collins—armed, some said, with a crowbar—broke into the sanctorum and ordered Arnold out. Patterson asked Shafroth to call out the Guard to restore order.[25]

After talking with police chief Hamilton Armstrong, a cool-headed Shafroth decided that the Guardsmen could stay in their beds. Had he sent the troops, he probably would have looked as foolish as Governor Davis Waite did in 1894 when he ordered the militia to oust Denver's police and fire commissioners. As it was, the skirmish at the assessor's office boomeranged against Speer, whose grip on power was already weakening. Reformers lionized Arnold and rallied around him. Speer's popularity plummeted, and he bowed out of the May 1912 mayor's race—which was won by Henry Arnold. "The Speer machine," wrote historian Edgar C. MacMechen, "so long dominant and triumphant, was scrapped as junk."[26]

Victory in 1912

Speer's fall and Arnold's rise joined Shafroth's long list of plusses. On July 13, 1912, he declared his candidacy for the U.S. Senate, seeking to fill the slot held by Simon Guggenheim, who had decided to retire. In the same election, former governor Charles Thomas, Shafroth's ally in many reform battles, sought the two years left on the term of Charles Hughes, Jr., whom the General Assembly had failed to replace after Hughes died in 1911.

Life could have been simple for Shafroth if his fellow Democrats—grateful for his reform record, appreciative of his political talents, sensitive to the progressive tenor of the times, and anxious to bask in the glow of his reputation—had done the sensible thing and presented him the Senate nomination on a silver platter. But that was a pipe dream, and Shafroth did not smoke.

The reality in 1912, as in 1908 and 1910, was that while ordinary Democrats liked Shafroth, the men who controlled the party preferred a more conservative candidate. Former governor Alva Adams was their man. At the 1912 Democratic state convention, Adams won more votes than Shafroth. The victory meant only that Adams's name would appear first on the Democratic primary ballot. Thanks to the new primary election system Governor Shafroth had engineered, his name would also appear, as would that of Denver attorney Thomas J. O'Donnell. Colorado's rank-and-file Democrats, not the party bosses, would determine the party's senatorial candidates. In September they made that choice, selecting Shafroth as the nominee for the six-year term and Charles Thomas for the two-year term.

Nationally, the Democrats smelled victory in 1912. For half a century they had largely been denied the presidency, but in 1912 conditions favored them. The Republicans were split. The old guard supported incumbent President William Howard Taft, while progressive insurgents, organized as the Bull Moose Party, flocked to Theodore Roosevelt. The Grand Old Party seemed to be breaking apart.

William Jennings Bryan suggested that Shafroth would make a good Democratic presidential nominee in 1912.[27] That was a high compliment but a stupid idea. Three times defeated in presidential contests, Bryan had demonstrated that the Democrats did not do well with a Western standard-bearer. Eastern states controlled huge blocks of electoral votes and could make or break a presidential candidate. Shafroth knew as much and wisely swatted the presidential bug before it bit him.

Instead he cheered for the Democratic nominee, Woodrow Wilson, former president of Princeton University, who as governor of New Jersey had compiled a reform record similar to Shafroth's. Wilson's free-trade policies did not appeal to some Coloradans, and Shafroth distanced himself from those ideas. But Wilson was an eloquent speaker, a dynamic man compared to Taft and, like Shafroth, a reasonable reformer. He was acceptable to Colorado's Democrats, who, despite the ongoing rift between reformers and the old guard, remained united in 1912.

The state's Republicans followed national trends and split into warring factions. Some supported Taft, the regular Republican nominee for president. Others—including Philip B. Stewart from Colorado Springs, Isaac N. Stephen from Pueblo, and Edward Costigan and Benjamin Barr Lindsey from Denver—championed Theodore Roosevelt's Bull Moose Party. Lindsey, who stood five feet in height and weighed around a hundred pounds, gained the nickname "Bull Mouse."[28] Shafroth had reason to fear both the mouse and the moose. In 1908 and 1910, some Republican progressives had supported him. In 1912, the question was whether their defection to Theodore Roosevelt would deprive Shafroth of the reform votes he needed to win.

A complex ballot, a large voter turnout, and the tendency of voters not to vote straight tickets made counting the votes cast on November 5, 1912, a nightmare. Denverites looked to the skies that evening, expecting to learn who had been elected by means of signal lights shining from the State

Capitol and from the city's highest building, the 372-foot Daniels and Fisher Tower. They waited in vain. Not until the next day did they find out that the Democrats had won a smashing victory.

The Bull Moose Party had not attracted many Democrats, but it had split the Republicans. Shafroth received 118,260 votes for the U.S. Senate. Clyde Dawson, the Taft Republican nominee, got 66,949, and Frank D. Catin, the Bull Moose Republican, secured 58,649. Shafroth was the easy victor, although he might not have been had all the Bull Moose Republicans stayed with the regular Republicans. Charles Thomas, similarly benefiting from the Republican split, won the two-year U.S. Senate term. Shafroth also had the satisfaction of seeing Democrat Elias Ammons chosen governor over Bull Moose candidate Edward Costigan and Taft Republican Clifford O. Parks.

The popular vote for U.S. Senate in 1912 was technically an advisory vote. The General Assembly still had the authority to name the senators. The Nineteenth General Assembly, dominated by Democrats, bowed to the people and selected Shafroth and Thomas. To have done otherwise in that reform-charged election would have been political suicide.

Shafroth owed his rise to the U.S. Senate to hard work, intelligence, and the reform tide that he seized at its flood. When he turned the governorship over to Elias Ammons, reform torches still brightly lit the path of progress. But within seventeen months, Ammons would see his administration and the state shamed after Colorado National Guardsmen accidentally killed women and children at Ludlow, a tent colony of striking miners in Colorado's southern coal field. Shafroth was fortunate to be U.S. senator, rather than governor, when that happened. His fortune, however, was likely misfortune for those Ludlow victims; they might have met a different fate had Shafroth, who refused to send troops into the northern Colorado coal fields during the 1910-1911 strike, been governor in 1914.

Shortly after his 1912 victory, Shafroth told *The Denver Post* that he would go to Washington to advance the interests of Denver and Colorado, that he would fight federal conservation policy, that he would bring home whatever federal bacon he could snatch, and that he would try to get the lame-duck session of Congress abolished.[29] Those were, as it turned out, small aspirations. During the next six years he won a more significant role on the national scene than he envisioned in 1912. Although his reputation would eventually rest mainly on his extraordinary achievements as Colorado's governor, his lone term in the U.S. Senate set him above Colorado's many run-of-the-mill senators. The years 1913 to 1919, crucial ones in the nation's history, would give John Franklin Shafroth additional scope for his talents.

Chapter Seven
Domestic
Affairs

The date: March 4, 1913. The place: the Senate Chamber in the United States Capitol. The occasion: the inauguration of Woodrow Wilson as twenty-seventh President of the United States and Thomas R. Marshall as vice president, along with the swearing in of senators, among them John Franklin Shafroth.

A big man, Shafroth must have felt like a giant sardine packed among hundreds of dignitaries, who so crowded the Senate that much of the regular furniture had to be removed. Even so, several members of outgoing president William Howard Taft's cabinet could not find seats. Taft himself was commodiously accommodated in a big leather armchair, next to a similar one occupied by Wilson. Lesser luminaries from the House of Representatives found themselves trumped for space by senators, justices of the Supreme Court, foreign ambassadors, and members of the new president's cabinet, including Shafroth's old ally, William Jennings Bryan, soon to be named secretary of state.[1]

By swearing senators in by groups, Vice President Marshall made quick work of the oath taking. John Franklin knew that his minute in the spotlight was only one small episode in a momentous day. Still, he must have relished the ritual, which not only put him in the company of Taft, Wilson, and Bryan but also made him a member of the U.S. Senate, the most powerful political club in the nation. Son of an immigrant shopkeeper, Shafroth had come far in his fifty-eight years. The small town of Fayette, Missouri, where he was born and grew up, was long behind him. So, too, was dusty Denver of the 1880s, where he first made his mark in politics. His ten years in the

U.S. House of Representatives and his two terms as Colorado's most successful reform governor also belonged to the past. By 1:35 P.M., his oath taking was behind him, and six years in the Senate lay ahead—as did Woodrow Wilson's inaugural address.

Speaking to a large crowd at the east portico of the Capitol, Wilson challenged the country to embrace reform. He urged tariff reduction so consumers might benefit from lower prices. He proposed overhauling the nation's antiquated banking system. He observed that "we have been proud of our industrial achievements but have not hitherto stopped thoughtfully enough to count the human costs, the cost of lives snuffed out." He recognized that laboring people were often "powerless to determine" the conditions of their work. He agreed with the conservationists: "We have squandered a great part of what we might have used, and have not stopped to conserve the exceeding bounty of nature." He asked for the nation's help as he concluded: "Men's hearts wait upon us; men's lives hang in the balance; men's hopes call upon us to say what we will do. Who shall live up to this great trust? Who dares fail to try? I summon all honest men, all patriotic forward looking men, to my side. God helping me, I will not fail them, if they will but counsel and sustain me!"[2]

Shafroth enthusiastically sustained the president on most issues, including reform of the banking system, assistance to labor, and protection of the weak. Indeed, in some respects the new senator from Colorado was more of a reformer than the new president. Shafroth no doubt wished that Wilson had included a call for women's suffrage in his inaugural address, which suffered from a surfeit of "men's hearts . . . men's lives . . . men's hopes." Just a day before the inauguration, suffragettes organized by militant Alice Paul paraded in Washington and found incredible opposition; thugs attacked them, while the police refused to intervene. "Rowdies Slap and Spit on Weeping Suffragettes Police of Washington Fail to Protect Marchers," ran the headline in Denver's *Rocky Mountain News.*[3] Wilson said nothing about that riot, which left hundreds hurt. Nor did he ask for fair treatment of Puerto Rico or independence for the Philippines, issues dear to Shafroth since his days in the House of Representatives, when he first opposed U.S. imperialism.

Shafroth recognized that lower tariffs would help Coloradans, who paid more than necessary for many manufactured goods because of high tariffs. But he also realized that several Colorado products—lead, wool and, most important, sugar—would suffer if denied tariff protection. Shafroth's misgivings over Wilson's tariff position, however, were nothing in comparison to the senator's heartburn over the rhetorical support the president gave conservationists, a species of reformer Shafroth judged more detrimental to Colorado's development than grasshoppers. Yet despite the president's talk, tailored to suit his Eastern constituents, Shafroth knew that Wilson could trim his conservation sails to fit Western political realities.

Much of what the president said in his inaugural, Shafroth had read in the 1912 Democratic platform.[4] Coloradans who had not digested that verbiage enjoyed a superb opportunity to learn Wilson's views on October 7, 1912, when he addressed more than 14,000 people at the Denver City Auditorium while 12,000 others waited outside hoping to be admitted.

Shafroth and the overflow audience cheered Wilson as he outlined the differences between his positions and those favored by William Howard Taft, running as the Republican nominee, and Theodore Roosevelt, the Bull Moose candidate. Neither Roosevelt nor Taft, Wilson charged, would do anything about lowering tariffs. Taft, Wilson said, seemed to have no effective policy to deal with the great business combines that increasingly dominated the nation. Roosevelt advocated accepting the monopolies as inevitable and then regulating them. Wilson damned the notion of making monopolies "permanent and legal."[5] Deriving his philosophy from the scholar and jurist Louis D. Brandeis, Wilson argued for a "New Freedom" under which government would use its power to break up monopolies.[6]

Shafroth, who had waged his own battles with big coal companies, big railroads, and big money, saw a kindred spirit in Wilson. He also found that Wilson could sugarcoat his conservation position, making it palatable to pro-development Westerners. "You know," Wilson told the auditorium crowd, "that you are fretful and dissatisfied because great forest areas, great water courses, great mineral resources, are held back from use by the government of the United States. Why does the government at Washington preserve this policy so stiff and rigid and unchangeable? The government of the United States dares not relax its grasp for fear these special powers [the trusts] . . . should become the master of your development and of the nation's development itself."[7] The inference was clear. If monopolies could be eliminated, then Westerners could be trusted with freer use of public lands. That was music to Coloradans' ears, and another reason for them to vote for Wilson. That they did on November 5, 1913, giving him the state's six electoral votes.

Wilson's victory was, however, less than overwhelming, because he won less than 43 percent of the national popular vote. Most of the rest of the electorate divided their ballots between Roosevelt and Taft. The Taft-Roosevelt split also helped the Democrats win both houses of Congress—the first time they held both the presidency and Congress since 1893-1895. Their power in

1913, however, was without much padding. With the Democrats holding only a six-vote advantage in the Senate, Wilson needed the backing of an overwhelming majority of the Democratic senators to enact his programs. As he well knew, not all Democrats agreed with him. Democratic senators saw that if they stuck together they could accomplish much, but if a handful wanted to block the president or the other Democrats, that handful could be successful.

Shafroth realized that if he were to influence the policies of the Democratic Party and the president—if he were to block measures he opposed and accomplish his own aims—he needed to work the levers of congressional power. He recognized that voting, giving speeches, dispensing patronage, and sending federal dollars home, although significant and necessary, were not the alphas and the omegas of the job. Having served ten years in the House of Representatives, he knew that attention to mundane

Presidential candidate Woodrow Wilson and U.S. Senate candidate John Shafroth campaign in downtown Denver in October 1912. Colorado Historical Society.

committee work often made the difference between legislative effectiveness and ineffectiveness; that, as his namesake Ben Franklin once wrote: "By diligence and patience the mouse bit in two the cable."[8]

Shafroth meant to be effective, even if he had to work overtime gnawing cables. With more than seventy committees, the Senate had plenty of assignments to give its ninety-six members. Some committees, such as Appropriations, Agriculture and Forestry, Banking and Currency, and Foreign Relations, were national in scope and fraught with work. Others, such as Fish and Fisheries or Mines and Mining, had more regional than national import; they were significant for some senators but of little value to others. Still others, such as the Committee on the Disposition of Useless Papers in the Executive Department, held scant allure for would-be Ciceros.

Shafroth gathered roses—committees of importance and interest to him. On March 15, 1913, he was appointed to four powerful bodies: Appropriations, Agriculture and Forestry, Banking and Currency, and Mines and Mining. And, despite his lack of seniority, he became chairman of the Committee on the Pacific Islands and Porto Rico (as Puerto Rico was then spelled), a position of interest to few senators. Shafroth, though, coveted it because of his long-held conviction that U.S. imperialism had to be checked. Later he added the Committee on Public Lands and the Committee on the Philippines to his portfolio, becoming chair of the latter in May 1918.

Tearing Down Tariffs

The Senate spent much of early March 1913 in housekeeping chores. On reconvening in early April it considered a novel request: Woodrow Wilson proposed to address a joint session of Congress personally. Not since John Adams's presidency, 112 years earlier, had a president spoken to Congress. Instead, the chief executive sent written messages, which clerks read to often bored legislators. Wilson, an eloquent speaker and deft political strategist, grasped the public relations advantage of appearing before Congress to urge a sweeping reduction in tariffs, a cornerstone of his 1912 campaign.

The president's proposal to address the lawmakers sparked a short debate in the Senate. John Sharp Williams, a Democrat from Mississippi, could not cotton to the idea. It reminded him, Williams said, of the British practice in which the sovereign gave "speeches from the throne." Henry Cabot Lodge, whose ancestral Massachusetts roots extended back to John Adams and before, did not mind the president's coming to Congress, but he tried to postpone Wilson's appearance, hoping, perhaps, to show that Lodge and his fellow Republicans were still a force to be respected.

Shafroth paused to give some senior senator a chance to respond to Williams and Lodge. When none did, John Franklin jumped to Wilson's defense. Recalling his years in the House of Representatives, Shafroth noted that presidential messages recited by droning clerks often went over with a thud. During his years as governor, he told his fellow senators, speeches he had delivered in person were more effective than those read by a stand-in. Finally, Shafroth argued that a presidential appearance before Congress would not be regal: "It is democratic in the extreme because it puts the president in personal contact with both Houses of Congress."[9]

Wilson hardly needed Shafroth's succor; the Senate dared not snub the president. Still, the Colorado senator's brief maiden speech was a smart move; it may have gained him a point with the president, and it simultaneously gave Shafroth an easy opportunity to introduce himself to his colleagues as a former governor and a man with previous congressional experience.

Wilson spoke to Congress on April 8, forcefully stating his case for tariff reduction. "It is clear to the whole country that the tariff duties must be altered. . . . We must abolish everything that bears even the semblance of privilege or any kind of artificial advantage. . . . [T]he object of tariff duties henceforth must be effective competition, the whetting of American wits by contest with the wits of the rest of the world."[10] Representative Oscar W. Underwood promptly introduced a bill to lower tariffs.

The president's logic was impeccable. If tariffs were lowered, prices would likely fall, thereby putting millions of dollars in the hands of consumers. Many of them would spend that money improving their lives and giving the economy a boost. If U.S. industry had to compete against foreign industry, then many trusts would lose their monopoly pricing power. Again, consumers would benefit. Moreover, tariff reduction was tantamount to tax reduction, because the government then derived much of its revenue from the tariff duties. Those duties were regressive, costing the poor and middle classes a greater percentage of their income than the rich. By proposing to replace tariff revenues with a graduated income tax, Democrats inched toward progressive taxation as a means of limiting the concentration of money and power in the hands of a few.

Logic, however, was not king in politics, and those with money and power were not asleep. The Underwood tariff, they argued, would hurt some U.S. industries. Stockholders might face dividend cuts. Workers might lose their jobs. Some producers might find that they lacked the wits to compete with foreign rivals. A chorus of dissent rose across the country, from both Republicans and Democrats—from the steel makers of Pennsylvania to the cotton growers of Mississippi to the sugar beet farmers of Colorado. To win the tariff contest and serve the common good, Wilson and his supporters had to fight those special pleaders at every turn. If one group were favored, others would demand similar preferential treatment. If that happened, soon none of the dominos would stand, and there would be no tariff reduction.

Shafroth and Colorado's other Democratic senator, Charles Thomas, had problems with Underwood. Practically all of their constituents had much to gain from lower tariffs on agricultural products, farm machinery, and a long list of other manufactured goods. Prune eaters in Pueblo looked forward to the duty on prunes being cut in half; lemon eaters in Limon delighted in the prospect of a 40 percent reduction in lemon duties; and bicyclists in Boulder rejoiced that the tariff on bicycles would fall by 20 percent. But many other Coloradans stood to lose from reduction of tariffs on sugar, wool, and lead.

Louisiana's two Democratic senators stood by the sugar producers of their state and vowed to vote against Underwood. Thomas Walsh of Montana, also a Democrat, threatened to do likewise. Had those balky lawmakers persuaded Shafroth, Thomas, and one or two other Democrats to join them, then Underwood might have become wormwood, a defeat that would have compromised the rest of Wilson's presidency. Wisely, the president fudged on sugar, allowing a penny-a-pound protection for three years, after which it was to enter duty-free. Shafroth and Thomas, for their part, were willing to compromise. They remained loyal to the president, though they risked losing some votes in Colorado because of that fealty.[11]

After five months of hearings and negotiations, Underwood became law in early October 1913. With it came the federal income tax to make up for lost revenue. Before he went to the U.S. Senate, Shafroth had supported the Sixteenth Amendment to the U.S. Constitution, ratified February 25, 1913, which made the income tax constitutionally permissible. In mid-February 1914, he had to take a little dose of the medicine he had concocted when he submitted his 1913 tax return. Shafroth reported making $7,000 in salary, almost $4,000 in rents and interest, and nearly $5,300 in stock dividends and corporate earnings. That put him among Colorado's substantial citizens but left him far behind the truly wealthy—men such as Colorado Springs copper millionaire Spencer Penrose and Denver industrialist Lawrence C. Phipps, a former partner of Pittsburgh steel magnate Andrew Carnegie. After deducting more than $9,000 in business costs and exemptions, Shafroth had a taxable income of $3,696.90, on which he paid 1 percent, or $36.96.[12]

By 1916 it was clear that the new income tax revenues were not sufficient to support the government. To make up the difference, Congress raised income tax rates and imposed a federal inheritance tax—both measures that mainly affected the very wealthy and met with Shafroth's approval. Also sweet, from his standpoint, was Congress's decision to maintain the penny-a-pound tariff on sugar. The tariff was kept because it yielded tens of millions in revenue; as a side-effect, it shielded Colorado's sugar beet industry from foreign competition.[13]

In the end, Shafroth lost little or nothing from his position on the sugar tariff. The 1913 decrease from 1.33 cents a pound to 1 cent a pound was acceptable to the sugar beet growers, and they applauded the maintenance of that duty after 1916. By backing the president in 1913, Shafroth gave Wilson the victory he needed. Perhaps he and other sugar senators worked out a deal whereby the administration agreed to revisit the sugar question in 1916—allowing protection to remain. If so, it was a piece of brilliant politics, a chess player's maneuver that let the sugar senators have their cake in 1913 and eat it again in 1916, a presidential election year.[14]

In supporting the Underwood tariff, the income tax, and the inheritance tax, Shafroth in his first seven months in the Senate participated in three major legislative events. Underwood was no ordinary tariff. It represented the first significant tariff reduction since before the Civil War, more than six decades earlier. During the twentieth century, low tariffs became the dominant trade philosophy of the United States, an approach that eventually led to a worldwide reduction in protectionism and a consequent increase in trade. By shifting from the regressive taxes created by high tariffs toward the more progressive income tax, the legislators of 1913 began a redistribution of the tax burden that limited the massive concentrations of wealth and power spurred by the rise of big business. In many respects, the twentieth century was to be the century of the middle class. Wilson's progressive supporters, including John Franklin Shafroth, willingly abetted the rise of that class.

Building the Federal Reserve

Several other progressive measures caused Shafroth far less angst than did the Underwood tariff. The Clayton Anti-Trust Act of 1914 was so watered down in going through Congress that it made few friends or serious enemies. Labor secured a rhetorical concession that the labor of a person was not a commodity, but such statements hardly protected unions against big business. Nor did Shafroth's support of the Federal Trade Commission accomplish much, because the commission was often ineffective in curbing unfair trade practices. By contrast, the Federal Tariff Commission, created as part of the 1916 income tax bill, initially promised to succeed in fine-tuning tariffs. By appointing Edward Costigan to the Tariff Commission, Wilson did Shafroth a favor because Costigan, the erstwhile leader of Colorado's Progressive Party and a potential rival to Democrats, was temporarily removed from the Colorado scene.

Shafroth's support of Clayton's pro-labor language was predictable. He had befriended labor in Colorado, had been elected with labor's help, and would continue to serve labor's interests in the Senate. Early in his term, in May 1913, he supported investigation of coal mining conditions in West Virginia. When his ally, Congressman Edward Keating of Pueblo, proposed a measure limiting child labor (the Keating-Owen Act), Shafroth backed it, even though Keating had to stretch the U.S. Constitution to make possible federal regulation of what many judged a state prerogative. Shafroth believed in states' rights, but he believed more strongly in protecting children. Keating-Owen became law in September 1916, only to be declared unconstitutional by the U.S. Supreme Court in 1918.

Shafroth also favored Wilson's efforts to limit railroad workers' shifts to eight hours a day, a stance Wilson took in 1916 to prevent a nationwide railroad strike. But Shafroth was willing, when necessary, to oppose the president in defense of labor's interests. In 1915 Shafroth backed the Burnett bill, which aimed to curtail immigration by forbidding entry to the illiterate. Many labor leaders and progressives supported the measure, but Wilson vetoed it. In 1917 Shafroth joined an overwhelming majority of senators to reenact the bill and override the president's veto.[15]

Usually, however, he stood with the president, as demonstrated by his support for the Owen-Glass Act, also known as the 1913 Federal Reserve Act.[16] In his April 8, 1913, address to Congress, Wilson told lawmakers he would eventually ask them to reorganize the nation's jerry-built banking system. He made that request in his second appearance before Congress, on June 23, 1913. The banking system, or lack thereof, badly needed fixing, as the panic and depression of 1893 and the bank crisis of 1907 had demonstrated. The depression of 1893 rocked the whole country; in Denver, half the city's eighteen banks failed in two days in July. Even when banks were not crumbling, they could not adequately expand the money supply to meet the needs of a growing economy. Critics also bemoaned the power of East Coast cities, particularly New York, where economic czars used their financial muscle to strangle rival entrepreneurs in the South, Midwest, and West.

In his superb study, *Woodrow Wilson and the Progressive Era: 1910-1917*, historian Arthur Link notes: "Bankers and businessmen and leaders of both parties agreed that the national banking system . . . was about as badly adapted to the financial needs of a great nation as any system could be."[17] But, says Link, the critics did not speak in unison, nor did they offer a solution mutually acceptable to private bankers and progressives; the former were anxious to keep the government out of what they considered their business, the latter just as anxious to make the banks answer to the government.

As a member of the Senate Banking and Currency Committee, Shafroth assumed an important role in shaping the nation's new banking landscape, a Herculean task for which he was well suited. Back in the 1890s, he had urged the federal government to buy more silver as a way of expanding the country's money supply. As Colorado's governor, he tried but failed to create a reserve pool to protect banks and their depositors. In early 1911 he saw his state's moguls shaken when David Moffat, president of Denver's most powerful bank, could not obtain credit in New York City and went bankrupt.

Not only did Shafroth know banking and understand the needs of ordinary people, he also was willing to wade through arcane financial details, minutiae which hypnotized most people. Nor did he flinch from the long hours and hard work the banking committee required. In September and October 1913, the committee listened to hundreds of expert witnesses and compiled a drier-than-dust report of more than three thousand pages. Then the committee drafted the Owen-Glass Act, patiently explaining its complexities to the Senate. Finally, a House-Senate conference committee ironed out differences in the respective bills. At every stage, including his service on the conference committee, Shafroth questioned witnesses, suggested improvements, and clarified points for his less banking-savvy colleagues.

The Federal Reserve system largely fixed the broken banking system. Although it did not directly insure depositors' money, it provided a pool of reserves upon which national banks could draw in crises. It gave the government considerable control over banking by allowing the president to name the Federal Reserve governors. It helped decentralize financial power by establishing a dozen Federal Reserve districts. It created mechanisms allowing banks to increase the money supply, including the use of short-term agricultural loans as backing for currency, a boon to the South, Midwest, and West. It gave the Federal Reserve the power to change interest rates. It probably went as far as politically possible to satisfy the old Populist demands for easier credit and decentralized banking.

Coloradans who hoped to see Denver designated one of the regional Federal Reserve centers found that their city was neither financially important nor centrally located enough to garner that prize. Instead the Colorado capital had to settle for becoming a branch of the Federal Reserve Bank in

Kansas City, Missouri. Most voters in the state probably did not realize the service Shafroth had done them. Banking, like tariff policy, was not an issue that raised people's passions except when their savings accounts were being gored. But Shafroth's involvement in crafting and enacting the Owen-Glass Act merits him a place in the history books. With some modifications, Owen-Glass stood the test of time, lasting through the twentieth century and into the twenty-first. The Federal Reserve Act, says historian Arthur Link, was "the greatest single piece of constructive legislation of the Wilson era."[18] William Gibbs McAdoo, Wilson's secretary of the treasury, credited Shafroth with doing much to ensure the passage of that legislation.

Puerto Rico and the Philippines

By December 1913 the Senate had been in almost continuous session since March. Shafroth's responsibilities were not discharged until a few days before Christmas, when the Owen-Glass conference committee adjourned. Much had changed in Congress since Shafroth first served as a representative in 1895. Sessions were longer, the workload heavier. Helping balance these burdens were better offices and more clerical help. Shafroth recalled that back in 1895 House members had no office accommodations at all: "[O]nly in the house wing of the Capitol building a committee composed of from fifteen or twenty congressmen had a long table and each one had a drawer in that table in which to keep his correspondence or other things he wished to preserve."[19] Becoming a senator had advantages, Shafroth explained in a letter to his older brother: "The Senators have a great deal better quarters than the Members of the House and a great deal better assistance in their work. We have an elegant Senate Office Building and each Senator has two large rooms, and some have three. Each Senator is provided with two stenographers and a clerk, which is of great assistance to him."[20]

His office pleased him, but not everything went well. Virginia had accompanied him to Washington, where, like so many congressional couples, they moved into a boarding house. His letters to William expressed no complaint about that arrangement, but he must have missed his comfortable Denver home with its well-stocked library—places he would see little of between 1913 and late 1921. Jennie left muggy Washington in early August 1913 and returned to Denver to help care for her elderly mother. In late December, after months of grueling work on the banking bill, John Franklin looked forward to her return to Washington. In January they traveled to New York and thence by ship to Puerto Rico, which he visited in his capacity as chairman of the Senate committee that oversaw the island's affairs.[21]

After his return in mid-January 1914, Shafroth met with Wilson. In mid-February the president wrote to his secretary of war, Lindley M. Garrison, stating that something should be done "about the liberalization of government arrangements in Porto Rico. . . . I have had an interesting talk with Senator Shafroth who has just returned from Porto Rico, and found that his ideas and ours ran along the same lines."[22]

Shafroth and Wilson both knew that the government of Puerto Rico, hastily created by the 1900 Foraker Act, was, like the banking system and tariff policy, badly in need of reform. Though not of great public concern, the issue was critically important to more than a million Puerto Ricans. Ever since 1898, when the United States snatched Puerto Rico and the Philippines from Spain at the end of the Spanish American War, the denizens of those islands had been without meaningful self-government and denied U.S. citizenship. The 1912 Democratic platform had condemned "colonial exploitation" and decried "the experiment in imperialism as an inexcusable blunder which has involved us in enormous expense . . . and laid our Nation open to the charge of abandonment of the fundamental doctrine of self-government."[23] Despite that denunciation of imperialism, Congress, bogged down in other matters, put Puerto Rico and the Philippines on back burners.

Few senators were as attuned to the nation's "abandonment of the fundamental doctrine of self-government" as was Shafroth. He stood among the handful of congressmen who had opposed the colonial experiment at the time of the Spanish American War. By 1913 most Democratic policy makers had at least partially come around to his way of thinking. They more or less agreed that someday the remote Philippines should become independent, but nobody knew when that day would come.

Puerto Rico presented a thornier problem, one entwined with national defense and the Panama Canal, which opened August 15, 1914.[24] If Puerto Rico, strategically located a thousand miles east of Panama, should fall into hostile hands, the United States might pay dearly. U.S. self-interest aced out Puerto Rican self-determination. Independence was not in the cards.

Working within the limits of the possible, Shafroth and a few other congressmen, cheered on by Woodrow Wilson, began a long process to give Puerto Ricans greater self-government and U.S. citizenship. Progress was slow. Most senators and representatives considered Puerto Rico far less important than tariffs, banks, and federal pork for their home states. There were no Puerto Rican senators or representatives in Congress to fight for their interests. To build a fire under Shafroth's committee, Wilson sent him a note in June 1916: "I believe I have more than once expressed to you my

Senator Shafroth in the study of his York Street home in Denver. Denver Public Library, Western History Collection.

deep interest and concern in this matter."[25] Along with it he included a request for action from Arthur Yager, Wilson's appointee as governor of the Puerto Rico. In early July the president again wrote Shafroth: "I am heartily glad that the Puerto Rican Bill is on the ways and hope that it may soon be launched as a seaworthy ship."[26]

Those congratulations turned out to be premature. In late July, Newton Baker, who had replaced Lindley Garrison as secretary of war, told Wilson the Puerto Rican bill was "still hanging fire in the Senate." There was danger in delay, he added, because Jose de Diego, a Puerto Rican politician, was agitating for restoration of Spanish power. If the bill did not pass, Baker warned, "further internal disturbance may result."[27] The Senate moved glacially. Not until January 31, 1917, was Shafroth able to cajole his colleagues into considering the Jones-Shafroth bill.

Named after Shafroth and House sponsor William A. Jones, the legislation drew some criticism. Senator James Martine of New Jersey, an enemy of women's suffrage, did not like it because if gave the Puerto Rican legislature the right to determine whether women could vote. Senator Wesley L. Jones of Washington state, a pro suffrage man, did not like it because it did not guarantee women the right to vote. Other senators carped about the $8,000 salary for the U.S.-appointed governor of Puerto Rico. Finally the bill, which had already cleared the House, passed the Senate. On March 2, 1917, nearly four years after Shafroth became chairman of the Committee on Porto Rico, Woodrow Wilson signed the measure into law.

Jones-Shafroth extended U.S. citizenship to more than a million Puerto Ricans, and although those who wished to reject that citizenship could do so, few did. In that regard the act was a giant step forward, the greatest expansion of U.S. citizenship since 1868, when the Fourteenth Amendment made ex-slaves citizens. However, Puerto Ricans still could not elect U.S. senators or representatives—they remained without representation in Congress—nor could they elect their own governor. The act gave Puerto Ricans the same civil rights enjoyed by mainland Americans, with the significant exception of the right of trial by jury. It permitted Puerto Ricans to elect a senate to help govern the island, along with an elected house of representatives. It allowed for the possibility that the appointed governor would be a Puerto Rican. But it granted that governor total veto power and kept many governmental functions under U.S. control.

Some Puerto Ricans accepted Jones-Shafroth as an improvement over the Foraker Act.[28] Others, anxious for real self-government, saw it as a weak measure that fell far short of doing justice. Shackled by the reality that the

United States had no intention of giving up control of Puerto Rico, Shafroth, in the most important piece of legislation to bear his name, had helped improve the government of Puerto Rico. But he received scant thanks either from most Puerto Ricans, who resented their continued political bondage, or from mainland Americans (including Coloradans), who cared little, if at all, about Puerto Rico.

U.S. occupation of the Philippines, another thorn in the body politic, was in theory an easier burr to remove. The Democrats' 1912 national platform had promised independence to the nine and a half million Filipinos, and Shafroth took that pledge seriously. He scolded the Senate in March 1915: "We have continually promised these people not only self government but independence. It comes with poor grace from Senators who believe in the principles enunciated in the Declaration of Independence that we should in any manner attempt to prevent the passage of such a measure as the one working to the independence of the Philippine Islands."[29]

Nearly a year later, in January 1916, with the foresight of a champion chess player, Shafroth told his colleagues that Japan regarded the U.S. presence in the Philippines as a provocation, much as the United States saw the interference of other major powers in Latin America as a threat. "The holding of the islands," he warned, "is a perpetual irritation to Japan, and will be the underlying cause of war if we have a contest of arms with her." He also pointed out that by keeping the Philippines the U.S. was exposing the islands to attack and occupation "by any nation that might get into a conflict with us."[30] That chilling prospect came true late in late 1941 and early 1942, when Japan swept down upon the Philippines and captured thousands of U.S. and Filipino troops, many of whom perished during the infamous Baatan death march.

Unwilling to heed the horrors swirling in Shafroth's crystal ball, Congress refused to fix a date for Philippine independence, although it paid lip service to the idea of eventual independence. When Shafroth became chairman of the Senate Committee on the Philippines in May 1918, he wrote to Manuel L. Quezon, president of the Philippine Senate: "I wanted the chairmanship so that I could be of assistance in carrying out the promises of independence our Government gave to your people."[31] In the hectic months leading up to the end of World War I, he was unable to deliver on that promise. It was a blow to the Philippines and a potential blow to Colorado, because, as Shafroth had noted in 1912, the state's sugar industry was threatened by competition from Filipino producers.[32] Not until July 4, 1946, did the islands become a sovereign nation.

Public Land Policy

Shafroth's failure to produce a speedy resolution on the Philippines demonstrated something he already knew: It was much easier for Congress to do nothing than to take action. Conservative Southern Democrats sometimes bickered with the party's more progressive Northerners. Republicans stood ever ready to take advantage of Democratic divisions. The Senate's heavy workload and complex rules further hamstrung the body. Shafroth wanted the United States to adopt the metric system. The idea died. He wanted to abolish the lame duck session of Congress. The measure died. He wanted the federal government to grant some of its forest lands to the states to help finance road building. The proposal died. He wanted the president to serve a single six-year term. The idea died. He constantly pressed for measures giving women the right to vote. They all died.

The Senate's inability to get things done sometimes worked in Shafroth's favor. He had promised Coloradans that he would fight conservationists. When some senators proposed the leasing of federal coal lands in Alaska, he objected that the federal government should not control the resources at all. Far better, he argued, for the government—"the worst landlord on earth"— to give its lands back to the states, which then could collect taxes from the resources when they were developed.[33] Shafroth gave a long speech on the issue in late September 1914, copies of which he sent to many senators. Charles Thomas, like Shafroth a foe of federal ownership and leasing, judged the address a "corker."[34] Other senators politely promised to read it.

Shafroth failed to stop the leasing of Alaska coal lands; coal companies and promoters of an Alaskan railroad were too powerful for him. But after that defeat, he allied with other anti-leasing senators to beat back similar proposals. Some of his comrades shared Shafroth's view that the federal government should return its lands to the states. Others were conservationists of the deepest green who opposed leasing because they did not want any development. And some progressive senators, such as the Republican Robert La Follette of Wisconsin, feared that leasing would benefit big businesses.[35]

Senator Thomas Walsh of Montana, an avid pro-leaser, complained about Shafroth to Wilson in March of 1916, suggesting that Shafroth lusted after the taxes the states could pick up from developers of federal lands: "While governor of Colorado he [Shafroth] was no doubt embarrassed in finding the revenue with which to meet the necessary expenditures of the state."[36] That assessment was partly true. Shafroth did want to increase state revenues. Moreover, opposing federal ownership of huge chunks of Colorado land got Shafroth votes at home.

But he based his anti-leasing stand on more than a lust after taxes and votes. He cogently argued that the residents of all states should be treated equally. In Eastern, Midwestern, and Southern states, land that once had belonged to the U.S. government now belonged to private citizens. Therefore, it was unfair for the government to lock up huge tracts in Western states. In Colorado, for instance, more than thirty thousand square miles—an area larger than Massachusetts, Vermont, and New Hampshire combined—belonged to the national government. In a letter to William Jennings Bryan, Wilson commented on the Colorado senator's arguments. Giving federal lands to the states, said the president, would be "a very difficult step to justify." He admitted Shafroth was "sincere and impressive, but I must admit he has not convinced me."[37]

Nor did Shafroth convince Gifford Pinchot, the leader of the conservation movement, that the federal government should relinquish its forests, mountain lands, and hydroelectric sites in the West. In a legislative standoff, Shafroth and his allies were able to block leasing, while Pinchot and his friends prevented the states from getting control of federal lands. The senator had little use for Pinchot, claiming the forester "promulgated and found many adherents to a policy that is very detrimental to the Western states."[38] However, if Colorado stood to benefit, Shafroth could cooperate with conservationists. Such was the case with Rocky Mountain National Park.

For years the naturalist Enos Mills, who had the odd habit of lashing himself to the tops of pine trees during intense thunderstorms, had tussled with windy bureaucrats as he fought for protection of more than 350 square miles of scenic splendor, located about 70 miles northwest of Denver. Dominated by 14,259-foot Longs Peak, the area contained eighty summits over 13,000 feet and another seventy 12,000-foot cloud scrapers. In 1912 the newly formed Colorado Mountain Club, led by James Grafton Rogers, joined Mills in his campaign. Rogers, a partner in the Rogers and Shafroth law firm, worked with Morrison Shafroth, John's son, to draft legislation establishing Rocky Mountain National Park.[39]

Years earlier, Congressman Shafroth had supported creation of Mesa Verde National Park based on its merits as a treasure trove of ancient Indian ruins and its potential to attract tourist dollars. Mills's proposal for Rocky Mountain National Park also promised to rake in money from visitors, whose access to northern Colorado was made easier by improved roads. With Senator Shafroth's support, Congress approved the new park, the nation's thirteenth. In 1919 it drew more than 170,000 tourists, a stunning statistic for the time, greater than the visitor numbers for Yosemite, Glacier, and

Yellowstone combined.[40] Ironically, a man who went to Congress to oppose conservation helped create one of the country's most successful parks. If nothing else, his support for Rocky Mountain demonstrated that Shafroth was pragmatic and flexible, with common sense and a nose for the dollar.[41]

In one of his last speeches in the Senate, in early March 1919, Shafroth for the umpteenth time attacked Senator Walsh's proposal for leasing federal lands. Shafroth had opposed federal land leases since the beginning of his term, and it must have seemed to him that he was leaving the Senate at about the same point he entered it—fighting for his constituents' rights to control their own lands. Between March 1913 and March 1919, however, he did far more than stand up for Coloradans. He played a part in enacting the Underwood tariff, the Federal Reserve Act, and the revenue laws establishing the income and inheritance taxes— some of the most important pieces of domestic legislation of the twentieth century. He had shepherded the Jones-Shafroth Act through the Senate, a bill that attracted little attention in the United States but carried great import in Puerto Rico. He had proven himself a true friend to labor. Farmers, too, had reason to applaud him. In 1916 he had backed a series of measures benefiting agriculturalists, including one that made it easier for them to borrow on their farms, an amendment to the Federal Reserve Act to expand farm credit, and a warehousing bill that gave farmers some protection from unscrupulous grain dealers.

Shafroth also dealt with scores of other matters, great and small. He pushed for appropriations for Colorado's two national parks; supported an unsuccessful bid to get a national park established in the Mount Evans area, near Denver; tended to his constituents' requests for pensions; prodded the U.S. Treasury to purchase silver; urged the Senate to sanction an amendment to the Constitution prohibiting the sale of alcohol; fought for women's suffrage; sought money to protect migratory birds; looked for ways to eliminate coyotes; and advocated federal funds for highway building.

Between 1913 and 1917, domestic affairs, the Philippines, and Puerto Rico kept Shafroth amply busy. When he went to the Senate, he had expected to spend his time protecting Colorado's interests and advancing progressive reforms. He had not foreseen the massive breakdown in the old world order that plunged Europe into war in August 1914. That titanic conflict, which the United States finally entered in April 1917, claimed millions of lives, while millions of others—including John Shafroth—found their lives profoundly changed.

Chapter Eight
War

On Sunday morning August 2, 1914, *The Denver Post* headlined: "World War On," announcing an exchange of shots between Germany and Russia. By late August, Austria-Hungary, Serbia, Germany, Russia, France, Great Britain, Belgium, Montenegro, and Japan had entered the conflict.

The tragedy took the United States by surprise. Two weeks before the Old World went mad, *The Denver Post*, finding little news to report, heralded the arrival in Denver of a water treatment plant engineer. Nor were the nation's politicians anticipating war. The Democratic platform of 1912 concentrated almost exclusively on home affairs, paying more attention to post roads and rural credits than to foreign policy. Before mid-1914, nations that would soon capture the public's attention—Bosnia, Serbia, Belgium—were to most Americans inconsequential little places in big geography books.

John Shafroth, too, had focused almost exclusively on domestic issues. In late April 1914 he made a brief foray into foreign relations when he read the Senate a short telegram from Colorado veterans of the Spanish American War, offering to help the United States in its simmering dispute with Mexico. Senator Boies Penrose of Pennsylvania complained that the few seconds Shafroth spent on the telegram wasted the Senate's time and then characterized Wilson's Mexico policy as "wicked." Shafroth shot back: "Making slurring remarks about the 'watchful waiting' policy of the United States in this matter, the object of which was to avoid war and to avoid bloodshed and referring to those matters in connection with a little telegram, it seems to me is unworthy of the Senator from Pennsylvania." And, said Shafroth, Penrose, who had earlier supported the president, "has developed an inconsistency and taken a position of which he himself should be ashamed."[1] Writing to his brother William, Shafroth repeated his defense of Wilson's handling of the strained relations between the United States and Mexico. "It would be almost criminal for us to have war with Mexico. It would create a distrust in all of the South American Republics that we were attempting to seize property."[2] Never a flag-waving jingoist of Theodore Roosevelt's ilk, Shafroth searched for peaceful means to settle international disputes.

In September 1914 he read into the *Congressional Record* Wilson's proclamation designating October 4, 1914, as a day of prayer for peace. Fifty thousand Denverites heeded the president's call. At the Cathedral of the Immaculate Conception, the Reverend Hugh McMenamin blamed the war on "materialism, infidelity, lust," on the atheistic philosophy "vomited" from Germany's schools and universities, on "the commercialism which caused England to forsake God for mammon." Preacher Billy Sunday, who was in Denver leading a temperance gathering, took a few minutes to pray for peace. At the Central Christian Church, the Reverend George B. Van Arsdale hoped the nations of Europe would call upon the United States to mediate.[3]

For most of 1914 and 1915 the war contributed only marginally to Shafroth's heavy workload. In February 1915 he wrote his brother, William: "We have had all night sessions for three nights. . . . We have been in continuous session almost two years and the Senators are all very tired. . . . I have a large accumulation of articles pouring in on me nearly every day relating to measures that are before the Senate."[4] Sometimes he received a welcome guest. Will, his nineteen year-old-son, a senior at the University of Michigan, visited Washington at Easter 1914. Son Morrison also visited for a couple weeks in 1914. Jack, his eldest son, a naval lieutenant, was often at sea, earning (the senator bragged) $2,400 a year. Our boys, John Franklin told William, "are the best boys on earth, none of them has ever given us a particle of trouble." Helping assure that good behavior, he promised to pay them each $10 a month if they abstained from tobacco and alcohol.

Shafroth was also down on meat, advising his brother against eating too much of it: "I have . . . avoided eating heavily of meats. I have always thought they are breeders of a good many ills of the human frame."[5] Evidently his diet agreed with him. "My health has been very good," he wrote William in 1915, "while I know I am getting old, yet I do not feel any serious effects from the results of the passing years."[6] A year later, however, after dining with Vice President Marshall, Shafroth suffered an attack the newspapers blamed on gallstones.[7]

In May 1915, after adjournment of the marathon 63rd Congress, John, Virginia, and Will accompanied a congressional delegation on a tour of Hawaii. Businessmen angling for congressional favor treated the ten senators and more than forty representatives to a luau under a banyan tree, a visit to Pearl Harbor, an outing at Waikiki Beach, a chowder supper, a birthday party for former Speaker of the House Joe Cannon, and a visit to a pineapple cannery. The Shafroths then went on to the Philippines and spent five weeks there, after which they toured Japan and Korea for a month and spent a short time in China. "We had a delightful trip," John Franklin wrote his niece, Ethel Bridgman, "had a splendid rest and saw a great deal of what is very interesting and instructive."[8]

In Washington, Shafroth occasionally shook off his usual early-evening drowsiness and stepped out for a social function. He wrote his brother in April 1916: "This has been a very gay winter for society. . . . Mrs. Wilson, the wife of the President, is a very beautiful woman and many entertainments have been given by her and for her." Shafroth added, "I do not care for these things myself, but Jennie seems to want to see what is going on and so I go with her, although we do not attend all of them by any means."[9]

John Franklin was probably not overly interested in the cascade of chatter unleashed when Wilson married Elizabeth Boling Galt in December 1915, sixteen months after the death of his first wife, Ellen. Jennie, however, was attuned to the buzz. In March 1916 she wrote Morrison: "Last Tuesday evening we went to the White House and heard some fine playing and singing from two men of whom I had not heard; as we sat in the beautiful East Room ablaze with the other Mrs. Wilson. People still talk bitterly of his taking unto himself a bride in such short order."[10]

By March 1916 the Shafroths had changed lodgings, moving into an "elegant three story house owned by Mrs. Bradford." Other portions of the house were rented to a congressman and an assistant secretary of the interior. "We have splendid eating," Shafroth told his brother, "and all the rooms are nice and pleasant." Jennie seemed to enjoy the capital, although the climate made her "feel limp."[11] She felt torn between her duty to John and her desire to be back in Denver to help care for her mother, who lived in the Shafroth's York Street home with Jennie's sister, Susanne. For Jennie, as for John, there were not always enough hours in the day to do everything. She wrote Morrison: "A whole drawer full of socks to darn for your father reproaches me, but it will have to remain undisturbed for a few days more."[12]

The death of Jennie's eighty-four-year-old mother on February 24, 1917, broke one more of the Shafroth family's links to Fayette. The death of John's brother, William, in July 1916, severed another hometown tie. It also brought additional burdens, as John struggled with the complexities of his brother's estate.[13] Shafroth's Denver house, vacant by late 1917, also worried him. When it failed to rent at $100 a month, he told his agent to lower the price to $75 and instructed him to light the gas jet in the bathroom and partially open the front shades so the house would look occupied.[14]

The Road to War

In March 1916, in one of his last letters to his brother, Shafroth told him there was an "enormous amount of work before Congress this year."[15] Increasingly, that work centered on the war in Europe—a war that divided Americans between those such as William Jennings Bryan, who wanted to keep out of it, and those such as Theodore Roosevelt, who urged the United States to enter the bloody fray. Between the doves and the hawks lay a large middle ground of shifting opinion that gradually tilted toward preparedness and tended to favor the English and French. Denver's *Rocky Mountain News* said that it "believes in peace most sincerely. But not the peace that comes from national weakness and unpreparedness, not peace with dishonor."[16]

More than any other single factor, German submarine attacks pushed the United States into war. In May 1915 a German submarine sank the *Lusitania*, a passenger ship, killing 1,198 people, including 128 U.S. citizens.[17] Disagreeing with Wilson's tough diplomatic response to Germany, William Jennings Bryan resigned as secretary of state. Fearful that another attack could draw the nation into the war, some senators in early 1916 backed the McLemore resolution, which warned U.S. citizens to stay off armed belligerent ships. Others argued that kowtowing to the Germans was unwise. Wilson did not want to issue a warning. "There has been great excitement during the past week over the controversy as to warning passengers to keep off belligerent ships," Shafroth told William. "I fear very much that war may result from not warning the people. It seems to me, however, that people reading the newspapers and the agitation would have sense enough to keep off such ships."[18] Putting aside his fears, John Shafroth, as he usually did on major foreign policy issues, backed Wilson and voted against McLemore.

Neither Wilson nor Shafroth favored war. Democrats portrayed Charles Evans Hughes, the 1916 Republican presidential nominee, as a man likely to enmesh the United States in the conflict. Bryan talked of peace and stumped for Wilson. "Bryan's speeches at Pueblo last night and Colorado Springs tonight were masterpieces in argument and power," former Colorado governor Alva Adams told Senator Thomas Walsh.[19] Running on a "he kept us out of war" platform, Wilson won Colorado in 1916, as he had in 1912. Democrats also secured a comfortable margin in the U.S. Senate, where they out-numbered Republicans by fifty-four to forty-two. But, in an ill omen for 1918, they lost the House.

From December 1916 through January 1917, Wilson frantically tried to prod the Europeans into negotiating. In May 1916 Shafroth had backed a constitutional amendment giving the president authority to negotiate a treaty that obligated the United States to use its military to enforce a peace agree-ment as long as the Senate agreed. In late December 1916, Shafroth warned Wilson against assuming that he had the constitutional power to enforce peace. On January 3, 1917, Wilson responded to Shafroth, saying that while he believed the president and the Senate could decide on arrangements for maintenance of peace, he understood the need to consider the constitutional question.[20] But, pressured by events in Europe, Wilson did not wait for slow constitutional change. He addressed Congress on January 22, 1917, outlin-ing the foundations of an enduring peace—a "peace without victory"—and suggesting that the United States help enforce the peace.[21]

On February 1, 1917, Germany announced that its submarines would start sinking U.S. ships en route to Europe. Their offer to allow safe passage to one unarmed U.S. ship a week hardly placated Americans. If the United States had bowed to German tactics, it would have walked away from much of its trade. Moreover, the country would have abandoned its long-held position that the seas should be free, a principle vital to its economic well-being. During February and March German submarines snuffed out American lives, and the United States learned of a German proposal to ally with Mexico in the event of a German-U.S. war.

On April 2, 1917, Wilson asked Congress to declare war on Germany. Two days later Shafroth joined eighty-one other senators approving the war declaration. Colorado's other senator, Charles Thomas, was absent but said he favored the measure. On April 6, the House followed suit. Benjamin Hilliard, Denver's congressman, cast one of fifty votes against the declara-tion, as did Representative Edward Keating of Pueblo. "When Congress de-clares war," Keating said, "it does not mean that Congressmen are ordered to the front." Reminding his colleagues that many of them had campaigned in 1916 on a platform that stressed U.S. neutrality, he asked: "[W]ho among you last October and November, when you were asking for the votes of your constituents, dared to suggest to them that if elected you would send their boys to Europe? . . . Why, my friends, Woodrow Wilson running on that kind of a platform could not have carried a single state in this Union."[22]

Shafroth did not need to be reminded that congressmen were not ordered to the front. He had three sons of military age, one of whom, Jack, was already in the navy. Nor did he need to be scolded about broken Democratic campaign pledges. He had long advocated peace, and despite the events of February and March 1917 he clung to the belief that war could be avoided almost until it was actually declared. On March 28 his sister-in-law, Susanne Morrison, recorded in her diary: "John went to Washington Monday—he hopes for peace."[23] William Jennings Bryan, also hoping for peace, wrote to Shafroth: "Don't vote for war. You'll never forgive yourself if you do."[24]

Yet Shafroth did vote for war. Why? In May 1917 he explained his position in a speech supporting war bonds. The United States, he said, entered the war to secure freedom of the seas, to provide for the integrity of nations, and to promote democracy.[25] Like Wilson, Shafroth had wanted to stay out of the European conflict, which he regarded as senseless and fated to bankrupt the combatants.[26] But when Wilson, prodded by German submarine warfare and public opinion, finally concluded that war was necessary, Shafroth followed his leader. Susanne Morrison noted in her diary on April 6 that her brother-in-law had voted for war: "This in a degree justifies the measure for me, for I know what a good man John is."[27]

Shafroth was also, as always, a practical politician. With his chess-player's instinct for thinking several moves ahead, he probably sensed that antiwar congressmen would pay a high price for a symbolic gesture. Soon after the vote was taken, the *Rocky Mountain News* attacked Keating, Hilliard, and Thomas: "We are not proud of Colorado's part in the roll calls on the war resolution."[28] The *News* suggested that had the vote been secret Shafroth would have sided with the peace bloc. Had Shafroth opposed the war, as Bryan wanted, the measure would still have passed, and he would have assured himself a place on the ash heap of politics, along with Hilliard and Keating.

For Shafroth, the war declaration was both gratifying and distressing. "I will be one of the youngest officers in command of a destroyer," Jack, then thirty, wrote in announcing that he was to command the *Terry*. "If we meet the enemy I hope to give a most illustrious account of the Terry and add a little more luster to the name Shafroth."[29] Sons Will and Morrison also answered duty's call. Both joined the army and became captains.

Proud of his sons, Shafroth also worried about them. His brother-in-law James Seager wrote: "It is an awful thing that the best blood of all the world should be sacrificed to exterminate a generation of ambitious and ruthless paranoiacs."[30] And Jennie could hardly stand to have her three sons at risk. Her sister, Susanne, reported: "Jennie is so distressed and nervous. How could she be otherwise to give such a costly offering to her country." Jennie may have taken some comfort from a letter from President Wilson recognizing "the great sacrifice which this involves."[31] Keeping occupied also helped her. John wrote to his niece, Caroline Bradley, in Fayette: "Jennie . . . is busy nearly all the time studying French and doing a lot of knitting and other things."[32] The few surviving letters from John to Morrison suggest that the elder Shafroth kept a stiff upper lip. He could occasionally lighten up, though. In one letter he advised Morrison, who was courting Abby Staunton Hagerman of Kansas City, to take care what he wrote to her because censors were scrutinizing military mail. "It would be awfully embarrassing to you to have a letter opened which began 'divine enchantress of my soul.'"[33]

Work also helped the senator keep his mind off the dangers that faced his sons. "I am glad Jennie is soon to be with you," Seager, wrote early in the war; "it surely is not good for you to plod along there in your humdrum fashion."[34] Shafroth wrote John B. McGauran in Denver in early 1918: "Ever since the war began we have been exceedingly busy in Congress. All the Senators are nearly snowed under with enormous correspondence. It looks as if the session will last until October."[35]

Homefront Victories

Shafroth's humdrum labor paid off. In August 1917 a Colorado delegation including banker William Gray Evans, wealthy flour miller John K. Mullen, and Alva B. Adams (son of former governor Alva Adams) visited Washington, D.C. They sought to persuade the army to build a tuberculosis recuperation hospital near Denver, renowned as a place where people recovered from the often-fatal lung disease. Shafroth shepherded the delegation through the oppressive Washington heat to visit the appropriate functionaries. Official wheels ground slowly. Shafroth wrote Denver automobile dealer Finlay McFarland on March 17, 1918:

> On yesterday, after no less than 20 calls upon the Secretary of War, the Chief of Staff, the Surgeon General of the Army and others, we at last got the promise of the Acting Secretary of War to approve permanent construction of the tubercular hospital at Denver under an estimate of $1,700,000. As our Army will always be much larger than it has been, I am satisfied that in time we will get the hospital increased to three or four times the size of 1,000 beds, which it is now proposed to erect.

By the summer of 1918 a thousand men were at work on the hospital, later named Fitzsimons, in the hamlet of Aurora on Denver's eastern outskirts.[36]

Although he initially favored a negotiated, peaceful resolution to World War I, Senator Shafroth ultimately voted for the Declaration of War that committed U.S. troops to the conflict. His sons Jack, Morrison, and Will served as officers during the war. Colorado Historical Society.

In his letter to McFarland, Shafroth reported on other bacon he had snatched for Colorado. Some, such as the contract for $2 million worth of marble from Marble, Colorado, for the Lincoln Memorial, predated the war.[37] Other expenditures, including a $1,250,000 contract for winches and other ship equipment, were prompted by the war. Irrigators in western Colorado benefited from the nearly $2 million Shafroth helped secure for the Uncompahgre and Grand Valley reclamation projects. Veterans of the Indian Wars owed him thanks for helping them get pensions.

Shafroth watched out for Colorado's farmers. Accused of not doing enough for sugar beet growers in early 1918, he pressured the federal government, which was controlling farm prices as a war measure, to pay beet farmers more. His record in supporting agriculture, Shafroth bragged, was exceedingly strong: "I have voted for many millions of appropriations in aid of agricultural interests, not only in one bill but in every bill that has been presented." The senator then named a dozen measures he had supported, including one to provide agents in each farm county to promote scientific methods, and a statute allowing "loans at a very low rate of interest."[38]

During 1917 and 1918 Shafroth could have filled much of his senatorial plate with Colorado matters, but the times would not allow it. Larger issues demanded his attention. He voted to increase the size of the military establishment. He favored punishing seditious talk but opposed censoring the press. He continued to push for progressive legislation, including one bill to establish a minimum wage for women and children in the District of Columbia and another allowing the Hawaiian legislature to give the vote to women. And he trumpeted national prohibition, telling senators that after Colorado went dry on January 1, 1916, arrests for drunkenness decreased, tourism increased, the penitentiary population went down, savings went up, and 1,615 saloons and 17 breweries ceased to be. Perhaps that information helped move a few lawmakers to support prohibition. On December 18, 1917, Congress referred the Eighteenth Amendment to the states for ratification, and on January 29, 1919, it was declared ratified.[39]

Shafroth also tended to constituent requests, including one from Captain Morrison Shafroth of the 341st Field Artillery. Morrison trained at Camp Funston, Kansas, under the command of Major General Leonard Wood, who was in charge of the 89th Army Division. Many Coloradans served in the 89th and, like Morrison, revered Wood. When the division was sent to the East Coast to embark for France, the War Department told Wood that he was to be removed from command. Morrison phoned his father, asking him to intercede with President Wilson to reinstate the general. Morrison and his wife, Abby, also made a quick trip to Oyster Bay, Long Island, to see Theodore Roosevelt. He received them graciously but confessed that he had no influence with Wilson, "that it would only do harm if he attempted to intervene."[40]

Shafroth intervened, telling Wilson that Wood was popular among the Colorado troops, that it would be "a great mistake as to them not to permit General Wood to command them in engagements in France."[41] Wilson responded that Wood "is serving the country very much better in training men on this side than he could serve it in any other way at this juncture." Wood himself believed that General John J. Pershing, the overall commander of U.S. forces, feared the competition Wood would have given him in Europe. Or perhaps Wilson, who had found Wood incorrigible during the preparedness debate in 1916, did not want the outspoken general becoming more popular by winning battles in France. Wood stayed home.[42]

William Jennings Bryan also reluctantly stayed home. In January 1918 he wrote Shafroth: "On the theory that I might be called upon to act upon the Peace Commission, I am giving my time this winter to the study of the important peace treaties of the past and a history of the political relations between the leading European countries now engaged in war."[43] Shafroth responded in late January that a number of Democratic senators hoped Bryan would be appointed: "I believe that you are the one man of all others in the United States that will make the most favorable terms of peace in behalf of the common people."[44] In early November, Shafroth was still lobbying to get Bryan onto the peace commission. In late November, he gave Bryan bad news: "Nothing in years has caused me so much distress as the situation concerning the peace commission." Bryan's friends, Shafroth reported, remained his friends but "it would not do to start a contest on the peace commission; that it would create a storm that would make it impossible to accomplish the purpose and at the same time would embarrass the President immensely."[45] The message was clear: Wilson did not want the headline-grabbing Bryan in Europe, and Bryan's "friends" were not going to push the president on the issue.

By then Shafroth was in no position to help Bryan. In November 1918, after more than a quarter-century in politics, his career was brought to an abrupt end by a narrow defeat in his race for re-election. Not inclined to cry over his wounds, he wrote Bryan on November 8, 1918: "As you have noticed, we had an election and the result was unfavorable to us. Various advantages were taken, but I do not want to burden you with my tale of woe."[46] That tale, however, richly reflected the complexities of Colorado politics and society in the second decade of the twentieth century.

Chapter Nine
Crucible
of Politics

W hen John Shafroth returned to Colorado in mid-October 1918 to campaign for re-election to the U.S. Senate, he found the state reeling from an influenza epidemic. In less than three weeks, it had killed seventy-eight people in Denver alone. To control the contagion, officials closed schools, banned church services, and prohibited public meetings, forcing Shafroth to conduct a limited hand-shaking campaign in Denver and outstate communities such as Olathe, Grand Junction, and Leadville.[1] Describing his low-key politicking to Senator Charles Thomas, he said: "I have just returned from a stop over on the Western Slope where I have spent a week. We have done nothing in the way of speaking. We simply get out at a station and have the chairman of the county committee take us to all the stores and to the people in the town and we are introduced to those whom we see."[2]

Shafroth badly needed to shake more than a few hands. He needed to use his booming voice to trumpet his accomplishments to large crowds. He had to promote himself vigorously because Lawrence Cowle Phipps, his wealthy Republican opponent, had plenty of money with which to buy newspaper ads. Some said he also bought votes, even "hiring whole families, ostensibly to do election work."[3] During his six years in the Senate, Shafroth had spent little time in Colorado, imprisoned in Washington by long congressional sessions and several days' train travel from home. In 1912 strong reform winds had blown him to victory. In 1918 the winds were blowing the other way.

The uneasy alliance between conservative and reform Democrats that elected Shafroth to the U.S. Senate and Elias Ammons governor of Colorado in 1912 was wrecked on April 20, 1914. That day at Ludlow, south of Walsenburg, state militiamen battled with striking coal miners, killing five men and a child, and ignited a fire that killed two women and eleven children. The "Ludlow Massacre" polarized Coloradans. Law-and-order advocates and corporation toadies sided with Ammons and the militiamen. Other Coloradans sympathized with the workers. For Shafroth it was a political minefield. He dared not denounce Ammons, his friend and fellow Democrat; he dared not contribute to Colorado's national humiliation. But he could not appear unsympathetic to labor, upon whose support he counted. In that dilemma, Shafroth kept a low public profile.

Shafroth's secretary, John I. Tierney, a member of the Colorado State Senate, took a different tack. He returned to Denver from Washington, D.C., to attend the special session of the General Assembly that Ammons called in early May 1914. The governor asked for money to finance the militia. Tierney and a few other pro-labor insurgents wanted to impeach Ammons, branding him and others "weak, corrupt, or incompetent."[4] Historians may never know for certain if Tierney served as Shafroth's surrogate, saying for the sake of Shafroth's labor constituency what the senator dared not say himself. But John Franklin at least tacitly endorsed his secretary's views, because he continued to employ Tierney even after pro-Ammons conservatives demanded Tierney's dismissal.

Ammons survived the impeachment talk, but the Democratic Party was torn apart. Thomas Patterson, publisher of the *Rocky Mountain News,* ran as the Democratic nominee for governor in 1914 without the support of some conservative Democrats, who voted for the Republican George Carlson. Other Democrats backed Progressive Party candidate Edward Costigan. Patterson and Costigan split the reform vote, and Carlson waltzed into the governor's office. In July 1916 Patterson died, depriving Shafroth of one of his most effective advocates. He had already lost the support he once received from the *Rocky Mountain News,* which Patterson sold in October 1913 to John C. Shaffer, a Chicago millionaire. That left Shafroth largely dependent for newspaper backing in Denver on *The Denver Post* and its flamboyant publishers, Frederick G. Bonfils and Harry H. Tammen.

Democrats found 1916 more to their liking than 1914. Some voters from the moribund Progressive Party drifted to the Democrats, prompted by Costigan's endorsement of Wilson and Democratic gubernatorial candidate Julius C. Gunter.[5] Both Wilson and Gunter won, while Democrats

Benjamin C. Hilliard, Edward Keating, and Edward Taylor took seats in the U.S. House of Representatives. But the reformers' victories were partially eclipsed by the resurrection of Robert Speer. Hounded out of office in 1912, he bided his time while Denver experimented with commission government. In May 1916 he regained the mayor's office with "the remnants of the old machine . . . solidly behind him on election day."[6] It was, as Shafroth knew, a machine with a long memory and without affection for him.

Early in 1917, anti-reformers connived with Governor Gunter to gut the state's initiative and referendum statutes and to destroy the system that allowed candidates to petition their way onto the primary ballot. To save those instruments of democracy, which Shafroth had struggled for and won when he was governor, reformers staged a mass meeting at City Auditorium in Denver on March 14. Despite his busy congressional schedule in the weeks leading up to the declaration of war against Germany, Shafroth wired his son Morrison in Denver: "Inconvenient to leave here but will attend mass meeting next Wednesday if you think necessary . . . wire answer."[7]

The senator decided to return. He had a strong personal stake in maintaining the primary system, because if it were destroyed the Democratic political convention would have the exclusive power to name the party's U.S. Senate candidate. Simply put, the machine bosses could ax him. Rumor had it that Robert Speer and attorney Gerald Hughes, two of the most powerful men in the Democratic Party, were joining forces against the senator and that Gunter and the conservative Democrats were aiding Hughes and Speer by getting rid of the direct primary.[8]

At the auditorium, Shafroth roasted the anti-reformers for an hour. "Who do these legislators think they are?" he thundered. "Do they think we have ceased to believe and to hold that 'governments derive their powers from the consent of the governed'?" Shafroth had more than his own strong voice to help him in his fight. His secretary, John Tierney, went to the White House on March 14, seeking Wilson's help. Told that the president was ill and could not be disturbed, Tierney rushed to the nearby Treasury Department, where he roused William G. McAdoo, the secretary of the treasury and Wilson's son-in-law. McAdoo reached the president, who wired Shafroth: "No legislation should be enacted by the general assembly of Colorado to repeal, directly or indirectly, the initiative and referendum or the direct primary laws. These are instrumentalities by which the government is brought nearer the people and should be preserved."[9] Under pressure, the antireformers temporarily slunk away, and "the interests" depicted by *The Denver Post's* cartoonist were "Foiled Again! Curses!"[10]

Dirty Politics in 1918

Speculation that Shafroth would face a primary opponent in 1918 came to nothing. Speer may have coveted the nomination, but he died of pneumonia in May 1918. Hughes evidently saw little chance of taking the plum from Shafroth. Instead he supported the Republican nominee, Lawrence Phipps. A faction within the Democratic Party, cheered on by the *Denver Democrat* and its editor, John Barkhausen, followed Hughes and supported Phipps.

Colorado Springs millionaire Spencer Penrose (brother of Senator Boies Penrose, a Pennsylvania Republican) and Bulkeley Wells, a sworn enemy of labor, urged Phipps to run. Phipps, who had never held a significant elective office, staked his claim to the Senate seat on his experience seventeen years

A reformer never rests: When Colorado legislators tried to repeal the initiative and referendum laws in 1917, Senator Shafroth traveled from Washington to Denver to lead a rally against the proposal. The measure failed. Colorado Historical Society.

earlier as a vice president of Carnegie Steel and on the relief work he was doing in 1918 for the Red Cross. One of his campaign advertisements in the *Denver Labor Bulletin* claimed that he had "started his career in overalls, as a night weigh clerk in a small iron mill in Pittsburg [sic], working a twelve-hour shift for $1.00 per night. By sheer pluck and ability he rose among his fellow workers until he was recognized as one of the most successful and best-trained businessmen in America." The blurb did not mention Lawrence's uncle, Henry Phipps, one of Carnegie's partners, who might have had something to do with young Lawrence's "sheer pluck" rise.

Fleeing Pittsburgh's foul air, Phipps found Denver's climate pleasing and settled in the city in 1901. He established a tuberculosis sanitarium on the fringe of the east Denver neighborhood of Montclair, gaining favor with Denverites, who were happy to have the revenue. In 1904 he and his wife, Genevieve, separated. Gossips said she had wronged him by being overly friendly with her doctor, Thomas J. Gallagher.[11] Genevieve said, "Differences have existed between me and him [Lawrence] for several years. For the honor of the Phipps name, which my children bear, I trust that I may never find it necessary to state the nature of those differences."[12] Seven years later Lawrence, then forty-eight, again arched a few eyebrows when he married twenty-two-year-old Margaret Rogers, daughter of Platt Rogers, Shafroth's law partner. Fortunately a fortune covered a multitude of arched eyebrows, and Phipps by all accounts had millions, perhaps tens of millions.

By 1908 Phipps was listed among the supporters of the railroad David Moffat was building from Denver to Salt Lake. Moffat, president of Denver's First National Bank, hoped ultimately to extend the line to the West Coast, creating a rival to the great transcontinentals.[13] But he died in early 1911, ruined by his inability to get financing in the East. His railroad, meanwhile, died in Craig, Colorado, far from Salt Lake—and far from being profitable. Senator Charles Hughes, Moffat's attorney, died early the same year. Moffat and Hughes' collaborator William Gray Evans, the Napoleon Bill of Denver politics and the major force behind Speer, suffered a nervous breakdown in 1913. Gerald Hughes, Charles's son, was left to salvage the Moffat-Evans empire, a job that would be easier if Hughes could get his man, Lawrence Phipps, into the U.S. Senate. Allied with Phipps financially, Hughes was also close to him personally. When Margaret and Lawrence had a son in 1915, they named him Gerald Hughes Phipps.

Phipps and Hughes were gentlemen, so they left dirty political work to lesser men. Of these, Thomas J. O'Donnell, a leading Democrat, and John Barkhausen of the *Denver Democrat* were two of the most vitriolic and, because they were Democrats, two of the most dangerous. Shafroth did not need to take seriously O'Donnell's old allegation that the senator ate his pie with a knife, nor O'Donnell's jibe that John Franklin tied his tie outside his collar.[14] People had poked fun at his unkempt appearance for years; it had done him no harm. To the vague claim that "Colorado would be as well represented if it had a clothes pin stuck on the back of his chair in the senate," he could counter, when he got a chance, with a record of solid achievement.[15] To the often repeated charge that he failed to get Colorado any army bases, he could reply that the army had rejected the state for training camps because of its cold winter nights. Moreover, the army tuberculosis hospital he had helped secure would keep pumping money into the state's economy after the war ended. Vapid statements from Phipps such as "Men with backbone instead of wishbone needed in Washington" probably did Shafroth little harm.[16]

More damaging, given the anti-German temper of the times, was the accusation made in the *Rocky Mountain News* and the *Denver Democrat* that Shafroth was pro-German before April 1917 and remained so after the United States entered the war. Before April 1917, Shafroth had not taken sides, heeding Wilson's request that U.S. citizens remain neutral in thought, word, and deed. Shortly after the United States entered the conflict Shafroth read into the *Congressional Record* a letter from Godfrey Schirmer, president of Denver's German National Bank, stressing the loyalty of German Americans.

Loyalty did not save German Americans from bigotry. The German National Bank quickly changed its name to the American National Bank in response to the anti-German witch hunt that raged in Colorado. German books were burned in Boulder. Denver schools stopped teaching German. In eastern Colorado, an Austrian American was threatened with hanging. In western Colorado, a German American superintendent of schools was, as historian Lyle Dorsett reports it, "tarred and feathered for using a book that said favorable things about Germany."[17]

Shafroth, whose Swiss-born father spoke German, became a target of the xenophobia. Sometimes the denigration was subtle, as when Atterson W. Rucker, a former Colorado congressman, recalled his boyhood in Fayette, Missouri. He had gone to school with Shafroth and knew him well, said Rucker, but had not known his parents because they spoke little English.[18] Often Shafroth's detractors were more blunt. Shafroth partly owned the Welton Street Realty Company, which owned the land under Denver's Kenmark Hotel—known as the Kaiserhoff before 1917. Shafroth neither owned nor managed the hotel; he and his partners merely leased the land to the Kenmark's proprietors. Yet that did not stop the *Denver Democrat* from wailing: "The senator's German mind was shown when he named his hotel at Seventeenth and Glenarm the Kaiserhoff and had he Kaiser's coat of arms burned into its china, etched on its bar-room glassware and woven into its bed linen. . . . In paying tribute to the kaiser, he was expressing the natural feeling that came from his German blood."[19]

The more widely read *Rocky Mountain News* chimed in: "Mr. Shafroth is of German blood and antecedents. Naturally he is in sympathy with the German nation; and his temperamental shortcomings are all in the line of giving way, compromising. He did not want war. He will be very glad when it is at an end."[20] Shafroth wrote Morrison on November 1: "They . . . have been telling more lies about me than in any previous campaign."[21]

Shafroth's enemies could not find that he had ever said a word favoring Germany. They did dredge up some of his old votes in Congress, votes made before the United States entered the war, and twisted them to imply he was anti-military and pro-German. For example, in July 1914, a month before the war broke out in Europe, he had voted to build one new battleship for the U.S. Navy, instead of two. Nearly a year before the United States entered the war, he opposed putting state national guard units under federal control because he judged it "would injure the national guard organizations of the states and perhaps cause their disintegration."[22]

Shafroth rightly pointed out "these votes were cast . . . before the war and were intended for peace conditions."[23] However, more than a year after the United States entered the war, he blundered by accepting an invitation from William Randolph Hearst to attend 1918 Fourth of July festivities in New York City. Hearst, a powerful newspaper publisher widely suspected of pro-German leanings, asked 250 senators and representatives to attend the New York bash. All but thirty-four, realizing that Hearst was a "political typhoid carrier," declined. Unfortunately Shafroth—some said frugal John could not pass up a free meal—decided to go. Whisked to New York in a special train at Hearst's expense, the legislators enjoyed the day, which included a nine-hour-long parade. Afterward, the publisher treated the politicians to dinner at the Astor Hotel and entertainment at the Cocoanut Grove nightclub and the Ziegfeld Follies.[24] It was great stuff for the *Rocky Mountain News* cartoonist, who sketched a rumpled Shafroth sitting in a theater box with Hearst watching Ziegfeld girls shake their legs.[25] The *Denver Democrat* also savored the spectacle: "It was German money which paid for everything Shafroth eat [sic] and for the free bed in which he slept as Hearst's guest."[26]

When the *Denver Democrat, Rocky Mountain News, Denver Times,* and other papers were not jabbing Shafroth, they were gouging other reform

Democrats. Thomas Tynan, a Shafroth protégé and warden of the state penitentiary, defeated Julius Gunter in a bitter contest for the Democratic gubernatorial nomination. Edward Keating, despite his vote against entering World War I, won renomination to Congress in southern Colorado. Benjamin Hilliard, Denver congressman, also voted against war and as a result lost Democratic support in Denver, so he ran for re-election to Congress as an independent. Shafroth, closely connected with all three, suffered from his association with them.

Much of Shafroth's opposition came from predictable places: from conservative Democrats, who had opposed him since he was governor, and from Republicans. But some came from an unlikely source—from women, a group Shafroth had consistently befriended. Suffragist Alice Paul and President Wilson played large roles in estranging Shafroth from part of the women's movement, and Shafroth himself inadvertently took part by sponsoring the Shafroth-Palmer Amendment.[27]

Paul, a twenty-seven-year old-militant suffragist, arrived in Washington in December 1912 to prod Congress into proposing a woman's suffrage amendment. On March 3, 1913, the day before Wilson's inauguration, Paul focused national attention on women's lack of voting rights by staging a parade in Washington. For a year she worked under the umbrella of the National American Woman Suffrage Association (NAWSA), a group with nearly half a million members. Although it favored a constitutional amendment, NAWSA was concentrating on state suffrage campaigns. Paul thought women's time would be better spent pressuring Congress. Unlike many of the polite ladies in NAWSA, she was willing to picket, go to jail, and endure hunger strikes in prison. She also disagreed with NAWSA's nonpartisan stand, which urged women to vote for candidates who favored suffrage regardless of party. Paul demanded that the party in power be held responsible for getting the suffrage amendment passed.

Her strategy was simple. If Democrats, the party in power after March 4, 1913, got Congress to refer a women's suffrage constitutional amendment to the states, Paul would support them. But if they did not, she would oppose every Democrat who was up for re-election, even those—like John Shafroth—who were pro-suffrage. By their willingness to sacrifice a few good men, Paul and her supporters hoped to show Democrats that they must support suffrage if they wanted to retain control of Congress. By early 1914 Paul had broken with NAWSA and had become chairman of the Congressional Union for Women's Suffrage, which evolved into the National Woman's Party in 1917.

Shafroth stumbled into the civil war raging in women's movement on March 2, 1914, when he proposed the Shafroth-Palmer Amendment to the U.S. Constitution. For decades NAWSA had advocated the so-called Susan B. Anthony Amendment, a straightforward statement that "the right of citizens of the United States to vote shall not be denied or abridged by the United States or any station on account of sex."[28] In 1914 NAWSA, in a fit of temporary political insanity, deviated from that position to push a new scheme. It wanted Congress to propose a constitutional amendment that would require each state to hold a referendum vote on the issue of women's suffrage whenever 8 percent of a state's voters requested it. Some NAWSA leaders believed that such a proposal might overcome states'-rights objections to the Susan B. Anthony Amendment. Shafroth, trying to do what he thought women wanted, placed the idea before the Senate, while Representative A. Mitchell Palmer introduced it in the House. But the proposal backfired badly. Alice Paul and many others thought Shafroth-Palmer a stupid notion that would delay equal suffrage. Shafroth thus ran afoul of a vociferous and powerful segment of the women's crusade—and all for nothing, because the Shafroth-Palmer resolution failed to get the needed two-thirds vote.

Even had he not sponsored Shafroth-Palmer, John Franklin would have been targeted by Paul and the National Women's Party in 1918. In 1914 the Paul faction had campaigned against Charles Thomas in his Colorado race for the U.S. Senate, not because he did not favor equal suffrage but because Wilson and many other Democrats were not on the suffrage bandwagon. For the next four years Paul and her militant supporters hounded the president to pressure Southern Democrats in Congress, who opposed equal suffrage at least in part because it would give the vote to African American women. Shafroth strongly supported the Anthony Amendment when it came before the Senate in the summer of 1918, but he would not agree to water it down by excluding African-American women. Pressed by Senator John Sharp Williams of Mississippi to deny the vote to black women, Shafroth argued: "I think we must recognize democracy. That is what you have got to do, and you must recognize it in everybody."[29]

As the 1918 election approached, Wilson belatedly made equal voting rights for women one of his top priorities. In late September he personally asked the Senate to pass the Anthony Amendment, declaring: "We have made partners of the women in this war; shall we admit them only to partnership of suffering and sacrifice and toil and not a partnership of privilege and right?"[30] Perhaps if the president had matched his fine words with equal deeds and done more arm-twisting he could have picked up the two votes by which the measure fell short. As it was, twenty-two of the thirty senators who defeated the Susan B. Anthony Amendment on October 1, 1918, were Democrats. A couple more Republican votes could have saved the measure, but Republicans recognized that by withholding their support they would damage the Democrats, who would be blamed for the defeat.

Shafroth had gone to see Wilson shortly before the president spoke to Congress.[31] The senator knew that if the president failed in his quest for equal suffrage, Shafroth would face the wrath of Alice Paul. On October 1, the day the Senate shelved the Anthony Amendment, the *Rocky Mountain News* editorialized: "Those who believe in woman's right to vote . . . will vote against the party responsible for the defeat of suffrage, vote against the party as a party and as a whole without respect to the vote of an individual member of that party."

The National Woman's Party was ready to pounce. "Women on Shafroth's Trail Declare He Has Failed Them" ran a headline in the *Rocky Mountain News* on July 27, 1918. The article reported that Iris Calderhead of Kansas, an organizer for the Woman's Party, had arrived in Denver and opened an office in the Metropolitan Building. Gathering around her an influential coterie, including wealthy Democrats such as Mrs. Verner Z. Reed and Mrs. Horton Pope (whose attorney husband served the Guggenheims' smelter combine), Calderhead urged women to reject Shafroth.[32]

The October 16 edition of the *Denver Times* headlined: "Shafroth Fails to Champion Suffrage," charging that "suffrage has been Shafroth's strongest card, and yet he has come home to acknowledge defeat of the one thing he has been willing to admit he stands for." On November 2, the National Woman's Party ran a large front-page ad in the *Denver Labor Bulletin* showing women picketers being harassed by Washington police and asking Colorado women to dump Shafroth. On November 3, two days before the election, the National Woman's Party ran a full-page ad in the *Rocky Mountain News* with a similar anti-Shafroth message.[33]

Shafroth appealed to Ellis Meredith at the Democratic National Committee in Washington, D.C., asking her to get endorsements for him from NAWSA. "Nearly everything that has been published so far here has been treating me as if I were an enemy to the cause," he said.[34] Meredith, a leader in the 1893 campaign that secured equal voting rights for Colorado women, wired the senator that she would come to Denver to help him if needed.[35] Carrie Chapman Catt, NAWSA's president, told the *Denver Times:* "We have considered him [Shafroth] the most all-around hard worker for the suffrage amendment in the Senate."[36] In a letter to Mrs. George A. Bass, chairman of the National Democratic Woman's Committee, Catt was even more eloquent: "Two battles for Democracy are in progress, one in the western and southern fronts of Europe for world freedom, the other in the United States for Democracy at home. In the home struggle, Senator Shafroth is a fearless able general."[37] Shafroth thanked Catt in a telegram: "Your Times letter and telegram magnificent—just the thing needed."[38] More than Catt's letter was needed, as the election results would show, but Shafroth did not realize it until it was too late.

The 1918 Election

The senator also boasted a satchel full of other testimonials. "In view of the dastardly and dirty fight that has been made upon this faithful public servant, the people of the state should roll up for him an unprecedented majority," said Benjamin Barr Lindsey, Denver's juvenile court judge.[39] Franklin Lane, secretary of the interior, wrote Governor Gunter praising Shafroth as a "champion of those policies which the west believes in."[40] William Gibbs McAdoo, secretary of the treasury, sent his endorsement. Senator Key Pittman of Nevada told Philip Hornbein, the Colorado Democratic Party's state chairman, that Shafroth "stood as an impassable human barrier to the efforts of certain nature fakers and theorists in the far East in their effort to take away from the people of the West their lands, their mines and their timber for the purpose of constituting them into a grand park for the amusement of the effete East."[41] President Wilson, whose workload kept him from visiting Colorado, pleaded with voters: "I ask you to return John Shafroth to the United States Senate. I need him, the country needs him, and I ask the patriotic people of Colorado to vote for him."[42]

Senator Charles Thomas brought a bit of levity to an intensely serious campaign by writing a column in the style of humorist Peter Finley Dunne:

> Well said Mr. Dooley, "I see that the Republicans have trotted out a feller named Fips to run dawn the road behind old Jawn Shafroth . . . His [Fips's] platform is lyelty to the old flag and he guarantees to pull Uncle Sam's leg for Dinver. Ye know the fellers in Pittsburgh are still on the job. A fine little manicured Sinitor right after the war wud cum in mighty handy maybe. . . . It's a grate thing for bisniss . . . when U.S. Steel and U.S. Senator mean the same thing. . . . I've known old Jawn Shafroth since Hays was President. He ain't much for looks and wudn't know what to do with a valet if Larry lind him won . . . . He isn't illigent but he's always on the job."[43]

All those endorsements would not have meant much, if Shafroth had not had a means of getting them widely circulated. Fortunately and unfortunately, he had the support of the gorilla of Colorado newspapers—*The Denver Post*. With a Sunday circulation of nearly 120,000—more than twice that of its major rival, the *Rocky Mountain News*—the *Post* gave Shafroth a vehicle to get the public's attention. Consorting with a hairy ape, however, was dangerous business.

For nearly a quarter of a century the *Post's* buccaneer publishers, Frederick Bonfils and Harry Tammen, had used their paper to enrich themselves. Merchants who hesitated to advertise in the *Post* were coerced into doing so, lest the paper publish an exposé on their businesses. Nor did Bonfils stop at blackmail. Once he beat up *Rocky Mountain News* publisher Thomas Patterson. In February 1914 he brutally attacked prominent Democratic attorney Thomas J. O'Donnell while Mike Delaney, Bonfils' bodyguard, kept O'Donnell helplessly pinned. Morrison Shafroth wrote to his mother: "I just missed the battle at the court house the other day between O'Donnel [sic] and Bonfils. O'Donnel with his face all cut up got in the court house elevator as I got out. Bon and Tam and Mike Delaney and a big crowd were standing around the hall. It was pretty bad business. I guess they all had guns."[44]

The shrillness of the *Post's* 1918 electioneering reflected Bonfils' slash-and-burn tactics. The paper helped Shafroth by citing his record, featuring the endorsements he received, and exposing his detractors' lies. It cushioned the attacks on Shafroth's patriotism by noting that his three sons were serving in dangerous theaters of the war, while Phipps's son, Lawrence Phipps, Jr., "does his fighting from a swivel chair in front of a mahogany desk in a fire-proof, bomb proof, dynamite proof building in Washington . . . and the only danger that could possibly happen to young Mr. Phipps in this war, is the danger from over eating, over smoking or over resting."[45]

The *Post* harped on Phipps's big spending on votes, comparing him to Simon Guggenheim, who had virtually purchased one of Colorado's U.S. Senate seats in 1907. It nicknamed Phipps and Colorado Springs oil millionaire Oliver H. Shoup, who was running for governor, the "gold dust twins" and depicted them in political cartoons as toddlers in girls' skirts. It blew the whistle on Denver city officials for allegedly pressuring city hall workers, policemen, and firemen to vote for Phipps—or face losing their jobs. It belittled Phipps as "a good simple minded fellow, with some political ambition, and a barrel of money," a "Child in the Wilderness," a "Babe in the Woods," and putty in the hands of Gerald Hughes. It told voters that "a vote for Phipps and Shoup and the Republican congressmen means the prolonging of the war, the losing of many lives; it means the strengthening of Germany's determination to fight on, as they will understand it to means the repudiation of President Wilson and his war policies."[46]

Sadly for Shafroth, the *Post* overstepped even the wide boundaries that journalists then enjoyed. Ernest Morris, a Democratic candidate for the University of Colorado's Board of Regents, had incurred Bonfils and Tammen's wrath by successfully suing them. Morris, said the *Post*, was "born a Prussian, and is still a Prussian by instinct and birth and by arrogance and impudence." Morris was "so marked with the curse of Prussianism that even if he lived in a civilized country and grew to be as old a Methuselah, the Prussian curse would ever remain with him and stamp his acts." Such daily bilge eroded the paper's credibility and wasted space that could have been devoted to supporting Shafroth.[47]

By accepting Bonfils' support, Shafroth attracted enemies within the Democratic Party, among them Bonfils' punching bag, Thomas O'Donnell. "I know that his [O'Donnell's] animosities are very bitter," Charles Thomas wrote Shafroth, "and that he hates the *Post* proprietors most intensely."[48]

Lawrence C. Phipps (center) strolls past Denver's Brown Palace Hotel, where he celebrated his 1918 election to the U.S. Senate. Denver Public Library, Western History Collection.

The *Julesburg Advocate* summed up Shafroth's danger: "*The Denver Post* has come out into the open in support of Shafroth. That defeats Shafroth."[49]

That was an overstatement. The *Post*'s support was a mixed blessing, not a total curse. Nor was the senator totally dependent on Bonfils. Labor strongly backed him. Alice Paul and the National Woman's Party opposed him, but Carrie Chapman Catt and NAWSA supported him. Many farmers liked him, although the *Rocky Mountain News* carped about government prices for wheat.[50] In western Colorado, Representative Edward Taylor's popularity helped Shafroth, who also enjoyed the support of the *Grand Junction Sentinel*. In Pueblo, Colorado's second-largest city, the *Chieftain* opposed the senator, but the more widely circulated *Star-Journal* supported him. The *Boulder Camera* was with him; the *Colorado Springs Gazette*, against him.

A small band of federal office holders such as George Hosmer, Denver's customs collector, were beholden to Shafroth for their jobs and worked for him out of a combination of principle and self interest. Some old supporters from his days as governor also rallied around him. His former messenger, Oliver T. Jackson, founder of the African American farm community of Dearfield, wrote: "I am doing what I can single-handed and pledge you that Dearfield Settlement will show their appreciation of your interest in our settlement."[51] Another African American ally, John D. Harkless, composed "An Appeal to the Colored People of Colorado," in which he recalled Governor Shafroth's fast action in 1911 to prevent the lynching of Bob Harris in La Junta. Harkless also reminded voters of Shafroth's subsequent suggestion that Harris appeal his jail sentence with "the result . . . [that] Bob Harris today is a free man and Bob Harris's old mother and father were also saved from prison."[52]

Across the state, local Democratic organizations did what they could to return the senator to Washington. But the flu epidemic not only kept their candidate from speaking to large groups, it also often hit Shafroth's backers. On October 26, 1918, F.J. Bawden, the San Juan County treasurer, told Shafroth the Telluride area was overrun with the pestilence: "I will do all I can, but the election in this county from the looks of it now will not amount to much, we seem to have the plague, there were 45 or so deaths up to yesterday . . . and there were six more last night . . . It is simply awful."[53] In Washington, the flu sidelined Jack Tierney for two weeks and hobbled other members of Shafroth's staff, keeping them from distributing campaign literature.

The flyers that were sent out included a photo of Shafroth looking kindly, avuncular, and, unlike the trim and handsome Phipps, old. Like the photo, Shafroth's accomplishments were solid and significant but wrinkled by time and not particularly exciting. Coloradans cared little about the Philippines and Puerto Rico, places that had absorbed much of Shafroth's attention in the Senate. His disquisitions on banking and his continued support for silver may have moved a few voters, but silver was no longer a hot issue in Colorado and banking was hard to understand. Nor did most voters take an interest in adoption of the metric system or changing the date of the president's inauguration, two of the senator's pet projects.

Early in October, Shafroth wrote his brother-in-law James Seager that Phipps was an "exceedingly rich man, and I understand he is spending a good deal of money in this campaign, but money has not the powerful influence it used to have when Senators were elected by legislators."[54] October wore on. Phipps's money flowed. Shafroth's optimism waned. "We ought to win hands down," he told Senator Key Pittman, "but the Republican press, stimulated no doubt by the money of the opposition, are putting forth more lies than I have ever heard in a campaign before."[55] To Ellis Meredith he admitted: "[A]s they [Republicans] have unlimited money they have considerable advantage in the campaign."[56]

Contributing to the senator's gloom was a piece of news he received in late October: Morrison, serving in France with the 341st Field Artillery of the 89th Army Division, had been wounded. Morrison reported the injury was not serious, but Shafroth feared his son was minimizing his wound to spare the family worry. The concern proved correct. Shrapnel had smashed into Morrison's head, causing him to lose his sight in one eye.[57]

"Men Are Made and Unmade"

The tight race in Colorado concerned the national Democratic leadership, whose narrow control of the Senate could be lost if Shafroth were defeated. Homer S. Cummings, chairman of the National Democratic Committee, wrote to Wilson on November 4: "With reference to Colorado, the fight there seems to be a desperate one and somewhat in doubt."[58] Shafroth's old associate William Jennings Bryan, with no hint of pessimism, wired his good wishes on November 4, the day before the election.

When Coloradans went to the polls on November 5, Shafroth knew he might lose. As the precinct returns trickled in through the night, it appeared he might win, but when all the votes were counted, his hopes evaporated. The official count gave Phipps 107,726 votes to Shafroth's 104,347. Had 1,690 voters switched from Phipps to Shafroth, John Franklin would have gone back to the Senate, giving Democrats control of that body in the crucial period after World War I, which ended on November 11, 1918.

For Lawrence Phipps and his handler, Gerald Hughes, the result was most satisfactory. Benjamin Lindsey wrote to George Creel, who then headed the Office of War Information in Washington: "Gerald Hughes appeared with Mr. Phipps the night of election at the Brown hotel, and smilingly marched in arm in arm at the great congratulatory ceremonies held there, making himself quite conspicuous as having been the 'cause' for the success of Mr. Phipps of the steel trust against Mr. Shafroth of the State of Colorado."[59]

The closeness of the race makes explaining Shafroth's defeat both fascinating and frustrating. A variety of reasons can explain the result. For example, the Socialists fielded a candidate, as they had in Colorado elections for many years, and drew some votes away from the major-party candidates. Because it was unlikely that any socialist would vote for Phipps, a capitalist times ten, it is likely that Shafroth was hurt by the 5,606 votes that went to the Socialist U.S. Senate candidate, P.A. Richardson. Had Shafroth taken a few thousand of those votes, he would have been re-elected. But then, if he had pitched his message to socialists, other voters would have likely voted against him for being too radical.

Alice Paul and the National Woman's Party wanted to take credit for Phipps's victory, because Shafroth's demise bolstered the perception of their power. Certainly it is possible that 1,690 women, including former supporters of the Progressive Party as well as some Democrats, may have been swayed by Paul's logic and voted for Phipps rather than Shafroth. Inez Haynes Irwin, in *The Story of the Women's Party* (1921), wrote: "The defeat of Shafroth is universally ascribed to the Women's Party."[60]

Strangely, Shafroth and his friends did not emphasize the impact of the National Woman's Party, perhaps because a Goliath could not grasp being defeated by a David. In June 1918, Shafroth had warned Samuel E. Burris, one of his supporters: "We should be on the alert. Men are made and unmade in 60 days during these war times."[61] It was good advice that Shafroth did not heed when it came to Alice Paul. He underestimated her and the National Woman's Party. He may have mistakenly believed that his support for women's suffrage would protect him from the pebbles slung by what he probably considered a fringe organization. After the election it was, no doubt, hard for him to admit that women had helped defeat him. It was probably doubly difficult for him to realize that venerable suffrage leaders such as Carrie Chapman Catt and Anna Howard Shaw had, in less than six years, been overshadowed by militants who, as Senator Charles Thomas saw it, engaged in "much tumult and vociferous braying, all for notoriety's sake."[62]

Shafroth could find other explanations for his defeat, including the overall weakness of the Democratic ticket. Thomas Tynan, the Democratic candidate for governor, had alienated many conservative Democrats by striking out against Governor Gunter. In the general election, Tynan lost to Republican Oliver Shoup by more than 10,000 votes. Nor did Edward Keating and Benjamin Hilliard, two of the Democratic congressmen running in 1918, aid Shafroth's cause. In 1916, Keating had carried his southern Colorado congressional district by more than 9,000 votes. In 1918, after he voted against going to war with Germany, he lost his seat by 2,640 votes. Denver voters even more severely punished Hilliard. In 1916 Hilliard had won his seat in Congress by more than 4,000 votes. After he voted against war in April 1917, Democrats refused to re-nominate him for Congress. Running as

During his 1918 re-election bid, Shafroth's allies at The Denver Post *lampooned the well-funded Republicans as lackeys of the monied class. Colorado Historical Society.*

an independent in 1918, he gathered only 6,112 votes—24,134 fewer than in 1916. Charles Thomas, Shafroth's fellow U.S. senator, was not up for election in 1918, but he too was tarred as a closet pacifist because he been absent from the Senate when the war vote was taken.

H. S. Marshall, clerk of the District Court in Otero County, summed up Shafroth's problem: "[Y]ou were in mighty bad company—first and foremost, *The Denver Post,* then Keating, Hilliard, Thomas and Tynan—one could hardly hope to win with such a combination."[63] Former governor Alva Adams suggested that paid Republican precinct workers hurt the Democrats. In his view the election was "a tidal wave—gold and treason." Benjamin Lindsey had his own thoughtful analysis of the election. Wilson's letter endorsing Shafroth, Lindsey said, had backfired because Republicans claimed that the president was insulting their patriotism. Wilson and Shafroth's enemies had successfully intimated that "Wilson was weakening in dealing with Germany and wanted a negotiated peace." The *Post*'s "most vitriolic [sic], vindictive, awful daily tirade" against Ernest Morris, added Lindsey, disgusted many voters. And perhaps most important, "both Democrats and Republicans most led by Gerald Hughes, openly and flagrantly supported the Republican millionaire candidates. . . . In a word it was the old bipartisan machine . . . that elected the Republican ticket."[64]

The influenza bug also voted Republican. In previous contests, Shafroth had bested well-heeled opponents through hard work, much traveling, and frequent speaking. But the ban on public meetings in October and November 1918 left much of the campaigning to the newspapers. Phipps could and did purchase ads and influence everywhere. Indeed, the Republicans were probably relieved that their candidate was spared traditional campaigning because he was, at best, a mediocre speaker. Shafroth, although he sometimes sounded like a talking encyclopedia, had learned how to move the masses. Morrison wrote his father that it was "too bad the influenza epidemic prevented meetings, because campaigning would have helped you a lot."[65]

The despicable little flu virus, a hundred thousand times smaller than the crows' feet around Shafroth's eyes and ten thousand times thinner than the thinnest of his gray hairs, harbored a deep political bias. Flu sufferers who were not overworked, who could take time to rest, and who could afford to hire help tended to get better. Miners living in crowded boardinghouses, frazzled steel workers, and the denizens of densely populated immigrant districts—in short, Democratic voters—stood less chance of resisting and recovering from the malady. In all, the epidemic killed nearly eight thousand Coloradans and made roughly fifty thousand seriously ill.

The flu's impact on voter turnout is reflected in statistics from Edward Keating's southern Colorado congressional district, which encompassed Pueblo and the coal fields to the south and included thousands of immigrant workers. In 1916 Keating tallied 40,183 votes, and his Republican opponent garnered 31,137. In 1918 Guy Hardy, the Republican candidate, racked up 31,715 votes, and Keating took 29,075. Overall, Keating's district had 10,000 fewer voters in 1918 than in 1916, but the Republican vote declined only slightly while Keating's numbers plummeted by 11,000. Not all of the missing voters were flu-sick Democrats, but it is possible that a few thousand were. A few thousand more votes would have re-elected Shafroth.

Shafroth, in a letter to treasury secretary William Gibbs McAdoo, noted that Phipps had cemented his support by donating $75,000 to the Red Cross and "was head of an organization of several thousand women, whose aid and assistance no doubt materially contributed to his election." A year after the election, Shafroth estimated that the Republicans had spent "hundreds of thousands of dollars" in the contest.[66] He also blamed his loss on "a split in the Democratic organization." City workers, he told McAdoo, "were instructed to go down the Republican ticket or lose their jobs. Therefore, money and treason were the most important elements that contributed to our defeat."[67] Denver election numbers bear out Shafroth's assessment. In his hometown, where he had been a pillar of Democratic strength for more than a decade, he lost to Phipps by a margin of 5,598 votes. Had the Denver Democrats remained loyal to Shafroth, he more than likely would have won the election despite Alice Paul, despite the flu, and despite Keating's loss in southern Colorado.

Denver Post publisher Frederick Bonfils saw even more treacherous forces than treasonous Democrats at work. He wrote Shafroth: "You badly defeated him [Phipps] in the state and you would have won over him by a substantial majority had he and his friends not used vast sums of money to buy votes with." Bonfils claimed the sellouts "were paid $10 a day in some cases and the heads of families as much as $25 a day."[68] He wanted John Franklin to contest the election, but Shafroth replied that because Republicans would control the new Senate, he would have no hope of successfully challenging the result.[69] With good grace, Shafroth sent Phipps a traditional message of congratulations, pledging to help him as he assumed his senatorial duties.

Ever since he had been a member of the House of Representatives, Shafroth had tried but failed to do away with the lame duck congressional session that followed the November elections. But now, as a lame-duck legislator himself, he benefited from Congress's refusal to take his earlier advice, remaining in office until the new Congress was seated on March 4, 1919. He used the extra time to pursue some of his favorite crusades. Alice Paul and the National Woman's Party had helped defeat him, but that did not cool his ardor for equal suffrage, and he continued to push for the Susan B. Anthony Amendment. He also kept on fighting attempts to let the federal government lease Western lands.

In his remaining months in office, Shafroth had a final opportunity to champion one of his favorite causes—the creation of an organization to preserve peace. He had been advocating such a body for years. On January 22, 1917, six weeks before the United States entered the war, President Wilson told the Senate of his "expectation that the United States will join the other civilized nations of the world in guaranteeing the permanence of peace.[70]" Shafroth hailed the speech as "the greatest message of a century."[71] Just a week earlier, Shafroth had proposed that the Senate support a constitutional amendment allowing the president, with concurrence of two-thirds of the Senate, "to negotiate treaties to make the United States a party to a World Court of Arbitration."[72] On January 24, Shafroth told his Senate colleagues: "The world is now being drenched with the blood of millions, and I believe we have to yield some of our sovereignty in order to prevent the wholesale slaughter not only now continuing but which is likely to recur at intervals for ages to come. . . . This is revolutionary—of course, it is revolutionary, there is no question of that."[73]

Woodrow Wilson harbored similar revolutionary ideas. In a speech to Congress on January 8, 1918, he presented his fourteen points for reshaping the world after the war, the last of which envisioned a "general association of nations . . . for the purpose of affording mutual guarantees of political independence and territorial integrity to great and small states alike."[74] At the end of the war Wilson went to France to help frame the Treaty of Versailles. There he pressured the other victors into backing creation of the League of Nations, a body designed, in part, to prevent another major war.

Wilson was in the midst of the peace negotiations in January 1919 when anti-League senators attacked him. On January 14, Republican Senator William E. Borah of Idaho charged that a League of Nations would likely require the United Sates to maintain a large military establishment. To thwart Wilson, Senator Philander Knox of Pennsylvania (a Republican) proposed deferring action on the League.

Shafroth strongly disagreed with Borah and Knox. "The President," Shafroth said, "is now in Europe endeavoring to negotiate a peace treaty that not only will settle the disputes . . . but will at least have a tendency to prevent wars in the future." The war, Shafroth argued, was "a war to end all war," and therefore the president should be allowed to proceed unfettered in his efforts to get a peace that would prevent future wars.[75] In mid-February, when the details of the League were clearer, Shafroth said he approved, "although I do not think it drastic and strong enough."[76]

What Shafroth thought soon did not make much difference; on March 4, 1919, his term expired, and he became a private citizen. He stood on the sidelines cheering Wilson as the president toured the Midwest and West late in the summer of 1919, seeking public support for the League. Shortly after speaking in Pueblo on September 25, Wilson became so ill that he had to cancel the rest of his tour. A week later he suffered a debilitating stroke that left the League's supporters without effective leadership. On January 5, 1920, Shafroth wrote his son Will: "The Senate is acting the fool in not ratifying the treaty containing the League of Nations provision. The opportunity is the opportunity of centuries and the world will regret it exceedingly if the League of Nations should fail."[77] The Senate disagreed with Shafroth, and the United States, to Shafroth's dismay, did not join the League.

Though disappointed in his failure to be re-elected, Shafroth was not inclined to sulk. Briefly he considered returning to Denver, dusting off his old law books, and practicing law with Morrison. But after six years in the U.S. Senate and four years as Colorado's governor, commanding staff and participating in grand public affairs, the mundane routine of a small private law firm held little appeal for him. Fortunately, ex-senators often can count on their friends. Before John Franklin Shafroth left Washington, he found another way to earn a living.

The Shafroth family home at 1537 York Street. John and Virginia built the home in 1894 and raised their four children here. After her husband died in 1922, Virginia continued to live in the house until her own death in 1950. The building was demolished in the 1960s. Colorado Historical Society.

Chapter Ten
Twilight
and Legacy

overnor of Puerto Rico. Federal judge. Secretary of the Interior. Attorney general. Secretary of the Treasury. President of the United States. These were some of the positions that Shafroth's friends thought fit his talents after Colorado voters rejected him in 1918. William Jennings Bryan's suggestion in 1920 that Shafroth would make a good president was of no great significance, because by then Bryan had little power in the Democratic Party. Of more importance was William Gibbs McAdoo's high opinion of Shafroth. McAdoo, Woodrow Wilson's son-in-law, told Senator Charles Thomas in early 1920 that he had suggested Shafroth's name to the president as a possible secretary of the Treasury.[1]

None of those grand prospects would pan out. A defeated one-term senator from a small state, Shafroth probably realized that he was not likely to get much reward for his loyal support of President Wilson. Displaying the common sense that had served him well for more than half a century, he decided in 1919 to accept the chairmanship of the three-member War Minerals Relief Commission, which operated under the auspices of the Interior Department. On the surface it was a minor job, but it suited Shafroth well. With his sense of duty and detail, he was well equipped to adjudicate the claims that mining companies had against the government for suddenly canceling wartime contracts. The position promised a chance to travel. It would not, he thought, tie him down for more than about six months. And it paid $9,000 a year, more than he had made as a U.S. senator.

Before he could begin his new duties, he had to finish his old. It took him weeks to close his Senate office, as constituents continued to ask his help.

Soldiers' parents and spouses, anxious to hasten the return of their loved ones after the war, demanded much of his attention. Shafroth dutifully wrote acting Secretary of the Navy Franklin D. Roosevelt, asking that Reese A. Potter be let out of the navy. Elias Ammons requested help in getting his son Teller out of the army, thereby giving Shafroth a chance to do a favor for a former Colorado governor (Elias) and a future one (Teller). John Franklin also took time to help other old friends, even Republicans. On April 15, 1921, he recommended to President Warren Harding that he make Archie M. Stevenson, a longtime mainstay of Denver's Republican machine, ambassador to Argentina.[2] Other work was more prosaic. Finding that he had been reimbursed for a telegram that had actually been sent at government expense, Shafroth explained to the company that had borne the cost: "[T]he 35 cents does not belong to me; therefore, I re-inclose [sic] the same to you in the package in which you inclosed [sic] it to me."[3]

Shafroth's estimate that he would spend six months on the War Minerals Commission proved far too short. In the summer of 1919 he and Jennie went to San Francisco, where he had claims cases. He wrote Morrison: "We put in every night taking rides or going to 'movies' or some other amusement." Later, Jennie opted out of traveling with John because she did not want to miss the Spanish and French lessons she was taking. Much of the time the commission worked in Washington, allowing the Shafroths to stay in the swim of politics and society. "Jennie and I went to reception to Vice President Marshall last night," John Franklin wrote to Morrison, "and had a good time, that is, she did. She had on a lovely new party dress and many commented that she looked like a girl, which, of course, pleased me as well as her."[4]

Early in 1920 Shafroth told Will that the War Minerals Commission involved "a great deal of hard work in it and I am putting in more hours per day into the position than I have in any other occupation."[5] As burdensome as that labor was, it still left John Franklin with time for politics. His name naturally surfaced as a possible candidate for the U.S. Senate in 1920. Shafroth's ambition for elective office had cooled to the point of freezing, but he did not close the door on the possibility of another campaign. Instead he privately encouraged his son Morrison to don the family's political mantle. "All my life," he told Morrison, "I have been the first to arrive at my office and the last to leave it. It has been a constant grind of work and I know that if I were elected I would have the same grind on." Besides wanting to rest, John Franklin cited two other good reasons for not running: "First, I no longer care for the office. Second, and most important, is that I would deprive you of holding any office for seven years."[6] He added: "I am satisfied that a great many of my enemies would be glad to support you in order to get me out of the way."[7]

The strategy worked. Morrison, who had never held an elective office, won the 1920 Democratic nomination for Colorado attorney general. John Franklin, for his part, withdrew from politics by announcing in *The Denver Post* on July 19, 1920: "After one has been in public life as long as I have, he has a right to retire. One grows tired of public life after such a period." The retiree reserved the right, however, to "make some campaign speeches in Colorado on the League of Nations and the damnable methods the Republicans have used in killing ratification of the treaty."[8]

The November 1920 election turned out badly for the Democrats, both nationally and in Colorado. Republican Warren G. Harding, one of Shafroth's former Senate colleagues, was elected president. In Colorado, Republicans kept the governorship, captured the U.S. Senate seat previously occupied by Charles Thomas, and retained three of the state's four seats in the House of Representatives.[9] They also defeated Morrison Shafroth in his bid to become attorney general. John Franklin consoled him: "I happened to run in lucky years, and you ran in an unlucky year. You should not feel chagrined at the result, you should be proud of it." Taking a long view, father urged son to stay in politics because one day the tide would turn. And he advised Morrison to accept the cost of being in public life: "Although some people regret having entered politics on the ground that it is not remunerative, yet I have always been satisfied with what I did and would not change my course if I had it to do over."[10]

"I Have Quit the Game for Good"

In early 1920, Shafroth learned that Abby and Morrison became parents of Virginia, a "girl baby." He sent his congratulations and approbation: "[T]he oldest child of every family ought to be a girl as she has such a restraining influence over younger brothers."[11] Later, after having seen a picture of Virginia, he wrote Morrison: "I think you have some foundation for your claim that you have the cutest baby in the world."[12] John Franklin probably tempered his words because he had another grandchild, Helena—the daughter of son Jack and his wife, Helena—who could also lay claim, in a doting grandfather's opinion, to the title "cutest baby in the world."

Being in Denver, Morrison bore much of the responsibility for watching over the family home. In April 1921 John Franklin heard that robbers in Denver were blowing up safes, so he told Morrison either to put a note on the safe at 1537 York stating that there were no valuables inside, or to post the combination for the robbers, thereby sparing the house from the damage of an explosion. Morrison also received gratuitous financial advice from his father: "The way to make a living when you income is not large is to save. It's what you save, not what you make that counts."[13]

Will, who at that time was in Poland working for the American Relief Administration, received a shipment of socks from his father, although the elder Shafroth fretted that couriers might not carry such bulky items from England to Poland. He also worried that Will might start drinking. He had made a contract with his sons years earlier, agreeing to pay them ten dollars a month if they did not touch liquor. In late 1920 he offered to renew the contract with Will. Because of Prohibition in the United States, however, frugal John stipulated that Will would only get the payments while he was in Europe. In the spirit of compromise that had served him as a politician, he eventually agreed to pay Will even if he had three glasses of light wine a day, as long as he did not "drink any whiskey, gin, rum, or other strong drink."[14]

Shafroth's generosity extended beyond his own sons. Like Benjamin Franklin, John Franklin understood that a principal sum could produce substantial results over time. Late in 1920 he gave the Denver School Board a $500 U.S. savings bond, the income from which was to provide an annual prize "as an incentive to young men to keep posted on public questions and to become proficient in the art of extemporaneous speaking."[15] In early 1921 he made a similar donation to Central College in Fayette, Missouri, to create a debating prize in honor of his brother William. These were marks of a man putting his affairs in order. In the summer of 1920 he outlined his plans to Morrison: "Jennie goes to Europe to visit Will and as soon as the work of this Commission closes I will meet her over in Europe where we will spend five or six months. Then I will arrive in Denver to practice law until I die so don't start anything for me."[16]

In June 1920, Shafroth thought the War Minerals Commission was on the verge of finishing its work. Jennie traveled to Europe that summer, but John could not because the commission's cases dragged on. Shafroth, *The Denver Post* reported on November 15, 1920, had saved the government lots of money: Of the $8.5 million appropriated to settle claims, the commission was likely to spend only $3 million. Finally, in mid-May 1921, after having settled 1,203 claims in two years, Shafroth tendered his resignation to Secretary of the Interior Albert Fall.[17] He then hurried to New York to embark for Naples, where he intended to meet Jennie. He had been to

Europe before and had already seen such places as Antwerp and Brussels. On the 1921 trip he and Jennie planned to visit Italy, Switzerland, Austria, Germany, France, Scotland, and England.

Frugal as ever, Shafroth decided to travel on a U.S. Mail Steamship Company vessel, the *Pocahontas*. He choose that ship, a former German liner the United States seized during the war, because he had been told it charged low fares and would not be crowded. One of 640 passengers aboard the *Pocahontas* when it left New York on May 21, 1921, he sailed in style, paying $180 for an entire stateroom. For the first time in years he had a chance to relax for days on end, to catch up on reading, as he looked forward to the twenty days it would take to reach Naples.

Cheap accommodations on a luckless liner turned out to be penny-wise and dollar-foolish. The *Pocahontas* left New York in the midst of a strike called by marine workers after ship owners reduced wages. Staffed by incompetent scab laborers, the ship took nine days to get to Boston. Repairs there took another eight days. The star-crossed *Pocahontas* then set out across the Atlantic, where its refrigerators failed, forcing the crew to throw spoiled food overboard and the passengers to subsist on preserved beef. Saltwater got into the fresh water, so passengers and crew choked down brackish water. Some crewmen even plotted to sink the feckless steamship, a threat the captain crushed by clamping the potential mutineers in chains. Forty days after it left New York, the poky *Pocahontas* finally reached Naples.[18]

Compared to the voyage, the rest of Shafroth's European tour apparently went smoothly. He had told Jennie to scout out the best masterpieces of Italian art so he would not waste time looking at the chaff: "I do not fancy spending a long period of time over any one picture or statue."[19] A keen observer of politics and economics, if not of art, John Franklin carefully studied postwar Europe. Unimpressed by European legislatures because they lacked decorum and their members were prone to fistfights, Shafroth had higher praise for the League of Nations.[20] He observed several sessions of the League assembly in Geneva and found the delegates dedicated, although sad, as he was, that the United States was not part of the organization.

Shafroth had predicted that the world war would wreck European economies, and what he saw on his trip confirmed his assessment. Shattered economies and collapsing currencies distressed him, but the consequent purchasing power of the U.S. dollar delighted him. After a dinner for five people at the Grand Hotel in Vienna, he was startled to get a bill for 3,100 crowns. His surprise turned to relief, even joy, when he calculated that this sum came to less than two dollars. "It is simply impossible," he later told *The Denver*

Post, "for one person to eat his fill of the most delicious of foods in Vienna and be charged more than forty cents."[21]

John and Jennie returned to the United States in late November 1921. On his trip back to Denver he visited Fayette to say hello to family and friends. It was in some respects a sad visit; his elder brother, William, was gone, and his favorite sister, Sophia Hale (who lived in Beatrice, Nebraska), had died in early 1921. One sister, Louisa, remained in Fayette, and another, Laura Seager, resided in Lansing, Michigan.[22] Returning to Denver in December 1921, Shafroth planned to go into law practice with Morrison, who had

Morrison Shafroth (center), Honest John's second son, ran unsuccessfully for Colorado attorney general in 1920. He remained politically active; here he poses with other delegates at the 1936 Democratic National Convention. Colorado Historical Society.

reopened the family law offices early in 1919. He was also pleased that Morrison and Abby and their two young daughters, Virginia and Ellen, lived at 1545 Vine, a ten-minute walk from the Shafroth family home on York.

In May 1921 Shafroth had written Morrison urging him to consider running for governor, adding: "Don't calculate at all upon me, for I have quit the game for good."[23] His political career was over, but he could not stop thinking and acting as a public man.[24] In late December 1921 he lectured a gathering at the Colorado State Capitol on the tragic economic plight of Europe. In mid-January 1922 he summarized his observations and sent them to President Harding, suggesting that the United States participate in an international conference to ease Europe's economic woes. Harding thanked Shafroth for his "illuminating" letter. The president said he realized things were awry abroad but feared getting drawn into European affairs: "The difficulty lies in the fact that many political questions are involved, and it has seemed to me that these political questions must be settled by Europe without our becoming involved."[25] Such isolationism, many historians have argued, proved a blueprint for disaster, but in a United States intent on returning to "normalcy" after World War I it was a widespread and unshakeable point of view.

Shafroth had little time to change isolationists' minds. A mid-December 1921 letter from Frank J. Kellogg of Battle Creek, Michigan, thanked Shafroth for ordering six boxes of Kellog's brown tablets and advised him "to take hold of your treatment with the determination that you are going to win." That suggests that John Franklin was ill, although other correspondence indicates that he kept his problems private. On February 5, 1922, he wrote to his brother-in-law James Seager, "We are all well—Morrison, Abby and her children took dinner with us yesterday. They live within two blocks of us and we see them every day."[26] A few days later he went to Colorado Springs to speak. On his return he took to his bed with what appeared to be a severe cold. His chest pains alerted doctors to the likelihood that he was suffering from heart failure. He rallied, then faded. On Monday, February 20, 1922, at 1:15 P.M., John Franklin Shafroth, age sixty-eight, died at his York Street home surrounded by his family.

In keeping with his wishes the family kept his funeral simple, almost Spartan. No flowers surrounded his flag-draped coffin as it lay in state at the Colorado State Capitol for two hours on February 23. One of the first mourners to file by, Mrs. S. M. Inman, a longtime acquaintance of Shafroth's, waved two U.S. flags over the senator's remains as troops from Fort Logan and the Colorado National Guard formed an honor guard. The list of dignitaries paying their respects and named as honorary pallbearers included three former governors—Alva Adams, Elias Ammons, and Julius Gunter—as well as Denver mayor Dewey Bailey and Thomas F. Dawson, formerly secretary to Senator Henry Teller. Demonstrating that Shafroth got along with his political enemies were the names of William Gray Evans and Archie Stevenson among the honorary pallbearers. Active pallbearers included younger men such as James Grafton Rogers and Henry and Oliver Wolcott Toll. After the ceremonies at the Capitol, services for Shafroth were conducted at the family home on York by his friend, Baptist minister George Vosburgh. His body was taken to Fairmount Cemetery and placed in a vault until son Will could return from Europe for the burial.

A Lasting Legacy

Paying tribute to Shafroth, historian Thomas F. Dawson wrote: "No man who ever lived in Colorado had more personal friends or exercised more influence than John Shafroth."[27] It was a high compliment because it came from a man who knew almost all the great figures in the state's political history—Henry Teller, Edward Wolcott, Thomas Patterson, Alva Adams, Charles Thomas—and still put Shafroth at the head of the list. The *Rocky Mountain News*, only a few years earlier among Shafroth's most rabid detractors, lauded him for his common touch: "Since the death of H. M. Teller . . . no one has ingrained himself in the hearts of Lincoln's plain people as Mr. Shafroth succeeded in doing." The *Boulder Daily Camera* offered similar praise: "Real leadership was Shafroth's and it was due to intrinsic ability, force of character, rather than to any attribute of personal good looks, voice, manner or fortune. He had no eloquence but he had lots of common sense."[28]

John Franklin Shafroth also had lots of political sense. In the 1890s, by shifting to the Democratic Party after it embraced silver, he saved his political career. By resigning from Congress in 1904 after questions about the validity of his election were raised, he ensured his political future. Sometimes he adroitly compromised, as in 1910, when he accepted a dual system of party conventions and petitions as a means of nominating primary candidates. In other instances, such as the battle for initiative and referendum constitutional amendments, he risked his political career and won. Unlike typically timid politicians, he was willing to take those risks. He knew how to play chess and was also skilled at poker.

Certainly Shafroth stood to benefit from some of the reforms he advocated. By breaking the stranglehold political bosses had on nominations, he became a U.S. senator. By getting the initiative approved, he made it easier to achieve other reforms on his agenda. Had he succeeded in curtailing the power of money in politics, he might have been re-elected to the Senate in 1918. Without question there was self-interest in much of Shafroth's reform.

But there was also principle and a desire to do the right thing. His anti-imperialism in the 1890s gained him few votes in Colorado, yet he kept fighting for the rights of Filipinos. As governor he probably could have made comfortable compromises with political hacks who thrived by scratching the backs of those who scratched theirs. But Shafroth stuck with his principles, a decision not without danger. In 1910 he barely won renomination for a second term as governor. As a U.S. senator he labored to craft the Federal Reserve system, a major contribution to the nation's financial stability but not a great vote-getter. Nor did he win plaudits in Colorado for his efforts to improve the political lot of Puerto Ricans.

When Shafroth left the Senate on March 4, 1919, he ended not only his political career of more than a quarter century but also an era in Colorado's political history. Of the state's high-ranking statesmen, only he and a handful of others—Charles Thomas, Alva Adams, and Billy Adams among them—had roots that went back to the days of Davis Waite and the rise of the Populists. Others lit the reform torches, but Shafroth more than any other Colorado politician made progressive proposals into concrete law. He had seen the reform movement grow from a Cherry Creek-sized rivulet into an unstoppable Colorado River-sized torrent. He rode that strong current to electoral success in 1908, 1910, and 1912. And, although he did not fully realize it at the time, he saw the reform waters slowly recede between 1914 and 1918.

Lacking a crystal ball, Shafroth could not foresee that the tide would continue to ebb; that after progressivism reached its high point in Colorado during his governorship, reactionary forces and men would rule the state for most of the next four decades; that one day Billy Adams, who had tried to thwart Shafroth's reforms, would be governor, and Alva B. Adams, Billy's nephew, would be a U.S. senator; that for nearly a quarter-century Benjamin F. Stapleton, Speer's successor as boss, would be mayor of Denver; or that almost every day until the early 1950s, Gerald Hughes would pull the political strings in Colorado.

Yet even had he known those things, Shafroth would not have had reason for pessimism. The reforms he fought for and achieved as governor—the initiative and referendum amendments to the state constitution, the direct primary, workers' compensation, safety regulations, and many others—would endure into the twenty-first century. Other progressive ideas that he backed, although not adopted in his lifetime, would stay on the reform agenda for the next ninety years. In 2002, for example, voters passed an initiated amendment to the state constitution to curb the influence of big money in political campaigns, and they considered but rejected an amendment to abolish the party caucus system of nominating candidates.

Many of the changes Shafroth championed as senator would also come to pass. One day the United States would enjoy tariffs even lower than those established by the Underwood tariff. One day the metric system would find favor among U.S. scientists and engineers; one day the lame-duck session of Congress would be eliminated; one day, after another major world war, the United States would take the lead in forming the United Nations. And one day—August 26, 1920, less than seventeen months after Shafroth left Congress—the Susan B. Anthony Amendment, giving women the right to vote, would be ratified as the Nineteenth Amendment to the U.S. Constitution.

Besides this legacy of public accomplishments, Shafroth could take pride in his family. The 1918-1919 *Who's Who in America* listed him as its only Shafroth. The 1941-1942 *Who's Who* listed three Shafroths: John Franklin Shafroth, Jr., Morrison Shafroth, and William Shafroth, all John Franklin and Virginia's children. From their parents they had learned to work hard, to value education, to do their duty, to act in accordance with their principles, to shun liquor and tobacco, to watch their pennies, and to be ambitious. From their father they also inherited a good start in life, because he willed each of them at least $25,000 in cash and property. That represented half of his estate, reportedly valued at $150,000 but probably worth substantially more. The other half went to Virginia.[29]

John Franklin Shafroth, Jr., the Shafroths' eldest son, enjoyed a distinguished naval career, rising through the ranks until he retired as a vice admiral. As chief of staff to Admiral William F. [Bull] Halsey, he helped direct naval action in the South Pacific during World War II. In the closing weeks of the war, he commanded an armada that included the battleships *Massachusetts*, *Indiana*, and *South Dakota* as they bombarded Honshu, the main Japanese island. On September 2, 1945, he stood on the deck of the *U.S.S. Missouri* to witness the surrender of Japan. After his retirement in 1949, he worked to clear the name of Admiral Husband Kimmel, who, Shafroth and others believed, had been unfairly blamed for lack of naval preparedness at Pearl Harbor in December 1941. John Franklin Shafroth, Jr. died in 1967 at age eighty and was buried at Arlington National Cemetery.[30]

Morrison, the Shafroths' second son, followed in his father's legal and political footsteps. Drowned by the conservative flood that doomed his fa-

One of Virginia Morrison Shafroth's joys was her granddaughter Virginia, who, as the wife of Mayor James Quigg Newton, would serve as Denver's first lady from 1947 to 1955. Courtesy Virginia and Quigg Newton.

ther in 1918, Morrison lost his bid to become Colorado attorney general in 1920. Running for the U.S. Senate in 1924, he lost to Republican Rice Means, the anointed candidate of Colorado's powerful Ku Klux Klan. In the wake of the 1929 stock market crash, progressive forces again stirred, but they favored Edward Costigan, who beat Morrison in the 1930 U.S. Senate Democratic primary and then won the U.S. Senate seat.

Morrison's successful legal career balanced his unsuccessful political ventures.[31] In 1927 he joined William W. Grant, Henry Wolcott Toll, Sr., and Erl Ellis to form the firm of Grant, Ellis, Shafroth, and Toll.[32] Henry Wolcott Toll was the grandson of Edward O. Wolcott, Republican U.S. senator from Colorado between 1889 and 1901. Early in John Shafroth's political career he and Wolcott were allies, but they parted ways in the mid-1890s when the Republican Party abandoned the cause of silver. Shafroth bolted the party; Wolcott remained a Republican.

In late 1936 Morrison left Denver to become chief counsel for the Internal Revenue Service in Washington, D.C. That job turned sour in mid-1937, when Morrison refused to bow to President Franklin D. Roosevelt's demand that the IRS release confidential information about taxpayers. He lost his post as a result. The *New York Times* saluted him: "[T]here are not too many men in public life who are willing to give up their jobs for the sake of principle."[33] Like father like son, the *Times* might have added, because "Honest Morrison" was following the precedent set by "Honest John," who put honor before position when he resigned his congressional seat in 1904.

For Morrison, though, principle did not translate into political advantage. After his tussle with FDR, Morrison returned to Denver and to private life, sallying forth on occasion to support others' ambitions, including those of James Quigg Newton, who was elected Denver's mayor in 1947 and again in 1951. Morrison had a personal stake in those campaigns because his daughter Virginia had married Newton in 1942.[34] Perhaps, too, Morrison enjoyed seeing Newton defeat Mayor Benjamin F. Stapleton in 1947, because Stapleton was once a cog in the Speer political machine that so often gave John Franklin Shafroth grief. Newton's eight years in office brought echoes of John Franklin's reform crusades; the mayor swept away the patronage-ridden City Hall fiefdom reminiscent of Speer's days and replaced it with an efficient, merit-driven, progressive municipal government.

Keeping fit by playing tennis, Morrison enjoyed a robust old age.[35] He spent many years on the board of directors of the Colorado Historical Society, an apt affiliation for the son of Governor John Shafroth, who had helped build the society's elegant neoclassical marble building just south of the State Capitol. Having outlived his father's political rivals and his own, he died in early October 1978 at age eighty-nine, in Denver.[36]

Will Shafroth, the youngest of the Shafroth children, stayed in Europe for more than four years after World War I, working most of the time for the American Relief Administration, directed by Herbert Hoover. In 1921, Will was in Poland serving, as he put it, as a "Baby Feeder" to save the lives of Polish children in the war-ravaged country. He found a few days that autumn to visit his parents in Berlin while they were touring Europe. Will then went to Riga (in Latvia), to Moscow, and finally to Samara, a Russian city on the Volga, where famine was so terrible that the living ate the bodies of dead. Dogs and cats disappeared, Will reported, rats grew adept at hiding so that they would not be eaten, and hungry people devoured the bark from trees. When one of the relief workers died and was eaten, garbled news stories suggested that Will had himself been devoured.[37]

The reports of Will's having been digested proved grossly exaggerated. From mid-September 1921 to mid-May 1922 he supervised up to twenty thousand local workers in a relief effort that, by some estimates, kept a million and a quarter Russians alive.[38] In 1922 he went to Turkey to continue his humanitarian work. He wrote to Morrison: "[R]eliefing [sic] might be a life occupation for anyone who wants it, but that does not include me. I expect to quit permanently November 1st."[39] After resigning, Will joined his mother and his Aunt Susanne, who were touring Europe that winter.

On returning to the United States, Will went into law practice with Morrison and in 1924 married Janet Durrie. His father had been among the organizers of the Denver Bar Association in the 1880s; half a century later, Will also took an interest in promoting legal standards, serving in a variety of posts for the American Bar Association, the American Judicature Society, and the National Conference of Bar Examiners during the 1930s. When the Office of U.S. Courts was established in Washington, D.C. in 1940 to supervise federal courts, Will became chief of its division of procedural studies and statistics. In 1960 was named the office's deputy director, and in 1964 he retired. He died in 1991 at age ninety-seven.[40]

Virginia Shafroth also was blessed with abundant years. Her husband's sudden death at age sixty-eight did not destroy her own avid interest in the world around her. In the autumn of 1922 she and her sister Susanne traveled to Europe, where they joined Will. In early December 1922 she asked Morrison, who was dutifully tending the family's affairs in Denver, to "send my money right away." She told Morrison: "Your Auntie [Susanne] and Will are reading up on how to break the bank at Monte Carlo."[41]

In Denver Virginia maintained her interest in politics, taking pride in 1941 that her sons were all Democrats but not Roosevelt New Dealers.[42] From the family home on York, she watched as Morrison and Will rose in the legal profession and John became an admiral. In 1944 she was named Colorado Mother of the Year, and in March 1949, on her ninety-fourth birthday, *The Denver Post* described her as "one of Denver's best loved and respected citizens."[43] She died the next year, at age ninety-five, survived by her sons, seven grandchildren, and ten great-grandchildren.[44]

Virginia, John Franklin, and their children (with the exception of John, Jr.) rest today in Denver's Fairmount Cemetery, near a handsome memorial proclaiming the shady spot sacred to the memory of the Shafroths. Susan

Shafroth's death brought a slew of tributes, including this one from The Denver Post. *Frank Shafroth Collection.*

(1882-1886), their daughter, nestles close to the big stone. Robert E. Lee Morrison (1865-1949), Virginia's brother, is tucked away to the right. John Franklin (1854-1922), Virginia (1855-1950), and son George (1891-1911) form a row immediately in front of the main memorial. In a second row, Morrison's wife, Abby Staunton Hagerman (1892-1975), Morrison (1888-1978), and Will (1894-1991) are buried. Will's stone also memorializes his wife, Janet Durrie (1897-1996), and their daughter Sylvia (1929-1988).

Within half a mile of the Shafroth tract, many of John Franklin's political friends and enemies enjoy their peace. Robert Speer is a couple hundred paces to the north; Henry Teller and Thomas Patterson, a little farther northwest. William Gray Evans and Gerald Hughes conspicuously consume two large plots a few thousand feet south of the Shafroths. Up on a hill to the northeast, Lawrence C. Phipps looks down on the others from the Fairmount Mausoleum.

The political hubbub of long ago is of no concern to the squirrels, strollers, and bicyclists who find a pleasant haven in that city of the dead. The oaks, elms, and spruce that offer shade matured as John Shafroth's political career came of age. They added rings as he fought for the right of ordinary people to control their government. They lost leaves and budded again as he struggled, season in and season out, to insure justice for women, working people, Filipinos, and Puerto Ricans. For a hundred years, the oldest among them have felt the hot winds of reform and the icy blasts of reaction. And when reform winds blow again, visitors to Fairmount who have read of "Honest John" may, with a little imagination, hear whispered in the rustle of those old trees the name Shafroth.

Notes

The official papers of Governor John Shafroth reside at the Colorado State Archives in Denver. The bulk of his private papers, as well as the papers of his wife Virginia [Jennie], sons John [Jack], Jr., Morrison, George, and Will, are in the Western History Collection of the Denver Public Library, carefully arranged by Michael Wolfe. A smaller Shafroth collection, including some correspondence and several large scrapbooks, is at the Colorado Historical Society in Denver. The division of the collection unfortunately separates related items from one another.

In the endnotes, box numbers are cited for the Denver Public Library collection. The smaller collection at the Colorado Historical Society is arranged by date, so the endnotes simply give dates. Denver Public Library is abbreviated DPL, Colorado Historical Society is CHS, and John Franklin Shafroth is JFS. The Christopher Gerboth, Donald Walker, and James Newton Dickson III manuscripts cited in these notes are in the law offices of Shafroth and Toll in Denver. These manuscripts, along with the Welch and Musselman M.A. theses at the University of Denver, contain considerable detail on various aspects of Shafroth's life not included in this work. The Shafroth family may eventually donate them to the Denver Public Library or the Colorado Historical Society.

Chapter 1

1
Congressional Record, 58th Congress, 2nd Session, February 15, 1904, 38:2, 1986-1987; *Rocky Mountain News*, February 15, 16, 1904; *Evening Post* [New York], February 27, 1904.

2
Morrison Shafroth, interview by David McComb, June 10, 1975, 17a, Oral History Collection, CHS (hereafter cited as Morrison Shafroth interview). See also Thomas Dawson Scrapbook, CHS, 61:453, for circumstances surrounding the March 4, 1885, resignation of U.S. Representative James F. Wilson in the last hours of the Congressional session.

3
Thomas F. Dawson, "The Passing of Senator John Franklin Shafroth," *The Trail* (February 1922), 18-19.

4
History of Howard and Cooper Counties, Missouri (St. Louis: National Historical Company, 1883), 406-407.

5
Biographical sketch of JFS, Shafroth Papers, DPL, Box 14; JFS to William Schaffrath, April 8, 1921, Shafroth Papers, CHS, ff. 123. JFS, evidently reponding to a genealogical inquiry, told William Schaffrath that Shafroth's father migrated to the United States "very young," that he was an orphan at the age of twelve, and that he had two sisters, one of whom married a man named Eimann.

6
Portrait and Biographical Record of the State of Colorado (Chicago: Chapman Publishing Company, 1899), 20-21; William C. Ferril, *Sketches of Colorado: Being an Analytical Summary and Biographical History of the State of Colorado, Volume I* (Denver: Western Press Bureau, 1911), 94-95.

7
History of Howard and Cooper Counties, 270.

8
Ibid., 406-407.

9
H. Denny Davis, March 3, 1995, interview by Christopher B. Gerboth, cited in Gerboth, "Honest John: The Life of John Franklin Shafroth (1854-1922)," typescript in the Denver law offices of Shafroth and Toll, 10. See also Michael Fellman, *Inside War: The Guerilla Conflict in Missouri During the American Civil War* (New York: Oxford University Press, 1989), 135, cited by Gerboth.

10
Rocky Mountain News, December 5, 1911.

11
John Franklin Shafroth, "Oration," Shafroth Papers, DPL, Box 14.

12
All quotations in this and following paragraphs from JFS college notebook, Shafroth Papers, DPL. Box 14.

13
JFS to Clara Berrick Colby, December 17, 1912, Shafroth Papers, DPL, Box 7.

14
Undated *Rocky Mountain News* clipping, Shafroth Scrapbook, I:323, CHS.

15
The 1875 *Illustrated Map of Howard County* shows Major's law office above the Boyd and Shafroth store in the Masonic Building on Main Street. The Fayette *Advertiser*, February 23, 1922, said the Shafroth home stood "where now [1922] is the Commercial Bank Building."

16
Biographical Directory of the American Congress, 1774-1971 (Washington, D.C.: Government Printing Office, 1971), 1287. James Hamilton Lewis (1863-1939) served with Shafroth in the House of Representatives (1897-1899) and Senate. In the House he served from Washington; in the Senate from Illinois.

17
For Denver's history, including the 1870s and 1880s economic booms, see Stephen J. Leonard and Thomas J. Noel, *Denver: From Mining Camp to Metropolis* (Niwot: University Press of Colorado, 1990).

18
Harry E. Kelsey, Jr. *Frontier Capitalist: The Life of John Evans* (Boulder: Pruett Publishing and Colorado Historical Society, 1969); Allen D. Breck, *William Gray Evans: Portrait of a Western Executive.* (Denver: University of Denver, 1964).

19
Elmer Ellis, *Henry Moore Teller: Defender of the West* (Caldwell, ID: Caxton Printers, 1941); Sibyl Downing and Robert E. Smith, *Tom Patterson: Colorado Crusader for Change.* (Niwot: University Press of Colorado, 1995).

20
Rocky Mountain News, October 8, 1879.

21
Rocky Mountain News, October 19, 1879.

22
Rocky Mountain News, October 14, 1879.

23
Agreement, Andrew W. Brazee and John Franklin Shafroth, October 20, 1879, Shafroth Papers, DPL, Box 8.

24
Rocky Mountain News, April 7, 1881.

25
Rocky Mountain News, August 14, 1881.

26
Rocky Mountain News, September 2, 1881.

27
Kansas City Star, January 16, 1977. Lilac Hill was placed on the National Register of Historic Places in 1969 as a significant example of the Federalist style of architecture, as the home of important people, and as a "haunted house."

28
JFS to John Morrison, July 20, 1881, and John Morrison to JFS, August 1, 1881, Shafroth Papers DPL, Box 14. Shafroth's salary is revealed in an undated *Rocky Mountain News* article in Shafroth Scrapbook, I:323, CHS.

29
Rocky Mountain News, July 1, 1950; Denver City Directories.

30
JFS to Morrison Shafroth, February 6, 1920, Shafroth Papers, DPL, Box 7.

31
Virginia Shafroth Newton, interview with Donald Walker, Jr., Denver, July 17, 2001.

32
"Berkeley Heights" promotional sheet, undated, Shafroth Papers, CHS.

33
JFS to Jack Shafroth, August 10, 1891, Shafroth Papers, DPL, Box 16.

34
Denver City Directories indicate that Luthe was district attorney in 1883. The *Rocky Mountain News,* January 10, 1882, reported that Shafroth had become assistant city attorney for the prosecution of criminal cases. John Stallcup was city attorney at that time. Shafroth's government jobs probably allowed time for a private law practice on the side.

35
JFS to James H. Seager, January 8, 1907, Shafroth Papers, CHS.

36
JFS to James H. Seager, Letterbook, January 8, 1907, Shafroth Papers, CHS.

37
Certificate of Incorporation, Broadway Realty Company, July 22, 1905. Shafroth Papers, DPL; Tom Noel interview with Frank Shafroth, Denver, January 8, 2002.

Chapter 2

1
Boulder Daily Camera, July 20 and October 14, 1894.

2
Rocky Mountain News, July 12, 1893; *New York Times,* July 12, 1893. James E. Wright, *The Politics of Populism: Dissent in Colorado* (New Haven: Yale University Press, 1974), 170.

3
Fort Collins Express, October 27, 1894.

4
Campaign Speech File, Shafroth Papers, CHS.

5
Colorado Transcript [Golden], October 17, 1894.

6
Colorado Transcript, October 31, 1894.

7
That Shafroth's relationship with the APA was not particularly strong may be inferred from an article in the *Colorado Catholic* on November 3, 1894, which named dozens of Republican office seekers as members or tools of the APA, but did not mention Shafroth. Further research may clarify Shafroth's relationship to the APA. *Colorado Catholic* noted that "the Populists have presented a state ticket on which there is not a single APA."

8
Robert H. Rhodes, a Prohibitionist, received 1,079 votes, and Democrat John T. Bottom garnered 975. *Rocky Mountain News,* November 9, 1894.

9
Quotation from Richard D. Lamm and Duane A. Smith, *Pioneers and Politicians: Ten Colorado Governors in Profile* (Boulder: Pruett Publishing, 1984), 90.

10
Denver Republican, May 22, 1895.

11
Congressional Record, 54th Congress, 1st Session, February 5, 1896, 28:7, Appendix, 174.

12
Ellis, *Henry Moore Teller,* 246-252.

13
William L. Hewitt, "The Election of 1896: Two Factions Square Off," *Colorado Magazine* 54 (winter 1977), 44-57, provides coverage of the Wolcott-Teller fight.

14
Ellis, *Henry Moore Teller,* 257.

15
Denver Republican, March 30, 1897, May 27, 1898; *Congressional Record,* 56th Congress, 1st Session, December 12, 1899, 33:1, 250-253; also *Rocky Mountain News,* April 24, 1900.

16
Congressional Record, 54th Congress, 2nd Session, January 8, 1897, 29:3, Appendix, 13; *New York Press,* December 7, 1900; E. K. MacColl, "John Franklin Shafroth, Reform Governor Colorado, 1909-1913," *Colorado Magazine* 29 (January 1952), 39; *Washington Post,* December 5, 1897.

17
G. Michael McCarthy, *Hour of Trial: The Conservation Conflict in Colorado and the West* (Norman: University of Oklahoma Press, 1972), 27; *Congressional Record,* 53rd Congress, 1st Session, May 10, 1897, 30:1, 982-985.

18
Chicago *Times-Herald,* January 28, 1898; *Denver Post,* June 14, 1902.

19
Congressional Record, 67th Congress, 4th Session, February 28, 1923, 64:5, 4945. William D. Rowley, *Reclaiming the West: The Career of Francis G. Newlands* (Bloomington: Indiana University Press, 1996) does not give Shafroth similar credit.

20
Congressional Record, 55th Congress, 1st Session, May 10, 1897, 30:1, 984.

21
See Edmund B. Rogers, "Notes on the Establishment of Mesa Verde National Park," *Colorado Magazine* 24 (January 1952), 16; JFS to Charles S. Thomas, January 25, 1900, Shafroth Papers, CHS; Jerome C. Smiley, *History of Denver, with Outlines of the Earlier History of the Rocky Mountain Country.* (Denver: Denver Times, Times-Sun Publishing, 1901), 59. Duane A. Smith, *Mesa Verde National Park: Shadows of the Centuries* (Topeka: University Press of Kansas, 1988), 55, adds that "Congressman John Shafroth's yeoman efforts on behalf of the park ... educated fellow House members sufficiently to change Congressional attitudes," leading to national park status for Mesa Verde.

22
Washington Post, December 29, 1903.

23
JFS, University of Michigan Papers, Shafroth Papers, DPL, Box 7.

24
Denver Post, Empire Magazine, February 16, 1958.

25
Morrison Shafroth to H. Ray Baker, January 7, 1958, Shafroth Papers, DPL, Box 13.

26
Henry S. Pritchett to JFS, March 23, 1901, Shafroth Papers, DPL, Box 5.

27
MacColl, "John Franklin Shafroth," 39.

28
Women's Journal [Boston], December 24, 1910.

29
Frank Friedel, *The Splendid Little War* (New York: Dell Publishing, 1962), 9. Friedel is quoting John Hay, at the time U.S. Ambassador to England.

30
Congressional Record, 55th Congress, 2nd Session, June 14, 1898, 31:8, Appendix, 637.

31
Congressional Record, 56th Congress, 2nd Session, December 5, 1900, 34:4, Appendix, 8.

32
Congressional Record, 57th Congress, 1st Session, June 24, 1902, 35:7, 7317.

33
Aspen Democrat, January 6, 1901.

34
Stuart C. Miller, *Benevolent Assimilation: The American Conquest of the Philippines, 1899-1903* (New Haven: Yale University Press, 1982), 134; *Congressional Record*, 56th Congress, 2nd Session, December 5, 1900, 34:4, Appendix, 5.

35
Miller, *Benevolent Assimilation*, 152.

36
Congressional Record, 57th Congress, 1st Session, June 24, 1902, 35:7, 7318.

37
Denver Times, October 6, 1901.

38
Aspen Democrat, January 6, 1901.

39
Congressional Record, 56th Congress, 1st Session, February 7, 1900, 33:2, 1624.

40
Congressional Record, 56th Congress, 1st Session, May 2, 1900, 33:8, 262-264.

41
See Miller, *Benevolent Assimilation,* 262; Carrie Chapman Catt to JFS, March 18, 1902; Irving Winslow to JFS, January 12, 1901, Shafroth Papers, DPL, Box 5.

42
Henry M. Porter to JFS, February 25, 1902; Harriet Burdick to JFS, April 15, 1902, Shafroth Papers, DPL, Box 5.

43
Denver Republican, November 2, 1900.

44
Edward Keating, *The Gentleman from Colorado: A Memoir* (Denver: Sage Books, 1964), 82.

45
Ibid.

46
Denver Republican, July 8, 1902.

47
Denver Republican, November 8, 1902.

48
Ibid.

49
Ibid.

50
New York Evening Post, February 27, 1904.

51
David J. Brewer to JFS, February 16, 1904, Shafroth Papers, DPL, Box 5.

52
Star [Cripple Creek], October 14, 1904, in Shafroth Papers, DPL, Box 38.

53
JFS to Dr. A. R. Shands, February 1, 1906, Lettterbook Volume 3, Shafroth Papers, DPL, Box 7. Aurelius Rives Shands was a prominent Washington, D.C., orthopedic surgeon.

54
George Shafroth, Diary, Shafroth Papers, DPL, Box 16.

55
Denver Post, November 1, 1904.

Chapter 3

1
James C. Morris to JFS, February 18, 1904; W. L. Clayton to JFS, February 22, 1904, Shafroth Papers, DPL, Box 5; *Rocky Mountain News,* September 21, 1904; *Denver Republican,* September 21, 1904.

2
Roland L. DeLorme, "Turn-of-the-Century Denver: An Invitation to Reform," *Colorado Magazine* 45 (winter 1968), 1-15, provides a summary of the relationship between corporations and politicians in Denver.

3
Marjorie Hornbein, "Three Governors in a Day," *Colorado Magazine* 45 (summer 1968), 259, quoting *Rocky Mountain News,* March 19, 1905. Hornbein gives an excellent account of the 1904 election. Her father, Philip, was a reformer in 1906 and 1908 and a Shafroth supporter.

4
Russell B. Nye, *Midwestern Progressive Politics: A Historical Study of Its*

Origins and Development, 1870-1958 (New York: Harper and Row, 1965), omits Colorado from his sophisticated elucidation of the progressive movement, but much of the discussion applies to Colorado.

5
Rocky Mountain News, September 9 and 13, 1906.

6
William D. Haywood, *The Autobiography of Big Bill Haywood* (New York: International Publishers, 1974, originally published 1929), 174-202. See also Thomas J. Noel, "William D. Haywood," *Colorado Heritage* (1984, Issue 2), 2-12.

7
Benjamin Barr Lindsey, *The Rule of Plutocracy in Colorado* (Denver: Hicks Printing House, 1908), 65.

8
Ibid., 43.

9
Benjamin Barr Lindsey and Harvey O'Higgins, *The Beast* (New York: Doubleday, Page & Co., 1910), 268.

10
Denver Post, April 29, 1909, cited in Gerboth, "Honest John," as being in Shafroth Papers DPL.

11
Rocky Mountain News, August 29, 1908.

12
Rocky Mountain News, September 9, 1908.

13
The *Rocky Mountain News* and *Denver Post,* September 6-13, 1909, have broad convention coverage. Rucker was elected to Congress in 1908 and 1910. In 1918 he opposed Shafroth's re-election to the Senate (see Chapter 9). A native of Fayette, Missouri, he knew Shafroth as a boy.

14
Ellis, *Henry Moore Teller*, 382-383.

15
Rocky Mountain News, September 10, 1908. See also Lloyd Keith Musselman, "Governor John Shafroth and the Colorado Progressives: Their Fight for Direct Legislation, 1909-1910" (M.A. thesis, University of Denver, 1961).

16
Denver Post, May 4, 1905.

17
JFS to Lafe Pence in Portland, Oregon, September 30, 1908, Shafroth Papers, CHS.

18
Rocky Mountain News, October 23, 1908.

19
Rocky Mountain News, October 28, 1908. The *News*, October 19-23, 1908, covered the trip extensively.

20
Advertisement, undated *Denver Republican* clipping, scrapbook, Shafroth Papers, CHS; *Denver Republican*, September 25 and October 3, 1908; invoice, South Platte Canal and Reservoir Company and Denver Union Water Company to JFS, June 1906, Shafroth Papers, DPL. All cited in Gerboth, "Honest John," 75.

21
Pueblo Chieftain, October 11, 1908.

22
George Shafroth, Diary, November 5, 1908, Shafroth Papers, DPL, Box 16.

23
Jack Shafroth to George Shafroth, November 19, 1908, Shafroth Papers, DPL, Box 16.

24
George Shafroth, Diary, January 11, 1909, Shafroth Papers, DPL, Box 16.

Chapter 4

1

Denver Republican, January 13, 1909.

2

Denver Times, December 18, 1908. Shafroth did not totally ignore Speer in making appointments. For example, in 1909 he named a judge whom the Speer faction endorsed (*Denver Republican*, January 16, 1909).

3

Robert G. Athearn, *The Coloradans* (Albuquerque: University of New Mexico Press, 1976), 219–220; *Rocky Mountain News*, December 18, 1910.

4

Rocky Mountain News, February 23, 1909, and July 30, 1910; see also *Denver Republican*, October 11, 1911.

5

Rocky Mountain News, February 23, 1909.

6

LeRoy Hafen, ed., *Colorado and Its People: A Narrative and Topical History of the Centennial State*, 4 volumes (New York: Lewis Historical Publishing Company, 1948), 3:396-398.

7

Denver Republican, December 29, 1909, and October 11, 1911; Gerboth, "Honest John," 82.

8

Rocky Mountain News, December 21, 1909; *Denver Republican*, December 8, 1911.

9

Gerboth, "Honest John," 86; *Rocky Mountain News*, January 12, 1909; Robert Shikes, *Rocky Mountain Medicine: Doctors, Drugs, and Disease in Early Colorado* (Boulder: Johnson Books, 1986), 144.

10

Rocky Mountain News, October 22, 1909, and March 31, 1910; *Pueblo Chieftain,* February 4, 1910.

11

Rocky Mountain News, January 10, 1911, printed Shafroth's message to the legislature summarizing his and its accomplishments from 1909 to 1911.

12

Rocky Mountain News, January 13, 1909.

13

Rocky Mountain News, June 14, 1948.

14

Rocky Mountain News, January 13, 1909. Shafroth indicated that he decided not to seek a second term for financial reasons, rather than on philosophical or political grounds.

15

Rocky Mountain News, August 9, 1910.

16

Rocky Mountain News, April 9, 1909, lists the measures the General Assembly passed.

17

Robert Perkin, *The First Hundred Years: An Informal History of Denver and the Rocky Mountain News* (Garden City, NY: Doubleday and Company, 1959), 415.

18

Rocky Mountain News, May 23, 1910.

19

Theodore Roosevelt, speech before the Republican National Convention, June 1912, quoted in Forrest McDonald, *The Torch Is Passed: The United States in the Twentieth Century* (Reading, MA: Addison Wesley, 1968), 132. In "Looking the World in the Eye" (*Atlantic Monthly,* December 2001, 68-82), Robert D. Kaplan cites political scientist Samuel Huntington's view of the "Populist Progressive" years as one of the many "creedal passion" periods in American history.

20
Rocky Mountain News, February 21, 1909.

21
Colorado State Archives, Records of the Office of the Governor: John F. Shafroth 1909-1913, Executive Record Book, Volume XIX, 1909, 116; *Rocky Mountain News*, March 23, 1909.

22
Rocky Mountain News, April 4, 1909, quoted in Musselman, "Governor John Shafroth," 52.

23
Rocky Mountain News, April 6, 1909.

24
See John Franklin Shafroth, "New Campaign Finance Law in Colorado," *Independent*, July 8, 1909, 83-84; MacColl, "John Franklin Shafroth," 50-51; *Rocky Mountain News,* April 28, 1909, October 11, 1910. James Newton Dickson III, "Progressivism in Colorado: The Reform Administration of John Franklin Shafroth 1909-1913" (M.A. thesis, Madison College, 1975), 34-35, has a good account of the campaign finance law.

25
MacColl, "John Franklin Shafroth," 42-43; also Dickson, "Progressivism in Colorado," 31.

26
Frank Merchant, "Colorado's First Highway Commission. 1910-1912," *Colorado Magazine* 32 (January 1955), 74-77.

27
George Shafroth Diary, March 31, 1909, Shafroth Papers, DPL, Box 16.

28
Rocky Mountain News, April 6, 1909.

29
Denver Republican, December 29, 1909.

30
Rocky Mountain News, March 4 and April 15, 1910; *Denver Republican*, March 4, 1910; *Denver Post*, April 17, 1910.

31
Rocky Mountain News, May 17, 1910.

32
Clyde King, *The History of the Government of Denver with Special Reference to Its Relations with Public Service Corporations* (Denver: Fisher Book Company, 1911), 252-253.

33
Denver Post, July 15, 1910.

34
Rocky Mountain News, August 10, 1910.

35
Rocky Mountain News, August 10, 1910.

Chapter 5

1
For a short treatment of Roosevelt's thinking in the summer of 1910, see G. Wallace Chessman, *Theodore Roosevelt and the Politics of Power* (Boston: Little, Brown and Company, 1969), 166-171.

2
Denver Post, August 29, 1910; *Rocky Mountain News*, August 30, 1910.

3
Rocky Mountain News, August 30, 1910.

4
Rocky Mountain News, August 30, 1910; Charles Larsen, *The Good Fight:*

The Life and Times of Ben B. Lindsey
(Chicago: Quadrangle Books, 1972), 120.

5
Cited from *Rocky Mountain News*, August
30, 1910—not a direct quote from Work.

6
Benjamin Barr Lindsey, "Uphold the Insurgents," *LaFollette's Weekly Magazine*,
2 (July 23, 1909), 7.

7
Rocky Mountain News, June 18, 1910.

8
Rocky Mountain News, August 10, 1909.

9
Rocky Mountain News, August 27, 1910.

10
Rocky Mountain News, August 30, 1910.

11
Ibid.

12
Rocky Mountain News, September 1, 1910.

13
Denver Express, April 12, 1910.

14
Rocky Mountain News, September 2, 1910.

15
Rocky Mountain News, September 9, 1910.

16
Unidentified clipping, Shafroth Scrapbook, 1:422, CHS.

17
Denver Republican, October 30, 1910,
for a brief biography of Stephen.

18
Washington Star, March 30, 1913, in
Dawson Scrapbook, 61:449, CHS.

19
Rocky Mountain News, October 25, 1910.

20
Creel reached the zenith of his career as
chairman of the Committee on Public
Information, the nation's main propa-
ganda agency during World War I. See
Perkin, *The First Hundred Years*, 414-417;
George Creel, *Rebel at Large: Recollections
of Fifty Crowded Years* (New York: G. P.
Putnam's Sons, 1947), 92.

21
Denver Republican, October 30-31, 1910.

22
Musselman, "Governor John Shafroth,"
121-125, details the election.

23
Rocky Mountain News, January 4, 1911.

24
Rocky Mountain News, January 11, 1911.

25
For Creel's remarks, see James Whiteside,
*Regulating Danger: The Struggle for
Mine Safety in the Rocky Mountain
Coal Industry* (Lincoln: University of
Nebraska Press, 1990), 100.

26
Quoted in ibid., 78. Whiteside reports
that miners could be blacklisted and fired
for accidentally damaging or killing a
mule.

27
Henry Dehman, *Ninth Biennial Report
of the Inspector of Coal Mines of the
State of Colorado, 1899-1900* (Denver:
Smith-Brooks, 1901), 8.

28
Rocky Mountain News, January 11, 1911.

29
Rocky Mountain News, February 16, 1911.

30
Denver Times, August 6, 1911.

31
MacColl, "John Franklin Shafroth," 48.

32
Rocky Mountain News, January 12, 1911.

33
Colorado Springs Gazette, May 7, 1911, quoted in Gerald D. Welch, "John F. Shafroth: Progressive Governor of Colorado, 1910-1912," (M.A. thesis, University of Denver, 1961), 103.

34
Denver Post, October 9, 1910.

35
Rocky Mountain News, March 21, 1911, quoted in MacColl, "John Franklin Shafroth," 43.

36
Rocky Mountain News, April 18, 1911.

37
Shafroth Scrapbook, 2:395, CHS.

38
JFS to Edward Taylor, December 16, 1911, JFS Correspondence, Colorado State Archives, quoted in Dickson, "Progressivism in Colorado," 89.

39
Denver Express, March 31, 1911, quoted in Welch, "John F. Shafroth," 106.

40
Rocky Mountain News, October 28, 1908. The governor remained friends with men such as his neighbor Archie Stevenson, one of Speer's major cat's-paws. Shafroth defeated Benjamin L. Jefferson for the 1910 Democratic gubernatorial nomination. After Shafroth was re-elected, he reappointed Jefferson to the State Land Board. *Denver Post,* January 10, 1910.

41
Pueblo Chieftain, August 3, 1912, quoted in Welch, "John F. Shafroth," 113.

42
The *Denver Post,* April 22, 1912, reported that 17,000 signatures were required to initiate each of the measures.

43
Denver Post, November 3-6, 1912.

Chapter 6

1
Denver Republican, November 1911, in Dawson Scrapbook, CHS, 61:475.

2
The *Denver Express,* April 29, 1911, reported that the wedding took place at New York's St. James Episcopal Church and said Shafroth did not attend because if he left the state the lieutenant governor would sign objectionable legislation.

3
Rocky Mountain News, April 6, 1911. The *Denver Times,* April 5, 1911, called George a hero and praised him for making "no complaint against what had befallen him."

4
Denver Post, January 19, 1941.

5
Rocky Mountain News, January 12, 1912.

6
Denver Republican, December 19, 1911.

7
Denver Republican, December 10, 1911.

8
Denver Post, February 17, 1910, in Shafroth Scrapbook 1:333, CHS.

9
Denver Express, July 13, 1909.

10
Rocky Mountain News, January 10, 1911.

11
Karen Waddell, "Dearfield, A Dream Deferred," *Colorado Heritage* (1988, Issue 2), 2-12.

12
Rocky Mountain News, August 30, 1910.

13
Rocky Mountain News, November 16, 1917.

14
Roy M. Robbins, *Our Landed Heritage: The Public Domain, 1776-1936* (Lincoln: University of Nebraska Press, 1962), 351.

15
Rocky Mountain News, June 21, 1907.

16
Canon City Times, October 20, 1910.

17
Denver Times, February 26, 1904.

18
Carl Abbott, Stephen J. Leonard, and David McComb, *Colorado: A History of the Centennial State* (Niwot: University Press of Colorado, 1994), 196.

19
New York Evening World, December 4, 1909, in Shafroth Scrapbook, CHS, Vol. 1.

20
Gerboth, "Honest John," 93, citing an unidentified newspaper clipping in Shafroth Scrapbook, CHS.

21
Lamm and Smith, *Pioneers and Politicians*, 91.

22
Morrison Shafroth interview, CHS, 32.

23
Denver Post, October 6, 1912; Phyllis Smith, *Once a Coal Miner: The Story of*

Colorado's Northern Coal Field (Boulder: Pruett Publishing, 1989), 103-118.

24
Denver Post, July 6, 1911.

25
Denver Republican, December 14, 1911.

26
Edgar C. MacMechen, ed., *Robert W. Speer: A City Builder* (Denver: Smith-Brooks Printing Company, 1919), 54.

27
Denver Express, September 27, 1910; *Pueblo Star-Journal*, February 26, 1912.

28
Creel, *Rebel at Large*, 102.

29
Denver Post, November 7, 1912.

Chapter 7

1
New York Times, March 5, 1913.

2
Congressional Record, 63rd Congress, Special Session, March 4, 1913, 50:1, 2-4.

3
Rocky Mountain News, March 4, 1913; *New York Times*, March 4, 1913.

4
For platform see *New York Times*, July 3, 1912.

5
Rocky Mountain News, October 8, 1912.

6
Arthur S. Link, *Woodrow Wilson and the Progressive Era: 1910-1917* (New York: Harper and Row, 1963), 18-22.

7
Rocky Mountain News, October 8, 1912.

8

Benjamin Franklin, *Poor Richard's Almanack* (Mount Vernon, NY: Peter Pauper Press, n.d.), 43.

9

Congressional Record, 63rd Congress, 1st Session, April 7, 1913, 63:1, 60.

10

Ibid., April 8, 1913, 132.

11

The *Rocky Mountain News*, a strongly pro-Shafroth paper until Thomas Patterson sold it in October 1913, was lukewarm toward Underwood—witness its editorial page of September 11, 1913. By the time the final vote on Underwood occurred, the defection of Thomas and Shafroth would not have made a difference because Thomas J. Walsh and two progressive Republicans supported it.

12

JFS to Mark Skinner, February 14, 1914, Shafroth Papers, DPL, Box 7, A copy of the tax return is in Shafroth Papers, DPL, Box 10. The *Rocky Mountain News* on September 10, 1913, noted that Skinner guessed that twenty thousand Coloradans (out of a population of more than eight hundred thousand) made more than $3,000 a year. The *News* estimated that only sixty people in Denver made more than $50,000.

13

An advertisement in the *Rocky Mountain News,* January 1, 1916, indicated that Colorado produced $22 million worth of sugar—more than twice the value of Colorado-grown wheat and seventeen times the value of wool.

14

Arthur S. Link, *Wilson: The New Freedom* (Princeton: Princeton University Press, 1956), 185, tells of a meeting on May 1, 1913, in which Wilson met with the sugar senators and implored them to support Underwood. Wilson claimed that no compromise had been struck at that meeting, but one may have been made tacitly then or at another time.

15

Denver Labor Bulletin, October 26, 1918, reviews Shafroth's labor record.

16

According to Howard W. Allen, "Geography and Politics: Voting on Reform Issues in the United States Senate, 1911-1916," *Journal of Southern History* 27 (May 1961), 216-228, Shafroth voted for 100 percent of the reform bills usually cited as "important" by historians (such as the Federal Reserve Act, the Clayton Antitrust Act, and the Federal Farm Loan Act), making him one of the seventeen most progressive senators. However, when Allen broadened his definition of "progressive" issues, he found that Shafroth voted against reform 58 percent of the time, making him far more progressive than most Southern Democrats but far less so than many Republicans. Allen's methodology is not totally clear. Shafroth's opposition to conservation measures probably explains his high anti-reform percentage. Moreover, Allen's list excludes all votes that were "partisan"—that is, that were primarily supported by members of one party. That exclusion may have led Allen to underestimate the reform records of Democratic senators, if we assume that the Democrats as a party supported reform more than the Republicans did.

17

Link, *Woodrow Wilson and the Progressive Era*, 43-44.

18

Ibid., 52.

19
JFS to William Shafroth, March 4, 1916, Shafroth Papers, DPL, Box 7.

20
Ibid., September 20, 1913.

21
Ibid., January 17, 1914.

22
Woodrow Wilson to Lindley M. Garrison, February 18, 1914, in Arthur S. Link, et al., eds., *The Papers of Woodrow Wilson* (Princeton: Princeton University Press, 1979), 29:269.

23
New York Times, July 3, 1912.

24
During this period, Puerto Rico was commonly spelled "Porto Rico." The "Puerto" spelling is used in this chapter except when referring to Shafroth's Senate committee or when quoting sources that used the "Porto" spelling.

25
Woodrow Wilson to JFS, June 26, 1916, Shafroth Papers, DPL, Box 7.

26
Woodrow Wilson to JFS, July 6, 1916, in Link, *The Papers of Woodrow Wilson* (Princeton: Princeton University Press, 1981),37:369.

27
Newton D. Baker to Woodrow Wilson, July 21, 1916, in ibid., 455-456.

28
In "Some Historical and Political Aspects of the Government of Puerto Rico," *The Hispanic American Historical Review*, 2:4 (November, 1919), 543-585, Pedro Capo-Rodriguez analyzes Jones-Shafroth and provides information on the Puerto Rican government before 1917.

29
Congressional Record, 63rd Congress, 3rd session, March 3, 1915, 52:5, 5343.

30
Congressional Record, 64th Congress, 1st Session, January 17, 1916, 53:1, 659.

31
JFS to Manuel L. Quezon, May 20, 1918, Shafroth Papers, DPL, Box 7.

32
Undated transcript, ca. September 1912, mentions a speech Shafroth gave in Arvada, Colorado, pointing out the dangers of competition from Filipino sugar. Shafroth Papers, DPL, Box 13.

33
Congressional Record, 64th Congress, 2nd session, February 1, 1917, 54:3, 2399.

34
Charles Thomas to JFS, November 28, 1914, Shafroth Papers, DPL, Box 7. William Gray Evans, often at odds with Shafroth when John Franklin was governor, commended him for his anti-leasing speech in a December 18, 1914, letter (Shafroth Papers, DPL, Box 7). Elias Ammons, Colorado's governor in 1914, also strongly opposed leasing. See G. Michael McCarthy, "Insurgency in Colorado: Elias Ammons and the Anticonservation Impulse," *Colorado Magazine* 54 (winter 1977), 26-43.

35
J. Leonard Bates, *Senator Thomas Walsh of Montana: Law and Public Affairs, from TR to FDR* (Urbana: University of Illinois Press, 1999), 204-207, provides a succinct account of the leasing controversy.

36
Thomas J. Walsh to Woodrow Wilson, March 16, 1916, in Link, *The Papers of Woodrow Wilson*, 36:328.

37
Wilson to William Jennings Bryan, December 29, 1914, in Link, *The Papers of Woodrow Wilson*, 31:547.

38
JFS to William Shafroth, March 14, 1916, Shafroth Papers, DPL, Box 7.

39
C.W. Buchholtz, *Rocky Mountain National Park: A History* (Boulder: Colorado Associated University Press, 1983), 135-136. James Grafton Rogers was not related to Shafroth's law partner, Platt Rogers.

40
Alexander Drummond, in *Enos Mills Citizen of Nature* (Boulder: University Press of Colorado, 1995), says Edward Taylor pushed the bill in the House, Charles Thomas in the Senate (223, 238-245). C.W. Buchholtz notes in *Rocky Mountain National Park* that the park's popularity was due largely to "its easy accessibility from the East and Midwest" (151).

41
In an August 16, 2002, conversation with Stephen J. Leonard, historian Michael McCarthy suggested that Shafroth might have supported the 350-square-mile park because it was smaller than some advocates wanted. Had it been extended into Wyoming, Rocky Mountain would have rivaled Yellowstone in size.

Chapter 8

1
Congressional Record, 63rd Congress, 2nd Session, April 22, 1914, 51:7, 7074.

2
JFS to William Shafroth, May 18, 1914, Shafroth Papers, DPL, Box 7.

3
Rocky Mountain News, October 5, 1914.

4
JFS to William Shafroth, February 28, 1915, Shafroth Papers, DPL, Box 7.

5
JFS to William Shafroth, June 13, 1914, DPL, Box 7. JFS proudly told his brother that son William would graduate at the age of nineteen on June 25, 1914.

6
JFS to William Shafroth, February 18, 1915, Shafroth Papers, DPL, Box 7.

7
Denver Post, December 21, 1916.

8
JFS to Ethel Bridgman, November 11, 1915, Shafroth Papers, DPL, Box 7. Ethel was a daughter of John's brother William. In an October 24, 1915, letter to his brother-in-law James Seager, Shafroth said his son Will "was delighted with the trip as it was the first ocean voyage he had ever taken."

9
JFS to William Shafroth, April 22, 1916, Shafroth Papers DPL, Box 7.

10
Virginia Shafroth to Morrison Shafroth, March 2, 1916, Shafroth Papers, DPL, Box 17. The first Mrs. Wilson died August 6, 1914. Wilson's engagement to Elizabeth Boling Galt was announced October 8, 1915. They married on December 18, 1915.

11
Washington Star, March 1, 1914, in Shafroth Papers, DPL, Box 39.

12
Virginia to Morrison Shafroth, January 18, 1915, Shafroth Papers, DPL, Box 17.

13
Reporting William's death, the *Denver Times* on July 27, 1916, named some of his relatives, including John Franklin and sisters Sophie Hale of Beatrice, Nebraska, Laura Seager of Lansing, Michigan, and Mrs. Lou Bradley of Fayette, Missouri.

14
JFS to W. H. Wolfersberger, December 29, 1917, Shafroth Papers, DPL. Box 7.

15
JFS to William Shafroth, March 4, 1916, Shafroth Papers, DPL, Box 7.

16
Rocky Mountain News, February 5, 1916.

17
The *Lusitania,* although a passenger ship, was carrying arms and other contraband.

18
JFS to William Shafroth, March 4, 1916, Shafroth Papers, DPL, Box 7.

19
Alva Adams to Thomas J. Walsh, October 13, 1916, quoted in Link, *Woodrow Wilson and the Progressive Era,* 243.

20
Woodrow Wilson to JFS, January 3, 1917, in Link, et al., eds., *The Papers of Woodrow Wilson,* 40:386.

21
New York Times, January 23, 1917.

22
Congressional Record, 65th Congress, Special Session, April 5, 1917, 55:1, 348.

23
Susanne Morrison Diary, March 28, 1917, Shafroth Papers, DPL, Box 28.

24
Bryan to JFS, undated letter (ca. April 1917), Shafroth Papers, DPL, Box 6.

25
Monte Vista Journal, May 19, 1917, in Shafroth Papers, DPL, Box 39.

26
JFS to James H. Seager, October 24, 1915, Shafroth Papers, DPL, Box 11.

27
Susanne Morrison, Diary, April 6, 1917, Shafroth Papers, DPL, Box 28.

28
Rocky Mountain News, April 7, 1917.

29
Jack Shafroth to JFS, March 28, 1917, Shafroth Papers, DPL, Box 6.

30
James H. Seager to JFS, May 22, 1917, Shafroth Papers, DPL, Box 6.

31
Woodrow Wilson to Virginia Shafroth, April 20, 1918, Shafroth Papers, DPL, Box 45.

32
JFS to Caroline Bradley, March 1, 1918, Shafroth Papers, DPL, Box 7.

33
JFS to Morrison Shafroth, July 8, 1917, Shafroth Papers, DPL, Box 17.

34
James H. Seager to JFS, May 22, 1917, Shafroth Papers, DPL, Box 6.

35
JFS to John McGauran, February 11, 1918, Shafroth Papers, DPL, Box 7.

36
Denver Labor Bulletin, November 2, 1918, describes Shafroth's efforts.

37
On September 30, 1913, ex-president William Howard Taft, who sat on the memorial commission, wrote Shafroth: "I

am very certain that Colorado marble is far and away the most beautiful marble that was presented to us for the Lincoln Memorial." See Shafroth Papers, DPL, Box 6.

38
JFS to John McGauran, February 11, 1918, Shafroth Papers, DPL, Box 7.

39
The amendment wasn't implemented for almost a year, until passage of the Volstead Act.

40
Morrison Shafroth interview, CHS; also in Shafroth Papers, DPL, Box 21.

41
JFS to Woodrow Wilson, May 28, 1918, Shafroth Papers, DPL, Box 7.

42
See Jack C. Lane, *Armed Progressive: General Leonard Wood* (San Rafael, CA: Presidio Press, 1978), 203-217.

43
William Jennings Bryan to JFS, January 8, 1918, Shafroth Papers, DPL, Box 7.

44
JFS to William Jennings Bryan, November 8, 1918, Shafroth Papers, DPL, Box 7.

45
JFS to William Jennings Bryan, November 23, 1918, Shafroth Papers, DPL, Box 7.

46
JFS to William Jennings Bryan, November 8, 1918, Shafroth Papers, DPL, Box 7.

Chapter 9

1
JFS to Morrison Shafroth, November 1, 1918, Shafroth Papers, DPL, Box 17. Shafroth told Morrison that he had returned to Denver "about October 10."

2
JFS to Charles Thomas, October 24, 1918, Shafroth Papers, CHS, Gerboth, "Honest John," 132.

3
Frederick G. Bonfils to JFS, December 26, 1918, Shafroth Papers, DPL, Box 13.

4
Rocky Mountain News, May 8, 1914.

5
Fred Greenbaum, *Fighting Progressive: A Biography of Edward P. Costigan* (Washington, D.C.: Public Affairs Press, 1971), 81-82. In March 1917, Wilson appointed Costigan to serve on the Federal Tariff Commission; see *Denver Post,* March 14, 1917.

6
MacMechen, ed., *Robert W. Speer,* 56.

7
JFS to Morrison Shafroth, March 9, 1917, Shafroth Papers, DPL, Box 17.

8
Rocky Mountain Herald, December 2, 1916; *Denver Labor Bulletin,* March 17, 1917, in Shafroth Papers, DPL, Box 39.

9
Denver Post, March 15, 1917.

10
Denver Post, March 14, 1917.

11
Denver Times, June 4, 1904.

12
New York Times, June 8, 1904.

13
Rocky Mountain News, January 12, 1908.

14
Denver Democrat, March 9, 1918, reprinting material from the *Oak Creek Herald.*

The comment was made by Thomas J. O'Donnell, whom Shafroth had defeated in 1912 in the Democratic preferential primary for the U.S. Senate.

15
Boulder Miner, reprinted in the *Denver Democrat*, March 23, 1918.

16
Denver Post, August 25, 1918.

17
Lyle W. Dorsett, "The Ordeal of Colorado's Germans During World War I," *Colorado Magazine* 51 (fall 1974), 284-285.

18
See Chapter 3 for the role Rucker played in helping make Shafroth governor.

19
Colorado Springs Gazette, October 30, 1918, quoting the *Denver Democrat*, October 26, 1918.

20
Rocky Mountain News, October 18, 1918, Shafroth Papers, DPL, Box 39.

21
JFS to Morrison Shafroth, November 1, 1918, Shafroth Papers, DPL, Box 17.

22
JFS to Tully Scott, July 14, 1918, Shafroth Papers, DPL, Box 7.

23
Ibid.

24
See W. A. Swanberg, *Citizen Hearst: A Biography of William Randolph Hearst* (New York: Bantam Books, 1963), 373-374.

25
Rocky Mountain News, October 23, 1918.

26
Denver Democrat, October 26, 1918.

27
A. Mitchell Palmer, later U.S. attorney general, sponsored the bill in the House.

28
Inez Hayes Irwin, *The Story of the Woman's Party* (New York: Kraus Reprint Company, 1971, originally published 1921), 55.

29
Congressional Record, 65th Congress, 2nd Session, October 1, 1918, 56:11, 10983.

30
Doris Stevens, *Jailed for Freedom* (New York: Schocken Books, 1976, originally published 1920), 290.

31
See David Morgan, *Suffragists and Democrats: The Politics of Woman Suffrage in America* (Lansing: Michigan State University Press, 1972), 125.

32
Rocky Mountain News, July 28, 1918; Mrs. Calderhead Walker to Alice Paul, November 27, 1918, in National Women's Party Papers, Auraria Library, Denver, Microfilm Reel 2.

33
The Woman's Party appeared to be well financed. It even took out a large advertisement in the *Denver Post* on October 27, 1918, despite the *Post*'s strong support for Shafroth.

34
JFS to Ellis Meredith, October 22, 1918, Shafroth Papers, CHS, ff. 21.

35
Ellis Meredith to JFS, October 27, 1918, Shafroth Papers, DPL, Box 6.

36
Carrie Chapman Catt to editor of the *Denver Times*, October 23, 1918, Shafroth Papers, DPL, Box 13.

37
Carrie Chapman Catt to Mrs. George A. Bass, October 11, 1918, Shafroth Papers, DPL, Box 13. Alice Paul's 1918 fight is more fully described in Doris Stevens, *Jailed for Freedom*, 280-300, and David Morgan, *Suffragists and Democrats,* 117-143.

38
JFS to Carrie Chapman Catt, undated, Shafroth Papers, DPL, Box 6.

39
Denver Post, October 27, 1918.

40
Franklin Lane to Julius Gunther, October 15, 1918, Shafroth Papers, DPL, Box 6.

41
Denver Post, October 24, 1918.

42
Denver Post, November 3, 1918.

43
Dawson Scrapbook, 61:439, clipping from *Durango Democrat*, October 27, 1918.

44
Morrison Shafroth to Virginia Shafroth, February 11, 1914, Shafroth Papers, DPL, Box 30. The Bonfils-O'Donnell fight is covered in Gene Fowler, *Timber Line: A Story of Bonfils and Tammen* (New York: Covici Friede Publishers, 1933), 388-391.

45
Denver Post, October 20, 1918.

46
Denver Post, November 5, 1918.

47
Denver Post, October 31, 1918. Morris was born in Prussia and came to America at age eight. His father was a U.S. citizen.

48
Charles S. Thomas to JFS, October 17, 1918, Shafroth Papers, DPL, Box 6.

49
Julesburg *Advocate* [sic] quoted in the *Denver Democrat*, July 13, 1918.

50
Thomas J. Knock, *To End All Wars: Woodrow Wilson and the Quest for a New World Order* (New York: Oxford University Press, 1992), 184. Knock suggests that the Wilson administration's low wartime wheat price angered Coloradans and hence affected the election. That may have been a factor, but only one of many in a tight race. Noting the close election results in other states, Knock concludes that the Democrats' loss of the Senate in 1918 did not result from voter disapproval of the president's international policies.

51
Oliver T. Jackson to JFS, October 24, 1918, Shafroth Papers, CHS.

52
John D. Harkless to JFS, October 23, 1918, Shafroth Papers, CHS.

53
F. J. Bawden to JFS, October 26, 1918, Shafroth Papers, CHS.

54
JFS to James H. Seager, October 4, 1918, Shafroth Papers, DPL, Box 11.

55
JFS to Key Pittman, October 24, 1918, Shafroth Papers, CHS.

56
JFS to Ellis Meredith, October 22, 1918, Shafroth Papers, CHS.

57
JFS to James H. Seager, December 28, 1918, Box 11. Shafroth Papers, DPL. Shafroth's letter indicates that a bullet struck Morrison above the right eye. Family tradition, which may be more

accurate, holds that Morrison was hit by shrapnel. Whatever the case, he lost his sight in the eye. Yet he continued his avid tennis playing for decades.

58
Homer S. Cummings to Woodrow Wilson, November 4, 1918, *The Papers of Woodrow Wilson* (Princeton: Princeton University Press, 1985), 51:589.

59
Benjamin Lindsey to George Creel, November 9, 1918, Lindsey Papers, Library of Congress, Box 59.

60
Irwin, *Story of the Women's Party*, 382.

61
JFS to Samuel Burris, June 11, 1918, Shafroth Papers, DPL, Box 7.

62
Stevens, *Jailed for Freedom*, 287.

63
H. S. Marshal to JFS, November 7, 1918, Shafroth Papers, CHS.

64
Lindsey to Creel, November 9, 1918, op. cit.

65
Morrison Shafroth to JFS, November 19, 1918, Shafroth Papers, DPL, Box 6.

66
JFS to F.L Vandergraft, *Pittsburgh Sun* editor, December 27, 1919, Shafroth Papers, CHS.

67
JFS to William G. McAdoo, November 20, 1918, Shafroth Papers, DPL, Box 7.

68
Frederick G. Bonfils to JFS, December 26, 1918, Shafroth Papers, DPL, Box 13.

69
JFS to Frederick G. Bonfils, January 2, 1919, Shafroth Papers, DPL, Box 13.

70
New York Times, January 23, 1917.

71
Ibid.

72
New York Times, January 14, 1917.

73
Congressional Record, 64th Congress, 2nd Session, January 24, 1917, 54:2, 1882.

74
Julius W. Pratt, *A History of United States Foreign Policy* (Englewood Cliffs, NJ: Prentice-Hall, Inc., 1961), 494.

75
New York Times, January 15, 1919.

76
New York Times, February 16, 1919.

77
JFS to Will Shafroth, January 5, 1920, Shafroth Papers, CHS.

Chapter 10

1
William Jennings Bryan to JFS, March 17, 1919, Shafroth Papers, CHS, ff 34. W. G. McAdoo to Charles S. Thomas, January 15, 1920, Shafroth Papers, CHS, ff. 74. McAdoo also suggested to Wilson that he appoint Shafroth secretary of the interior. See W. G. McAdoo to JFS, February 2, 1920, Shafroth Papers, DPL, Box 45.

2
JFS to Warren G. Harding, April 15, 1921, Shafroth Papers, CHS.

3
JFS to Emerson Buckingham Bank & Trust, May 12, 1919, Shafroth Papers, CHS.

4
JFS to Morrison Shafroth, December 16, 1919, Shafroth Papers, DPL, Box 7.

5
JFS to Will Shafroth, January 5, 1920, Shafroth Papers, CHS.

6
JFS to Morrison Shafroth, June 29, 1920, Shafroth Papers, DPL, Box 7

7
JFS to Morrison Shafroth, June 2, 1920, Shafroth Papers, DPL, Box 7. On April 20, 1920, JFS told Morrison that Denver's City Hall was controlled by Republicans who would "help you for many offices in order to get rid of me."

8
JFS to Morrison Shafroth, June 2, 1920, Shafroth Papers, DPL, Box 7.

9
Warren Harding served on the Senate Committee on Porto Rico and the Pacific Islands when Shafroth chaired that committee. Albert Fall, who became Harding's secretary of the Interior, was also a Senate colleague of Shafroth's.

10
JFS to Morrison Shafroth, November 17, 1920, Shafroth Papers, DPL, Box 7.

11
JFS to Morrison Shafroth, February 6, 1920, Shafroth Papers, DPL, Box 7.

12
JFS to Morrison Shafroth, March 8, 1921, Shafroth Papers, DPL, Box 7.

13
JFS to Morrison Shafroth, December 5, 1920, Shafroth Papers, DPL, Box 7.

14
JFS to Will Shafroth, February 1, 1921, Shafroth Papers, CHS.

15
JFS to Ben Jones, December 13, 1920, Shafroth Papers, DPL, Box 7. The Shafroth prize, first awarded in May 1923, has been given each year since then to a champion extemporaneous speaker in the Denver Public Schools.

16
JFS to Morrison Shafroth, June 29, 1920, Shafroth Papers, DPL, Box 7.

17
Fall accepted the resignation effective May 20, 1921. See Albert Fall to JFS, May 18, 1921, Shafroth Papers, DPL, Box 6.

18
New York Times, May 3, 1921; June 19, 1921; December 26, 1921. After Shafroth left the *Pocahontas,* its disasters multiplied, and it never returned to the United States. The ship was broken up for scrap; remnants of its crew reached New York City in late December 1921.

19
JFS to Caroline Bradley, May 5, 1921, Shafroth Papers, CHS.

20
Denver Post, November 24, 1921.

21
Denver Post, December 5, 1921.

22
The Fayette *Advertiser*, February 23, 1922, named the two surviving sisters but not Shafroth's sister Carrie Wright, who evidently pre-deceased him. Information on her is lacking in the genealogy accompanying the Shafroth Papers at the Denver Public Library. See "Shafroth Family Papers," typescript, Western History Collection, DPL, 1982, 2.

23
JFS to Morrison Shafroth, May 12, 1921, Shafroth Papers, DPL, Box 7.

24
The *Denver Democrat*, February 4, 1922, reprinted an article from the *Colorado Springs Democrat* saying that some Democrats wanted Shafroth to oppose Phipps in 1924. That, however, was improbable; Shafroth would turn seventy in 1924, and he had firmly closed the door on running again.

25
Warren G. Harding to JFS, January 22, 1922, Shafroth Papers, DPL, Box 6.

26
JFS to James Seager, February 5, 1922, Shafroth Papers, DPL, Letterbook, Box 7.

27
Thomas F. Dawson, "The Passing of Senator John Franklin Shafroth," *The Trail* (February 1922), 19.

28
Boulder Daily Camera, undated article ca. February 23, 1922, in Shafroth Papers, DPL, Box 39. On February 28, 1923, more than a year after his death, Shafroth's friend Edward T. Taylor paid tribute to him in the House of Representatives and inserted into the *Congressional Record* a succinct biography and eulogy of Shafroth by former senator Charles S. Thomas. *Congressional Record*, 67th Congress, 4th Session, February 28, 1923, 64:5, 4944-4946.

29
Denver Post, February 28, 1922. The value of Shafroth's estate may not have been stated accurately so soon after his death. A typewritten inventory titled "Estate of John F. Shafroth" in the Shafroth Papers, DPL, Box 14, lists real estate valued at $114,590, notes and mortgages valued at $60,430, and stocks and bonds valued at $134,950.

30
Denver Post, September 3, 1967.

31
Morrison's clients included Margaret Tobin Brown, better known as the "Unsinkable" Molly Brown for having survived the *Titanic* disaster.

32
Earlier Morrison had been in partnership with his father. After John Franklin Shafroth's death, Will Shafroth was associated with the firm. Erl Ellis left it in 1938 after he was convicted of involvement in a scheme to hide a surveillance microphone in Governor Teller Ammons' office. Eventually the firm evolved into Shafroth and Toll and included Frank Shafroth, a son of Morrison's, and Henry Wolcott Toll, Jr. By 2002, the Shafroth name had been on a Denver law firm for more than 120 years.

33
New York Times, September 18, 1937.

34
Newton's mayoral administration had many of the same reform hallmarks as Shafroth's gubernatorial administration. See Stephen J. Leonard, "Denver's Postwar Awakening: Quigg Newton, Mayor, 1947-1955," *Colorado Heritage* (spring 1997), 13-24.

35
Both Morrison and Will were top tennis players, having won the 1914 Colorado state doubles championship in 1914.

36
Rocky Mountain News, October 6, 1978.

37
New York Times, June 9, 1922.

38

Will Shafroth wrote a lengthy, fascinating eight-part series on Russian relief that appeared in the *New York Evening World* between July 17 and July 25, 1922. Dale Reed, archivist at the Hoover Institution, Stanford University, kindly supplied the authors of this study with copies of these articles, as well as other information on Shafroth's relief work. Also, the Hoover collection has a seventy-two-page typescript article, "The New Russia," which Will wrote in 1923. On Russian famine relief, also see Bertrand M. Patenaude, *The Big Show in Bololand: The American Relief Expedition to Soviet Russia in the Famine of 1921* (Palo Alto: Stanford University Press, 2002).

39

William Shafroth to Morrison Shafroth, October 13, 1922, Shafroth Papers, DPL, Box 17.

40

Rocky Mountain News, August 28, 1991.

41

Virginia Shafroth to Morrison Shafroth, December 11, 1922, Shafroth Papers, DPL, Box 17.

42

Denver Post, January 19, 1941.

43

Denver Post, March 23, 1949.

44

Rocky Mountain News, July 1, 1950.

Bibliography

Books

Abbott, Carl, Stephen J. Leonard, and David McComb. *Colorado: A History of the Centennial State*. Niwot: University Press of Colorado, 1994, originally published 1976.

Athearn, Robert Greenleaf. *The Coloradans*. Albuquerque: University of New Mexico Press, 1976.

Bates, J. Leonard. *Senator Thomas Walsh of Montana: Law and Public Affairs, from TR to FDR*. Urbana: University of Illinois Press, 1999.

Breck, Allen D. *William Gray Evans: Portrait of a Western Executive*. Denver: University of Denver, 1964.

Brundage, David. *The Making of Western Labor Radicalism: Denver's Organized Workers, 1878–1905*. Urbana and Chicago: University of Illinois Press, 1994.

Buchholtz, Curtis W. *Rocky Mountain National Park: A History*. Boulder: Colorado Associated University Press, 1983.

Chessman, G. Wallace. *Theodore Roosevelt and the Politics of Power*. Boston: Little, Brown and Co., 1969.

Cooper, John M., Jr. *Pivotal Decades: The United States, 1900–1920*. New York: W.W. Norton and Co., 1990.

Costigan, Edward P. *Public Ownership of Government: Collected Papers of Edward P. Costigan*. New York: The Vanguard Press, Inc., 1940.

Creel, George. *Rebel At Large: Recollections of Fifty Crowded Years*. New York: G. P. Putnam's Sons, 1947.

Dehman, Henry. *Ninth Biennial Report of the Inspector of Coal Mines of the State of Colorado, 1899–1900*. Denver: Smith-Brooks, 1901.

Denton, James A. *Rocky Mountain Radical: Myron W. Reed, Christian Socialist*. Albuquerque: University of New Mexico Press, 1997.

Denver City Directories.

Dorsett, Lyle W. *The Queen City: A History of Denver*. Boulder: Pruett Publishing Co., 1977.

Downing, Sibyl and Robert E. Smith. *Tom Patterson: Colorado Crusader for Change*. Niwot: University Press of Colorado, 1995.

Drummond, Alexander. *Enos Mills Citizen of Nature*. Boulder: University Press of Colorado, 1995.

Ellis, Elmer. *Henry Moore Teller: Defender of the West*. Caldwell, Ida.: Caxton Printers, Ltd., 1941.

The Federal Reserve System Purposes and Functions. Washington, D.C.: Board of Governors of the Federal Reserve System, 1961.

Fellman, Michael. *Inside War: The Guerilla Conflict in Missouri During the American Civil War*. New York: Oxford University Press, 1989.

Ferril, William C. *Sketches of Colorado: Being an Analytical Summary and Biographic History of the State of Colorado, Volume I*. Denver: Western Press Bureau Co., 1911.

Fowler, Gene. *Timber Line: A Story of Bonfils and Tammen*. New York: Covici Friede Publishers, 1933.

Greenbaum, Fred. *Fighting Progressive: A Biography of Edward P. Costigan*. Washington, D.C.: Public Affairs Press, 1971.

Hafen, LeRoy, R. ed. *Colorado and Its People: A Narrative and Topical History of the Centennial State*. 4 vols., New York: Lewis Historical Publishing Co., 1948.

Haywood, William D. *The Autobiography of Big Bill Haywood*. New York: International Publishers, 1974, originally published 1929.

Hill, Alice Polk. *Colorado Pioneers in Picture and Story*. Denver: Brock-Haffner Press, 1915.

History of Howard and Cooper Counties, Missouri. St. Louis: National Historical Company, 1883.

Hofstadter, Richard. *The Age of Reform: From Bryan to F.D.R.* New York: Vintage Books, 1955.

Irwin, Inez H. *The Story of the Woman's Party*. New York: Kraus Reprint Co., 1971, originally published 1921.

Keating, Edward. *The Gentleman from Colorado: A Memoir*. Denver: Sage Books, 1964.

Kelsey, Harry E., Jr. *Frontier Capitalist: The Life of John Evans*. Boulder: Pruett Publishing Co. and Colorado Historical Society, 1969.

King, Clyde. *The History of the Government of Denver with Special Reference to Its Relations with Public Service Corporations*. Denver: Fisher Book Company, 1911.

Knock, Thomas J. *To End All Wars: Woodrow Wilson and the Quest for a New World Order*. New York: Oxford University Press, 1992.

Lamm, Richard D. and Duane A. Smith. *Pioneers and Politicians: 10 Colorado Governors in Profile*. Boulder: Pruett Publishing Co., 1984.

Lane, Jack C. *Armed Progressive: General Leonard Wood*. San Rafael, Calif.: Presidio Press, 1978.

Larsen, Charles. *The Good Fight: The Life and Times of Ben B. Lindsey*. Chicago: Quadrangle Books, 1972.

Leonard, Stephen J. and Thomas J. Noel. *Denver: From Mining Camp to Metropolis*. Niwot: University Press of Colorado, 1990.

Lindsey, Benjamin Barr and Harvey J. O'Higgins. *The Beast*. New York: Doubleday, Page and Co., 1910.

Lindsey, Benjamin Barr. *The Rule of Plutocracy in Colorado: A Retrospect and a Warning*. Denver: Hicks Printing House, 1908.

Link, Arthur S., ed. *The Papers of Woodrow Wilson*. Princeton: Princeton University Press, 1966.

Link, Arthur S. *Wilson: The New Freedom*. Princeton: Princeton University Press, 1956.

———. *Wilson: The Road to the White House*. Princeton: Princeton University Press, 1947.

———. *Woodrow Wilson and the Progressive Era: 1910-1917*. New York: Harper and Row, 1963, originally published 1954.

MacMechen, Edgar C., ed. *Robert W. Speer: A City Builder*. Denver: Smith-Brooks Printing Co., 1919.

McCarthy, G. Michael. *Hour of Trial: The Conservation Conflict in Colorado and the West*. Norman: University of Oklahoma Press, 1972.

McDonald, Forrest. *The Torch Is Passed: The United States in the Twentieth Century*. Reading, Mass.: Addison Wesley, 1968.

McGovern, George S. and Leonard F. Guttridge. *The Great Coalfield War*. Boston: Houghton Mifflin Co., 1972.

Miller, Stuart C. *Benevolent Assimilation: The American Conquest of the Philippines, 1899-1903*. New Haven: Yale University Press, 1982.

Morgan, David. *Suffragists and Democrats*. Lansing: Michigan State University Press, 1972.

Noel, Thomas J. *The City and the Saloon: Denver, 1858-1916*. Lincoln: University of Nebraska Press, 1982/1984 Bison Book paper/ 1996 University Press of Colorado reprint.

Nye, Russell B. *Midwestern Progressive Politics: A Historical Study of Its Origins and Development, 1870-1958*. New York: Harper and Row, 1965.

Perkin, Robert. *The First Hundred Years: An Informal History of Denver and the Rocky Mountain News*. Garden City, N.Y.: Doubleday, 1959.

Portrait and Biographical Record of the State of Colorado. Chicago: Chapman Publishing Co., 1899.

Robbins, Roy M. *Our Landed Heritage: The Public Domain, 1776-1936.* Lincoln: University of Nebraska Press, 1962.

Rowley, William D. *Reclaiming the West: The Career of Francis G. Newlands.* Bloomington: Indiana University Press, 1996.

Shikes, Robert. *Rocky Mountain Medicine: Doctors, Drugs, and Disease in Early Colorado.* Boulder: Johnson Books, 1986.

Smiley, Jerome C. *History of Denver, with Outlines of the Earlier History of the Rocky Mountain Country.* Denver: Denver Times, Times-Sun Publishing Co., 1901.

Smith, Duane A. *Henry M. Teller: Colorado's Grand Old Man.* Boulder: University Press of Colorado, 2002.

———. *Mesa Verde National Park: Shadows of the Centuries.* Topeka: University Press of Kansas, 1988.

Smith, Phyllis. *Once a Coal Miner: The Story of Colorado's Northern Coal Field.* Boulder: Pruett Publishing Co., 1989.

Stanton, Elizabeth C. *History of Woman Suffrage.* 6 vols. New York: Source Book Press, 1970, originally published 1922.

Stevens, Doris. *Jailed for Freedom.* New York: Schocken Books, 1976, originally published 1920.

Stone, Wilbur F. *History of Colorado.* Chicago: The S. J. Clarke Publishing Co., 1918.

Swanberg, W. A. *Citizen Hearst: A Biography of William Randolph Hearst.* New York: Bantam Books, 1963.

Vickers, William B. *History of the City of Denver.* Chicago: O.L. Baskin, 1880.

Whiteside, James. *Regulating Danger: The Struggle for Mine Safety in the Rocky Mountain Coal Industry.* Lincoln: University of Nebraska Press, 1990.

Wright, James Edward. *The Politics of Populism: Dissent in Colorado.* New Haven: Yale University Press, 1974.

Government Documents

Biographical Directory of the American Congress, 1774-1971. Washington, D.C.: Government Printing Office, 1971.

Congressional Record. Washington, D.C.: Government Printing Office, 1894-1904; 1913-1919; 1923.

House Journal of the General Assembly of the State of Colorado, Nineteenth Session. Denver: Smith-Brooks, 1911.

Articles

Allen, Howard W. "Geography and Politics: Voting on Reform Issues in the United States Senate, 1911-1916," *The Journal of Southern History* 27 (May 1961): 216-228.

Bayard, Charles J. "The Colorado Progressive Split of 1912," *The Colorado Magazine* 45 (winter 1968): 61-78.

Capo-Rodriguez, Pedro. "Some Political and Historical Aspects of the Government of Puerto Rico," *The Hispanic American Historical Review* 2 (November 1919): 543-585.

Dawson, Thomas F. [a.k.a. "Uncle Tom"]. "The Passing of Senator John Franklin Shafroth," *The Trail* (February 1922): 18-19.

DeLorme, Roland L. "Turn-of-the-Century Denver: An Invitation to Reform," *Colorado Magazine* 45 (winter 1968): 1-15.

Dorsett, Lyle W. "The Ordeal of Colorado's Germans During World War I," *Colorado Magazine* 51 (fall 1974): 277-293.

Hornbein, Marjorie. "Three Governors in a Day," *Colorado Magazine* 45 (summer 1968): 243-260.

Hewitt, William L. "The Election of 1896: Two Factions Square Off," *Colorado Magazine* 54 (winter 1977): 44-57.

Kaplan, Robert D. "Looking the World in the Eye," *Atlantic Monthly* (December 2001): 68-82.

Latta, Robert H. "Denver in the 1880s," *Colorado Magazine* 28 (July 1941): 131-136.

Leonard, Stephen J. "Denver's Postwar Awakening: Quigg Newton, Mayor, 1947-1955," *Colorado Heritage* (spring 1997): 13-24.

———. "Swimming Against the Current: A Biography of Charles S. Thomas, Senator and Governor," *Colorado Heritage* (autumn 1994): 29-34.

———. "The 1918 Influenza Epidemic in Colorado," *Essays and Monographs in Colorado History*, Essays 9 (1989): 1-24.

Lindsey, Benjamin B. "Uphold the Insurgents," *LaFollette's Weekly Magazine*, July 23, 1909.

MacColl, E. K. "John Franklin Shafroth: Reform Governor of Colorado, 1909–1913," *Colorado Magazine* 29 (January 1952): 37-52.

McCarthy, G. Michael. "Insurgency in Colorado: Elias Ammons and the Anticonservation Impulse," *Colorado Magazine* 54 (winter 1977): 26-43.

Merchant, Frank. "Colorado's First Highway Commission, 1910–1912," *Colorado Magazine* 32 (January 1955): 74-77.

Mitchell, J. Paul. "Municipal Reform in Denver: The Defeat of Mayor Speer," *Colorado Magazine* 45 (winter 1968): 42-60.

Noel, Thomas J. "William D. Haywood," *Colorado Heritage* (Issue 2, 1984): 2-12.

Rogers, Edmund B. "Notes on the Establishment of Mesa Verde National Park," *Colorado Magazine* 29 (January 1952): 10-17.

Smith, Robert E. "Colorado's Progressive Senators and Representatives," *Colorado Magazine* 45 (winter 1968): 27-41.

Shafroth, John Franklin. "New Campaign Finance Law in Colorado," *Independent* (July 8, 1909): 83-84.

Snyder, J. Richard. "The Election of 1904: An Attempt at Reform," *Colorado Magazine* 45 (winter 1968): 16-26.

Waddell, Karen. "Dearfield. . . . .A Dream Deferred," *Colorado Heritage* (Issue 2, 1988): 2-12.

West, Elliot. "Dirty Tricks in Denver," *The Colorado Magazine* 52 (summer 1975): 225-243.

Theses and Dissertations

Dickson, James Newton III. "Progressivism in Colorado: The Reform Administration of Governor John Franklin Shafroth, 1909–1913." M.A. thesis, Madison College, Madison, Wisc., 1975.

Knautz, Harlan Ernest. "The Progressive Harvest in Colorado, 1910–1916." Ph.D. diss. University of Denver, 1969.

Musselman, Lloyd Keith. "Governor John Shafroth and the Colorado Progressives: Their Fight for Direct Legislation, 1909–1910." M.A. thesis, University of Denver, 1961.

Welch, Gerald Don. "John F. Shafroth: Progressive Governor of Colorado, 1910–1912." M.A. thesis, University of Denver, 1962.

Manuscripts

Benjamin Barr Lindsey Papers, Library of Congress, Washington, D.C.

Gerboth, Christopher B. "Honest John: The Life of John Franklin Shafroth, 1854–1922." Unpublished typescript, 1996, in offices of Shafroth and Toll law firm, Denver.

National Woman's Party Papers, 179 reels, Glen Rock, N.J.: Microfilming Corporation of America, 1977- , in Auraria Library, Denver.

Frank H. Shafroth Papers. Shafroth and Toll law firm, Denver.

The Governor John F. Shafroth Collection, Colorado State Archives, Denver.

Shafroth Papers, Colorado Historical Society Library, Denver.

Shafroth Family Papers, Denver Public Library, Western History and Genealogy Department.

Polhill, Dennis. "'Honest John' Shafroth: Colorado's Most Illustrious Citizen." Denver: Unpublished typescript, 1999, in offices of Shafroth and Toll law firm, Denver.

Scrapbooks
Thomas Dawson Scrapbooks, Colorado Historical Society, Denver.
John F. Shafroth Scrapbooks, Colorado Historical Society, Denver

Newspapers
Advertiser [Fayette, Mo.]
Aspen Democrat
Boulder County Miner
Boulder Daily Camera
Boulder News
Canon City Times
Colorado Catholic [Denver]
The Colorado Lawyer
Colorado Springs Gazette
Colorado Transcript [Golden]
Daily Camera [Boulder]
Daily Sentinel [Grand Junction]
The Denver Post
Denver Democrat
Denver Express
The Denver Labor Bulletin
Denver Republican
Denver Times
Durango Democrat
Evening Post [New York]
Fort Collins Express
Monte Vista Journal
New York Evening World
The New York Times
New York Sun
Oak Creek Herald
Post [Washington, D.C.]

Press [New York]
Public Forum [Denver]
Pueblo Chieftain
Pueblo Star-Journal
Rocky Mountain News [Denver]
Star [Kansas City]
Star [Washington, D.C.]
Times-Herald [Chicago]
Women's Journal [Boston]

Interviews

Davis, H. Denny, interview by Christopher B. Gerboth, March 3, 1995, Denver.

Newton, James Quigg, numerous interviews by Stephen J. Leonard and Thomas J. Noel.

Newton, Virginia Shafroth, interview by Donald Walker, Jr., July 17, 2001, Denver.

Shafroth, Frank, interview by Thomas J. Noel, January 8, 2001, Denver.

Shafroth, Frank, interview with Donald L. Walker, Jr., July 17, 2001, Denver.

Shafroth, Morrison, interview by David McComb, June 10, 1975, Oral History Collection, Stephen H. Hart Library, Colorado Historical Society, Denver.

Toll, Henry Wolcott, Jr., interview by Thomas J. Noel, May 6, 2002.

INDEX

COLORADO HISTORICAL SOCIETY
BOARD OF DIRECTORS

OFFICERS
W. Nicholas V. Mathers, *Chair*
Joseph W. Halpern, *Vice Chair*
Philip H. Karsh, *Vice Chair*
Dana H. Crawford, *Secretary*
Mary Lyn Ballantine, *Treasurer*
Georgianna Contiguglia, *President*

EX-OFFICIO DIRECTORS
Timothy E. Foster, *Executive Director,*
    Colorado Commission on Higher Education
John E. Moye, *Chair, Colorado Historical*
    Foundation
Frances Owens, *Colorado First Lady*

EMERITUS DIRECTORS
Janis H. Falkenberg
William H. Hornby
Frank A. Kemp
Myron D. Neusteter
Walter A. Steele

EXECUTIVE COMMITTEE
Ellen Kingman Fisher, Ph.D.
Jon N. Schler

DIRECTORS
Ronald G. Askew
Alice Bamford
W. Bart Berger
Virginia K. Berkeley
Martha Wright Cannon
Frederic K. Conover
Stanley Dempsey
Susan Drumm
F. A. Garcia, M.D.
Paul Kabotie
Vicky Kipp
Frank A. Kugeler
Virginia Morrison Love
Richard A. Marlar, Ph.D.
Jim McCotter
Mae McGregor
Douglas N. Morton
Robert J. Mutaw, Ph.D.
Tom Noel, Ph.D.
The Hon. Robert W. Ogburn
Ann Pritzlaff
James H. Ranniger
Bruce M. Rockwell

Jennie Rucker, Ed.D.
M. Edmund Vallejo, Ph.D.
Eleanor V. Vincent
Dottie Wham
Grant Wilkins

DIRECTORS COUNCIL
Ellen Kingman Fisher, *Co-chair*
Samuel P. Guyton, *Co-chair*
Katherine Beise
Tom Blickensderfer
Curtis E. Burton
Stuart P. Dodge
Joan Duncan
Ed Dwight
Walter C. Emery
Janis Falkenberg
Gael Fetcher
Carol K. Gossard
Edwin H. Grant, Jr.
James J. Hester
James P. Johnson
Frank A. Kemp
Roger D. Knight III
Walter A. Koelbel
Alma Kurtz
Dottie Lamm
The Hon. Carlos F. Lucero
Evelyn B. McClearn
Myron D. Neusteter
Martha J. Segelke
Walter A. Steele
Marcia Tate
Carol deB. Whitaker
Lee White
William F. Wilbur

EDITORIAL REVIEW BOARD

Vincent C. de Baca
Maxine Benson
Vine Deloria
William Gwaltney
David Fridtjof Halaas
Stephen J. Leonard
Patricia Nelson Limerick
Thomas J. Noel
Duane A. Smith